University Hospitals of Derby and
Burton NHS Foundation Trust
Library and Knowledge Service

KU-730-279
B32899

University Hospitals of Derby and
Burton NHS Foundation Trust
Library and Knowledge Service
This book is due for return on or before the last date shown below.

Comp
Langu

Sandra Stev
Assistant auth
Language con
Development

WITHDRAWN

University Hospitals of Derby and
Burton NHS Foundation Trust
Knowledge Service

Complete English as a Foreign Language

Sandra Stevens

Assistant author
Bismarck Vallecillo

Language consultant
John Shepheard

Development editor
Carolyn Burch

First published in Great Britain in 2001 by Hodder Education. An Hachette UK company.

This edition published in 2016 by John Murray Learning

Copyright © Sandra Stevens 2001, 2003, 2010, 2014, 2016

The right of Sandra Stevens to be identified as the Author of the Work has been asserted by her in accordance with the Copyright, Designs and Patents Act 1988.

Database right Hodder & Stoughton (makers)

The *Teach Yourself* name is a registered trademark of Hachette UK.

All rights reserved. No part of this publication may be reproduced, stored in a retrieval system or transmitted in any form or by any means, electronic, mechanical, photocopying, recording or otherwise, without the prior written permission of the publisher, or as expressly permitted by law, or under terms agreed with the appropriate reprographic rights organization. Enquiries concerning reproduction outside the scope of the above should be sent to the Rights Department, John Murray Learning, at the address below.

You must not circulate this book in any other binding or cover and you must impose this same condition on any acquirer.

British Library Cataloguing in Publication Data: a catalogue record for this title is available from the British Library.

Library of Congress Catalog Card Number: on file.

9781473601581

5

The publisher has used its best endeavours to ensure that any website addresses referred to in this book are correct and active at the time of going to press. However, the publisher and the author have no responsibility for the websites and can make no guarantee that a site will remain live or that the content will remain relevant, decent or appropriate.

The publisher has made every effort to mark as such all words which it believes to be trademarks. The publisher should also like to make it clear that the presence of a word in the book, whether marked or unmarked, in no way affects its legal status as a trademark.

Every reasonable effort has been made by the publisher to trace the copyright holders of material in this book. Any errors or omissions should be notified in writing to the publisher, who will endeavour to rectify the situation for any reprints and future editions.

Cover image © Shutterstock.com

Typeset by Cenveo Publisher Services.

Printed and bound in Great Britain by CPI Group (UK) Ltd., Croydon, CR0 4YY.

John Murray Learning policy is to use papers that are natural, renewable and recyclable products and made from wood grown in sustainable forests. The logging and manufacturing processes are expected to conform to the environmental regulations of the country of origin.

Carmelite House
50 Victoria Embankment
London EC4Y 0DZ
www.hodder.co.uk

Contents

Talking about length of time and prices; asking *who?* and responding using short answers; talking about the number of people using *how many*; talking about the same thing using *one, ones*; asking for an alternative, using comparatives; making negative comparisons, using *not as … as*; making decisions – buying things, using *I'll*; using the verb *hope* + present simple; talking about the past, using the past simple; talking about life experiences, using the present perfect

Vocabulary: hotel language; ordinal numbers

Pronunciation: *schwa* **/ ə/**

Credits

P157: © National Rail

P164: © Shutterstock.com

P164: © National Rail

P234: © Shutterstock.com

About the author

I have worked in English as a foreign language for over 40 years, as a teacher, teacher trainer, trainer of trainers, materials writer and consultant. Places of work have included the UK, France, Spain and Nicaragua with the British Council, ministries of education and private language schools. I have also made working trips to other countries, including Argentina, Hong Kong, Italy, Kuwait, Mexico, Poland and Uruguay. My experience has been with both children and adults.

Before becoming a teacher of English as a foreign language, I was an interpreter/translator (English/French) and a teacher of French. I have taught myself Spanish and have an understanding of German.

My current work includes specialist one-to-one teaching (e.g. pronunciation, grammar for communication and writing skills), together with the design, materials development and management of projects for both learners and teachers of English.

Having lived and worked in a number of countries and taught students from many parts of the world, I have developed both a practical knowledge of – and a theoretical framework to explain – how culture (the unwritten rules, beliefs and behaviours of a society) plays a part in international communication. As a result of this, linguistic and cultural mentoring have become a part of my current professional activities and an area of research.

Sandra Stevens

Introduction

How the course works

What is *Complete English as a Foreign Language*?

A complete self-access course to learn English without a teacher.

Who is *Complete English as a Foreign Language* for?

This course is for young and adult learners who want to understand and speak English with confidence. It teaches you how to use the language in real, everyday situations.

How much English do I need to use this book?

You can follow this course with very basic English.

What is special about this course?
The Discovery method: learn to learn!

There are lots of different ways of learning a language. Perhaps you have tried some methods, together with some learning techniques of your own. This course is based on the Discovery method. First you'll hear the language in context, then you are guided to work out the meaning, notice language patterns, understand grammar concepts, work on vocabulary and build your ability to understand, speak and write English. As a result of your own efforts, you will remember better what you have learned and use the new language with confidence. You will also be able to use these same learning skills to continue to learn the language after you have finished this course.

Everyone can learn another language – the key is **how** to learn it. Learning is more than just reading or memorizing grammar and vocabulary. It's about being an active learner, learning from real-life examples. If you work out a language point yourself, you can remember it more easily and you will be able to use it in your own situations.

And, because many of the essential details, such as grammar and pronunciation rules, are introduced through the Discovery method, you'll have more fun learning, too. Very quickly you will notice the progress you are making.

Enjoy yourself!

How do I use this course?

You learn English in English.

The course is flexible. You decide where, when and how long you study. Each exercise has a complete title, so you can stop and start at any time. We recommend that you study little and often. Some people find it fun and helpful to work with a friend.

The focus of the course is discovery of language and communication. You learn some grammar and you also learn how to do things in English, for example, *ask for information*, *offer to do something*, *accept or reject an invitation*, *make a suggestion*, etc. This book also teaches 'the little things', for example how to attract attention. These 'little things' help learners feel more confident with their English.

It also teaches you how, in English, speakers communicate their feelings and attitudes through language, stress and intonation.

It prepares you to talk about yourself, your life, your family, your work or studies, and your country.

At the end of the book we give you the answers to the exercises. You can check your progress as you go along.

What is in this course?

The complete course consists of this coursebook and audio with all the listening and pronunciation material.

The audio:
- ▶ gives you practice in listening and understanding
- ▶ is a model for pronunciation
- ▶ includes the guided pronunciation exercises.

The course contains this **Introduction**, ten units and a reference section. The **Introduction** includes a guide to **Key points of English pronunciation**, with exercises that you can do before you start Unit 1.

Each unit starts with a list of learning discovery points (**In this unit, you will learn how to ...**), so you know what you will learn in the unit.

The story conversations

The course follows a story, so you know the characters and the situation. The story is a conversation between the characters at the start of each unit (and sometimes within the unit, too). You start by doing a short exercise to check your understanding of key points of **the story**. Listening and reading exercises then help you to understand more detail.

An American English version of the conversations is available in audio form: an audio reference is given after each conversation transcript in the units. See the end the book for the American English transcripts.

The story conversations include examples of the new language in the unit. These examples then help you to discover and practise the language, under the following five main headings:

Language discovery

In these sections you listen and read examples from **the story** to discover how the language works. This is where you will learn important points of grammar and communication.

Vocabulary builder

In these sections you will find vocabulary and dictionary exercises. You'll also find some listening and reading for useful words and expressions.

Practice

Here you will practise language from the **Language discovery** sections and words and expressions from the **Vocabulary builder** sections. Some of the exercises have a special focus on developing your speaking and writing skills.

Listening, Reading, Speaking and Writing

These four skills are practised in all the units. **Listening** and **Reading** help you to learn and understand more language. In the **Speaking** and **Writing** sections you use the language you have discovered. At the end of each unit, before **Revision** and **Test yourself**, you will also practise these skills to:

▶ talk about the unit in relation to you, your life and your country: **About you**
▶ practise using your English in realistic situations: **What would you say?**

Pronunciation

Pronunciation is very important, especially for confidence. If you know how to pronounce English, this helps you to understand others and helps them to understand you. In these sections you will find guided practice and clear examples with lots of audio support.

In addition, there are also sections about British life, customs and habits.

Revision

At the end of every unit is a **Revision** section, which includes the following:

▶ **What is it in your language?** Here you translate into your language some examples of the main language points from the unit.
▶ A realistic **Writing** task.
▶ A **Speaking** task. Now it's your turn to join the conversation. This is another look at the first conversation in the unit. This time you participate.

Test yourself

There is a test at the end of each unit for you to check your progress.

Each test has two parts:

▶ In the first part, each question asks you to choose the correct or better option of two possibilities.

▶ In the second part, you write one side of a guided dialogue.

I can ...

This summary list is for you to check your own progress: can you tick all the learning discovery points from the unit?

Reference section

The reference section at the back of the book has four sections:

1 **A glossary.** The first time we use a grammar term, we provide a short definition in brackets. In the glossary we give full definitions, with more examples, of these grammar terms.

2 **A quick reference section of phrases for communication.** This is in alphabetical order, to help you find words and expressions quickly.

3 **A quick reference section of English grammar.** This gives clear explanations and examples of the main points of English grammar.

4 **A complete index.** With the help of the index, you can find a specific language point quickly.

I study English in a school. Is this book useful for me?

Yes, you can use this course at the same time as other books, for extra practice, revision and the 'little things'.

I'm a businessperson. Can this book help me?

Yes. This book emphasizes social competence in English in a variety of situations.

I want to travel. Is this book useful?

Yes. This book gives lots of practice in the language you need, for example, to order food and drink, find a hotel and use public transport.

I'm an English teacher. How can I use this book?

You can use this book:

▶ for reference

▶ as a coursebook

▶ as supplementary material

▶ for homework.

In addition:

- ▶ The **audio** can be used as a listening course.
- ▶ The **syllabus** and **exercises** can be used alone or in the combination you choose.
- ▶ The **Language tips** and **Common mistake** points are there to help with persistent problem areas.
- ▶ The **About you, your family and your country** sections can be used for personalization.
- ▶ The **Culture** sections can be starting points for comparisons with customs and habits in students' own countries and for fluency work.
- ▶ The **Revision** sections and the **Tests** can be used independently or as homework.

🎙️Key points about English pronunciation

English pronunciation has four areas you need to think about:

1 **Sounds.** This area is about consonants and vowels.

2 **Stress.** *Stress* means *emphasis*. There is both a) word stress, i.e. the stressed syllable in a word and b) 'sentence stress', the stressed syllable(s) in a sentence. Word stress is introduced in this section. Sentence stress depends on the context, so this is explained at various points throughout the course.

3 **Connected speech.** This is about the changes in sound that happen when we say words together in a phrase or sentence, e.g. an‿apple.

4 **Intonation.** *Intonation* is the music, or rise and fall of the voice. English often uses intonation to express feelings, e.g. *Hello* with a big fall sounds friendly, but with flat intonation it can sound rude or unfriendly.

This introduction to **Key points about English pronunciation** gives you important information about these four areas. It also includes guidance on pronouncing plural nouns in English, a key point which is difficult for many learners.

1 Sounds

Q How many letters are there in the alphabet?

A 26.

Q How many sounds are there in English?

A 44.

Q How many consonants are there in the alphabet?

A 21. But there are 24 consonant sounds in English.

Q How many vowels are there in the alphabet?

A Five – *a, e, i, o, u*. But there are 20 vowel sounds in English. Twelve of these are 'pure' vowels and eight are diphthongs (two vowel sounds together that make one).

Q How do I know how to pronounce an English word?

A English spelling and English pronunciation are sometimes different. This is why, in this course, I always suggest you listen to the audio several times before you read the words. Listening to English before you read it always helps with good pronunciation.

When you look up a word in a good English dictionary, you see the word in phonetics (e.g. course = /kɔːs/). At the front or at the back of a dictionary you will find a list of the phonetic symbols. Look at the vowels. Five of them have a / :/ mark after them. This means a long sound. Other vowel sounds are short. There are many pairs of words with similar sounds in English. They are different only in the vowel sound, one is short and the other long, e.g. *Sit* and *seat*. *Sit* is short /i/ and *seat* is long /iː/.

Q Which is the most common sound in English?

A The vowel sound, *schwa* /ə/. It's the only sound with a name and it means 'weak'.

Q Is there a difference in pronunciation between *no* and *know*?

A No. In English one pronunciation can have different spellings and different meanings. For example:
see and *sea*
right and *write*
meet and *meat*

There are many pairs like this in English.

1 Read and match.

For each word a–f, choose the word with the same pronunciation from list 1–6.

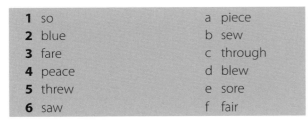

1	so	a	piece
2	blue	b	sew
3	fare	c	through
4	peace	d	blew
5	threw	e	sore
6	saw	f	fair

The alphabet

Do you know your *a*, *b*, *c* (alphabet) in English?

In English we very often have to spell words aloud for other people. This may be names, family names, addresses, email addresses, etc. We also need to understand when other people spell something for us. It is therefore important to learn the alphabet in English.

2 **00.01 Listen and repeat.**

Look at the columns of letters. The letters in each column have the same sound.
Listen and repeat the names of the letters. You will hear each letter twice.

a	b	f	i	o	q	r
h	c	l	y		u	
j	d	m			w	
k	e	n				
	g	s				
	p	x				
	t	z				
	v					

3 **00.02 Can you say the names of the letters?**
Listen to the first letter from each column.
Say the others with the same vowel sound.
Listen and check.

2 Stress

Q What is stress?

A Emphasis or accent. English has no written accents. It has stress on some words and syllables. This course explains and gives practice in stress.

Word stress

Q Where's the stress in words?

A In words with two syllables or more, one syllable has stress.

Q What's a syllable?

A Part of a word with a vowel sound.

 4 **00.03 Listen to the following words and find the syllable with stress.**

1 syllables
2 examples
3 conversation
4 above
5 important
6 information

Q Where's the stress on a word? How do I know?

A In some dictionaries, they show stress (ǀ) at the beginning of the syllable. For example, above /əǀbʌv/

Q Where's the stress in phrases and sentences?

A On the important or new information. For example, in *My name's Tom*, the stress is on *Tom*.

5 00.04 **Listen to the phrases and find the syllable with stress.**

1 Some Coke
2 To London
3 From David
4 Are they here?
5 Does it change?
6 Ask them.

When you learn a new word, make sure you learn where the stress is.

Weak forms

Q What about the syllables without stress?

A In these little words (for example *some*, *to*, *from*, *are*, *does*, *them*), sometimes the vowel sound changes to the first sound in the word – ***a***bout. It's the only sound with a name. It's called *schwa*. We write it like this /ə/. *Schwa* means 'weak'.

6 00.04 **Listen. How many /ə/ sounds are there – four, five, six or seven? Where are they?**

Q Is the pronunciation of the words above, for example *some*, *to*, always the same?

A No. Without stress the vowel sound is weak (*schwa*). When the word is important, the vowel sound is strong.

Q So, one word has two different pronunciations?

A Yes, that's right.

7 00.05 **Listen and repeat the phrases with these words. In a) the vowel is weak, in b) the vowel is strong.**

1 *Some*	weak strong	**a** *Some Coke*	
		b *Would you like some?*	
2 *To*	weak strong	**a** *to London*	
		b *Where to?*	
3 *From*	weak strong	**a** *from David*	
		b *Who from?*	
4 *Are*	weak strong	**a** *Are they here?*	
		b *Yes, they are.*	
5 *Does*	weak strong	**a** *Does it change?*	
		b *Yes, it does.*	
6 *Them*	weak strong	**a** *Ask them.*	
		b *Ask them, not me.*	

Q Is there a name for this, when one vowel has two different pronunciations?

A Yes, the weak pronunciation, /ə/, is called a weak form.

Q Why are weak forms important for learners of English?

A Learners often say *I can't understand English people – they speak very fast and swallow their words*. One reason for this is the weak forms. This course explains and gives practice in understanding and using weak forms.

3 Connected speech – linking words

 8 00.06 Listen and repeat.

Look at the link lines and stress in the transcript of the audio:

1 a <u>packet</u> of <u>crisps</u>
2 a <u>can</u> of <u>Coke</u>
3 a <u>bar</u> of <u>chocolate</u>
4 a <u>packet</u> of <u>chewing</u> gum
5 a <u>packet</u> of <u>biscuits</u>
6 a <u>bottle</u> of <u>water</u>
7 a <u>carton</u> of <u>fruit</u> juice
8 a <u>packet</u> of <u>sweets</u>

The word *of* **is weak in all the phrases, so the vowel is** *schwa* **/ə/.**

Listen again to the list of snacks, and repeat.

Pay special attention to:

a stress   **b** linking words   **c** weak *of* (əv)

4 Intonation

▶ Intonation is very important in English. What is intonation? The music or movement of our voice. Sometimes our voice goes up ➤ (a rise) – sometimes our voice goes down ➤ (a fall). This is intonation.

▶ Different languages express things in different ways. English uses intonation a lot for communication. A different intonation gives a different message. Is intonation important in your language? This course explains and gives practice in understanding and using intonation with confidence.

Intonation and feelings – voice movement

▶ In English we use intonation to express attitude (our feelings).

▶ In general, big voice movements express strong feelings.

▶ Flat intonation expresses that you are not interested or that your attitude is negative.

 9 00.07 Listen and repeat the words. You will hear each one twice.

a big movements = positive and interested
b small movements = not very positive, not interested, negative.

1a Yes?	b Yes.	4a OK?	b OK
2a This?	b This.	5a All right?	b All right.
3a No?	b No.	6a Sorry?	b Sorry.

Intonation in questions

 10   00.08 Listen and repeat the words.

a rises   **b** falls

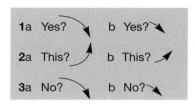 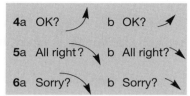

Q Is there a pattern here?

A Yes. A rise on a single word or phrase is generally a question.

Q Where exactly is this rise or fall?

A On the syllable with stress or emphasis. (A syllable is a word or part of a word with a vowel sound.)

Intonation in questions with *what?*, *where?*, etc.

 11   00.09 Listen and choose.

Read the questions.

Listen to the mini dialogues. Pay special attention to the important word in the question – the syllable with stress.

Choose a) or b) (the answer is the same for all the dialogues):

In questions with *what?*, *where?*, etc. the voice:

   a goes up on the syllable with stress ⬈   OR

   b goes down on the syllable with stress. ⬊

1 What's your <u>name</u>?	Monica.
2 Where are you <u>from</u>?	New York.
3 Where does he <u>work</u>?	In a school.
4 When do they arr<u>ive</u>?	At five o'clock.
5 Who can <u>drive</u>?	I can.
6 Which one's <u>yours</u>?	That one.
7 Why aren't they <u>here</u>?	Their train's late.
8 How's your <u>mother</u>?	She's fine.
9 Whose is <u>this</u>?	I don't know. It's not mine.

Common mistake

Many learners of English use an 'up' intonation with questions.

Questions with question words (*what*, *when*, etc.) go down. ⬊

12 00.09 Listen and repeat.

Listen again and repeat the questions.

Pay special attention to the fall on the syllable with stress.

Plural nouns with an extra syllable – *es*

In the sentence *Do you speak any foreign languages?*, how many syllables are there in *languages*?

Sometimes plural nouns have an extra syllable. For example, *language* has two syllables (*lang-uage*) but *languages* has three syllables (*lang-uag-es*). (A syllable is part of a word with a vowel sound.)

The pronunciation of the extra syllable is *is* /iz/.

 13 00.10 Count the syllables.

Look at the pictures and listen to the audio.

Write the number of syllables you hear.

1	One page	Two pages
2	One box	Two boxes
3	One bus	Two buses

4	One house	Two houses
5	One bridge	Two bridges
6	One sandwich	Two sandwiches
7	One slice	Two slices
8	One piece	Two pieces
9	One dish	Two dishes
10	One glass	Two glasses
11	One orange juice	Two orange juices
12	One kiss	Two kisses

Q How do I know when there's an extra syllable?

A After the letters *s*, *ss*, *sh*, *ch*, *ge*, *se*, *ce*, *x* there's an extra syllable.

Q Why these letters?

A Because after these letters it's difficult to pronounce the *s* without an extra vowel in the middle. An extra vowel = an extra syllable.

 14 00.10 **Listen again and repeat.**

1 *Saying* hello

In this unit you will learn how to:
▶ *start a conversation using question tags*
▶ *continue a conversation – short answers*
▶ *continue a conversation – saying more*
▶ *give invitations and make offers, using* Would you like ...?
▶ *use* a/some *with countables and uncountables*
▶ *offer more (food and drink)*
▶ *say* yes *and* no *to offers.*

VOCABULARY
▶ *food and drink*

PRONUNCIATION
▶ *question tags; rising intonation for offers; falling intonation for saying* yes *and* no *to offers*

CEFR: Can *ask people for things and give people things. Can understand and use familiar everyday expressions aimed at the satisfaction of needs of a concrete type (A1). Can understand sentences and frequently used expressions related to areas of most immediate relevance. Can agree and disagree. Can make and respond to suggestions (A2).*

The story

 01.01* *Our story begins on a plane.*

Listen to the conversation one, two or three times.

Choose the correct answer, a, b or c.

1 It's _____ in the plane.
   a cold
   b sunny
   c hot

2 The conversation is about ...
   a London.
   b a drink.
   c dinner.

3 The woman would like ...
   a some Coke.
   b to sleep.
   c to eat.

Man	It's hot, isn't it?
Woman	Yes, it is – very hot.
Man	Would you like a drink?
Woman	M'm, yes, please.
Man	What would you like?
Woman	Some Coke, please.

* For an American English version, listen to **11.1**.

Listening and reading

Cover the text of the story conversation.

Read the sentences.

 01.01 Listen and complete the words.

Then read the text of the story conversation to check your answers.

1 a The man starts the conversation.
       He says, *I __'s / h __ __ /, i __ n' __ / i __?*
   b The woman answers,
       Y __ __, i __ / i __ / – / v __ __ __ / h __ __.

2 a The man offers a drink.
       He says, *W __ __ __ __ d / y __ __ / l __ k __ / a / d __ __ __ k?*
   b The woman accepts.
       She says, *Y __ __ / p __ __ __ s __.*

3 a The man asks what drinks she wants.

He says, _W_ _ _ _ / _w_ _ _ _ _ / _you_ / _I_ _ _ _ _?

b The woman answers,

_So_ _ _ _e / _C_ _ _k_ _ _/, _p_ _ _ _ _ _e._

Ⓥ Vocabulary builder

DRINKS

1 Find seven drinks in this word search.

▶ The words go across → and down ↓. Use the pictures and your dictionary if necessary.

o	w	r	m	c	s	z
s	i	j	b	o	g	w
v	n	e	n	f	o	a
y	e	m	w	f	a	t
j	u	i	c	e	t	e
l	a	l	b	e	e	r
c	o	k	e	r	a	p

FOOD

2 Label these pictures. Use your dictionary if necessary.

4

Language discovery 1

STARTING A CONVERSATION – QUESTION TAGS

Example from the story

The man starts the conversation. He says, *It's hot, isn't it?*

Q What is 'isn't it?'?

A It's a question tag. Question tags are very common in English.

Q What are question tags?

A Question tags are short questions at the end of a sentence.

Meaning

Q Is this a real question?

A No. The man knows it's hot. The falling intonation also tells us it's not a real question. Here, the question tag starts a conversation.

Form

▶ We use the same tense in the main verb and the question tag.
▶ With a positive main verb, we use a negative question tag.
▶ With a negative main verb, we use a positive question tag.

1 Complete the table with the correct part of the verb *be*.

Grammar summary – question tags with verb *be*							
Positive verb + negative tag				**Negative verb + positive tag**			
I am right,	aren't I?			I'm not wrong,	_____ I?		
He She It	is English,	_____	he? she? it?	He She It	_____ English,	is	he? she? it?
We You They	are happy,	_____	we? you? they?	We You They	aren't happy,	_____	we? you? they?

Q And if there isn't a verb?

A That depends. Here are some examples.

Positive	Negative
It's good, isn't it?	It's not very good, is it?
OR	OR
Good, isn't it? *(informal)*	Not very good, is it? *(informal)*

With an adjective we use a negative question tag. With *not* + adjective, we use a positive question tag.

In informal spoken English, it is possible to start with the adjective. For example, *It's interesting, isn't it?* is correct and always appropriate. *Interesting, isn't it?* is correct and informal.

> **THE WEATHER**
> It is very common for British English speakers to talk about the weather. People often use the weather to start a conversation with people they don't know or don't know well.

2 Complete with the correct question tag.
   1 It's really cold today, _____ / _____?
   2 Nice and warm this morning, _____ / _____?
   3 The weather's not bad today, _____ / _____?
   4 Lovely day, _____ / _____?

 01.02 **Now listen and check your answers.**

How do you pronounce it?

STARTING A CONVERSATION

1 01.02 **Listen again and repeat the sentences.**

Pay special attention to the falling intonation on the question tag.

QUESTION TAGS WITH FALLING INTONATION

2 Match the pictures (1–9) with the correct sentence a–i and complete the question tags.

a It's a very good film, _____?

b You're David, _____? My name's Sam.

c This food's very nice, _____?

d This programme's not very interesting, _____?

e She's beautiful, _____?

f This isn't right, _____?

g It's not very warm in here, _____?

h They're lovely, _____?

i He's a good singer, _____?

 01.03 Now listen and check your answers.

 3 01.03 Now practise repeating these conversation starters.

Pay special attention to the falling intonation on the question tags.

Language discovery 2

CONTINUING A CONVERSATION – SHORT ANSWERS

Example from the story

| **Man** | It's hot, isn't it? |
| **Woman** | Yes, it is – very hot. |

'Yes, it is' is a short answer.

Meaning

The woman wants to continue the conversation.

Form

| **Man** | It's hot, isn't it? |
| **Woman** | Yes, it is – very hot. |

Here's a different example:

| **Man** | It's not very nice, is it? |
| **Woman** | No, it isn't. |

> **LANGUAGE TIP**
>
> **Contractions**
> *It's hot, isn't it?*
> *Yes, it is.* (Not: *Yes, it's.*)
> *It's* is the contraction (short form) of *it is*. It is not possible to end a sentence with a positive contraction.
> And in the negative?
> *It isn't very hot, is it?*
> *No, it isn't.*
> This is correct. It is possible to end a sentence with a negative contraction.

Q Can I just say *Yes*?

A *Yes* and *No* alone can sound impolite. It can mean you are not interested in the conversation.

Q The negative has two forms *No, it isn't* and *No, it's not*. Are they different?

A No, they are the same.

1 **Complete the short answers with expressions from the box.**

Example: They aren't here, are they? *No, they aren't.*

1	He's not there, is he?	No, _____
2	She's pretty, isn't she?	Yes, _____
3	This isn't difficult, is it?	No, _____
4	We're ready, aren't we?	Yes, _____
5	You're Paul, aren't you?	Yes, _____
6	They're in France, aren't they?	No, _____

I am   he isn't   it isn't   they aren't   she is   we are

CONTINUING A CONVERSATION – SAYING MORE

▶ It is very common to say more after short answers.

Look at these responses:

A Nice weather, isn't it?

B Yes it is.

OR	Yes, lovely.
OR	Yes, it's lovely.
OR	Yes, it is. It's lovely.
OR	Yes, it is, isn't it?

 2 **01.03 Listen to these conversation starter sentences one more time. Match sentences 1–9 with responses a–i and complete the responses.**

1 It's a very good film, isn't it?

2 You're David, aren't you?

3 The food's very nice, isn't it?

4 This programme's not very interesting, is it?

5 She's beautiful, isn't she?

6 This isn't right, is it?

7 It's not very warm in here, is it?

a Yes, _____ . They're beautiful.

b Yes, _____ . It's delicious.

c No, _____ . Not at all.

d Yes, _____ . I like him a lot.

e Yes, _____ . She's wonderful.

f Yes, it is. It's excellent.

g No, _____ . You're not too good at maths, are you?

8 They're lovely, aren't they?

9 He's a good singer, isn't he?

h Yes, that's right, _____ . And your name is …?

i No, _____ . The window's open.

INVITATIONS AND OFFERS – FOOD AND DRINK

Example from the story

The man suggests a drink.

He says, *Would you like a drink?*

 3 01.04 **Listen and practise your pronunciation and intonation.**

> Would you like a drink?
> W …
> Would …
> Would you …
> Would you like …
> Would you like a …
> Would you like a <u>drink</u>?

'A' OR 'SOME'?

Examples from the story

The man offers a drink. He says, *Would you like a drink?*

The woman chooses some Coke. She says, *Some Coke, please.*

Look at these examples:		
Would you like a sandwich?	a sandwich	singular (one)
Would you like some crisps?	some crisps	plural (more than one)
Would you like some bread?	some bread	uncountable (can't count it)

4 **Write *a* or *some* to complete the sentences.**

    a _____ is for plural things, for example *some grapes, some biscuits*, and for things we can't count, for example _____ *soup*, _____ *rice*.

    b _____ is for singular things, for example _____ *hamburger*, _____ *sandwich*.

5 **Choose the correct number for each picture.**

    1 an ice cream

    2 some ice cream

    3 some ice creams

    4 a cake

5 some cake

6 some cakes

7 a chocolate

8 some chocolate

9 some chocolates

10 a pizza

11 some pizza

12 a Coke

13 some Coke

6 Now write invitations for these pictures.

1 Example:

2

4   3

6   5

8   7

1 Example: Would you like a hamburger?

2 _____

3 _____

4 _____

5 _____

6 _____

7 _____

8 _____

01.05 **Listen and check your answers.**

 7 01.05 **Listen again and practise making these offers.**

> **LANGUAGE TIP**
>
> **Q** Can I say *Do you want a drink?*
> **A** *Do you want ...?*
> The grammar is correct.
> It is very informal.
> You can sound rude.
> Use: *Would you like ...?*
> Say: *Do you want ...?* only with people you know very well.
> **Q** Can I say *Do you like ...?* for offers and invitations?
> **A** No.
> *Do you like ...?* is a general question about likes.
> For example: *Do you like ice cream?* – a general question.
> *Would you like an ice cream?* – an invitation or offer.

OFFERING MORE – FOOD AND DRINK

Look at the table.

First offer	Second offer	
A sandwich?	Another sandwich?	singular
Some crisps?	(Some) more crisps?	plural
Some water?	(Some) more water?	uncountable

8 **Complete these offers with *another* or *more* or *some more*.**

   1 _____ drink?

   2 Would you like _____ / _____ crisps?

   3 _____ wine?

   4 Would you like _____ biscuit?

   5 _____ / _____ milk?

SAYING 'YES' AND 'NO' TO OFFERS

> **SAYING 'YES' AND 'NO' TO OFFERS**
> People say *please* and *thank you* a lot in English.
> It is the norm to say *Yes, please* or *No, thank you* (or *thanks*) to offers.
> *Yes* or *no* alone can sound rude.
> *Thanks* is a little more informal than *thank you*.

9 Look at these examples. Draw one, two or three ☺ symbols for each answer 1–4.

Saying *yes*

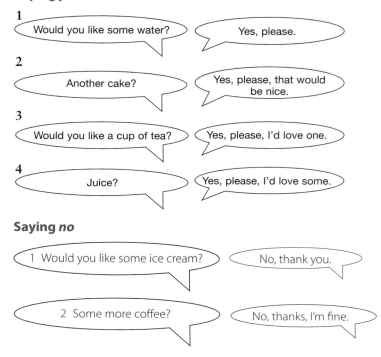

1

Would you like some water?

Yes, please.

2

Another cake?

Yes, please, that would be nice.

3

Would you like a cup of tea?

Yes, please, I'd love one.

4

Juice?

Yes, please, I'd love some.

Saying *no*

1 Would you like some ice cream?

No, thank you.

2 Some more coffee?

No, thanks, I'm fine.

LANGUAGE TIP

Q In an offer, for example *Would you like some tea?*, can I answer, *Yes, I would* or *No, I wouldn't*?
A The grammar is correct but they are not appropriate answers to offers. Say, *Yes, please* and *No, thank you* with offers.

How do you pronounce it?

RISING INTONATION FOR OFFERS; FALLING INTONATION FOR SAYING 'YES' AND 'NO'

01.06 Listen and repeat these offers and answers.

1 **A** Coffee?

   B Yes, please.

2 **A** Some more tea?

   B No, thanks.

3 **A** Would you like another drink?

   B Yes, please.

4 **A** More orange juice?

   B No, no more thank you. I'm fine.

5 **A** Would you like some more bread?

   B Yes, please, I'd love some.

Reading and writing

ABOUT YOU – FOOD AND DRINK

Answer these questions.

1 Are you hungry? Would you like something to eat?

2 What would you like?

3 Are you thirsty? Would you like something to drink?

4 What would you like?

Speaking

What would you say?

Situation 1   You are in the street.

            A person says to you, *Hello Chris*. You are not Chris.

            You say: _____

Situation 2   You are in a coffee shop.

            You want tea, your friend wants coffee.

            The waiter says to you: *Here's your coffee and tea for your friend.*

            You say: _____

Revision

WHAT IS IT IN YOUR LANGUAGE?

Here are some examples of the important points in this unit.

Translate the sentences into your language.

Remember – translate the idea, not the words.

1 It's hot, isn't it?
2 Yes, it is – very hot.
3 Would you like a drink?
4 Yes, please.
5 What would you like?
6 Some Coke, please.

Writing

1 **Write a shopping list of your favourite food and drink.**
Write a minimum of ten things, e.g. cheese, fruit juice.
Note: in a shopping list we don't use *a/an/some*.

2 **What is in your fridge or food cupboard?**

3 **Write a list. This time use *a/an/some* e.g. I've got some milk, a chicken, some eggs ...**

 Speaking

01.07 Now it's your turn to join the conversation.

Listen again to the story conversation at the beginning of the unit.

Say the man's words in the spaces.

 Test yourself

Which one is right?

Choose the correct sentence, a or b.

1 Starting a conversation   **a** Nice day, is it?
                                              b Nice day, isn't it?

2 Offering   **a** Would you like a drink?
                        b Do you like a drink?

    Saying *yes*   **a** Yes, I do.
                        b Yes, please.

3 Starting a conversation   **a** This food's not very hot, isn't it?
                                              b This food's not very hot, is it?

4 Starting a conversation   **a** This soup are delicious.
                                              b This soup's delicious.

    Responding   **a** Yes, it is, isn't it?
                        b Yes, it's.

5 Offering more   **a** Another bread?

                               b Some more bread?

       Saying *no*   **a** No, thanks, I'm fine.

                               b No.

 **Write a dialogue.**

Situation: You are in the street with a friend. It's cold.

You   **Your friend**

1 Start the conversation.

2 Respond.

3 Invite your friend for a drink.

4 Accept the offer.

OK, Let's go then!

SELF-CHECK

I CAN . . .
⚪ . . . start a conversation using a question tag with falling intonation
⚪ . . . continue a conversation using short answers and saying more
⚪ . . . give invitations and offer food and drink using *Would you like* plus *a* or *some*
⚪ . . . offer more food or drink, using *another* . . .? or *(some) more* ...? with rising intonation.

2 Asking for things

In this unit you will learn how to:
- ▶ *respond to offers*
- ▶ *make decisions, using* **I'll ...**
- ▶ *ask for things, using* **Could I have ... ?**
- ▶ *order drinks*
- ▶ *talk about availability, using* **have got**, **there is** *and* **some/any**
- ▶ *ask for and give opinions and make comparisons, using* **What's ... like?**, **smaller**, **more expensive**, *etc.*
- ▶ *ask for permission, using* **Is it all right if I ...?**

VOCABULARY
- ▶ *more food*

PRONUNCIATION
- ▶ *using intonation to sound polite*

CEFR: *Can ask people for things and give people things. Can understand and use familiar everyday expressions aimed at the satisfaction of needs of a concrete type (A1). Can understand sentences and frequently used expressions related to areas of most immediate relevance. Can use simple descriptive language to make brief statements about and compare objects. Can make and respond to suggestions. Can order a meal (A2).*

The story 1

 02.01* *The two passengers would like a drink …*

Listen to the conversation one, two or three times.

Choose the correct answer *Yes* or *No*.

1 The woman wants Coke.   Yes/No
2 The man wants water.   Yes/No
3 The woman wants ice.   Yes/No
4 The woman wants lemon.   Yes/No
5 The man wants ice.   Yes/No
6 The man wants lemon.   Yes/No

Man	Excuse me.
Flight attendant	Yes, sir?
Man	Could I have a Coke and some orange juice, please?
Flight attendant	Of course. Would you like the Coke with ice and lemon?
Woman	Yes, please.
Flight attendant	Ice for you, sir?
Man	No, thanks.
Flight attendant	Here you are. One Coke with ice and lemon and one orange juice.
Man and woman	Thank you./Thanks.

* For an American English version, listen to **11.02**.

Listening and reading 1

Cover the text of the story conversation.

Read the sentences.

 02.01 Listen and complete the words.

Then read the text of the story conversation to check your answers.

1 **The man wants the attention of the flight attendant.**

   He says, *E _ _ _ _ _ _ / m _.*

2 **The man asks for the drinks.**

   He says, *C _ _ _ _ _ / I / h _ _ _ _ / _ / Coke and / s _ _ _ _ / o _ a _ _ _ _ / j _ i c _, /*
   please?

3 **The flight attendant gives them the drinks.**

   He says, *H _ _ _ _ / y _ _ / a _ _ /. O _ _ / Coke with ice and lemon and / _ _ _ _ /*
   orange juice.

ATTRACTING ATTENTION

▶ In English we say *Excuse me* to attract attention.
Other ways, for example a sound like *ts, ts, ts*, are impolite.

Ⓥ Vocabulary builder

MORE FOOD

Label pictures a–f with the food names. Use your dictionary if necessary.

fish

chicken

beef

lamb

vegetarian

pork

The story 2

  02.02* *The flight attendant serves dinner to eight passengers.*

Listen to the conversation one, two or three times.

Choose the correct answer.

Passenger **1**	**a** chicken	**b** beef	
Passenger **2**	**a** beef	**b** vegetarian	
Passenger **3**	**a** fish	**b** pork	
Passenger **4**	**a** lamb	**b** fish	
Passenger **5**	**a** fish	**b** beef	
Passenger **6**	**a** fish	**b** beef	
Passenger **7**	**a** vegetarian	**b** chicken	
Passenger **8**	**a** fish	**b** chicken	**c** a sandwich

1	**Attendant**	Chicken or beef, sir?
	Passenger	Chicken, please.
2	**Attendant**	Beef or vegetarian, madam?
	Passenger	Beef for me, please.
3	**Attendant**	Would you like fish or pork, sir?
	Passenger	I'd like fish, please.
4	**Attendant**	What would you like to eat, madam, fish or lamb?
	Passenger	Could I have the lamb, please?
5	**Attendant**	Is it fish or beef for you, madam?
	Passenger	I'll have beef, please.
6	**Attendant**	And for you, sir?
	Passenger	The same for me too, please.
7	**Attendant**	Would you like vegetarian or chicken, sir?
	Passenger	I don't mind. I like both.
8	**Attendant**	Would you like fish or chicken, madam?
	Passenger	Nothing for me, thanks. I'm not very hungry. Could I have a sandwich instead?
	Attendant	Of course.

* For an American English version, listen to **11.03**.

Listening, reading and speaking

RESPONDING TO OFFERS – FOOD AND DRINK

1 **Complete the conversation.**

 Cover the text of the story conversation.

 Read the dialogues.

 02.02 **Listen and complete the words.**

 Then read the text of the story 2 conversation (passengers 1–5) to check your answers.

1	**Attendant**	Chicken or beef, sir?
	Passenger	Chicken, / p _ _ _ _ _.
2	**Attendant**	Beef or vegetarian, madam?
	Passenger	Beef / f _ _ / m _,/ please.
3	**Attendant**	Would you like fish or pork, sir?
	Passenger	I'_ / l _ _ _ / fish, please.
4	**Attendant**	What would you like to eat, madam, fish or lamb?
	Passenger	C _ _ _ _ / I / h _ _ _ / the lamb, please?
5	**Attendant**	Is it fish or beef for you, madam?
	Passenger	I'_ _ / h _ _ _ _ / beef, please.

2 02.02 **Now listen again to Passengers 1–5 and practise repeating these responses to offers.**

LANGUAGE TIP

Flight attendants and other people who work with food and drink don't always say *some*. They say *Tea?*, *Chicken?*, *Fish or beef?*, etc. for offers. This is practical and short.

Language discovery 1

RESPONDING TO OFFERS

Read the text of the story 2 conversation again for passengers 1–5.

1 Asking for the same.

Complete the sentence.

In the mini dialogues in the story, Passenger 5 wants beef.

Passenger 6 wants beef, too.

Passenger 5 says *I'll have beef, please.*

Passenger 6 says, *T _ _ / s _ _ _ _ / f _ _ / m _ / t _ _, please.*

2 Using the verb *mind*.

The flight attendant asks Passenger 7, *Would you like vegetarian or chicken, sir?*

He says, *I don't mind …*

Choose the correct meaning, a, b or c.

a He wants vegetarian.

b He wants chicken.

c It isn't important. He likes vegetarian and chicken.

3 Saying *no*; talking about alternatives.

Complete the sentences.

▶ The flight attendant asks Passenger 8, *Would you like fish or chicken, madam?* She isn't hungry. She says, *N _ _ _ _ _ _ _ / f _ _ / m _, thanks. I'm not very hungry. Could I have a sandwich i _ _ _ _ _ _?*

MAKING DECISIONS USING 'I'LL'

Example from the story

The flight attendant asks Passenger 5, *Is it fish or beef for you, madam?* The passenger says, *I'll have beef, please.*

LANGUAGE TIP
When you decide and speak, say *I'll ...*

4 Make decisions in these situations.

1 Would you like Coke or fruit juice?

_____'_____ / _____ fruit juice, please.

2 Which cake would you like, fruit or chocolate?

_____'_____ / _____ a slice of the chocolate one, please.

3 It's lunchtime … I think _____'_____ / _____ some bread and cheese.

4 Are you tired?

Yes, I think _____'_____ go to bed.

5 The supermarket is closed now. _____'_____ / _____ tomorrow.

LANGUAGE TIP

Negative decisions

Situation: It's time to go to work but you feel terrible. You decide to stay at home.

I don't think   **I'll** go to work. ✓

↑   ↑

Negative   Positive

NOT: **I think**   **I won't** go to work. ✗

↑   ↑

Positive   Negative

Put the negative with *think*, not with *I'll*.

ASKING FOR THINGS USING *COULD I HAVE …?*

Example from the story

The man in Story 1 asks for the drinks. He says, *Could I have a Coke and some orange juice, please?*

In Unit 1 we look at *a/an* and *some* with offers.

For example, *Would you like some coffee?*

▶ The use of *a/an* and *some* is the same for both offers and requests.

▶ *Please* is very common when you ask for something.

Look at the examples:

Singular

Offer	Would you like **a cup of coffee**?
Request	Could ⎫ I have **a cup of coffee**, please?
	Can ⎭

Plural

Offer	Would you like **some biscuits**?
Request	Could ⎫ I have **some biscuits**, please?
	Can ⎭

Uncountables

Offer	Would you like **some fruit juice**?
Request	Could ⎫ I have **some fruit juice**, please?
	Can ⎭

5 Complete the requests. Put the words in the right order.

1 A Would you like a drink?
   B Yes, _____, please?
      have/I/coffee/some/could

2 A Would you like something to eat?
   B Yes, _____, please?
      sandwich/have/can/I/a

3 A What would you like to drink?
   B _____, please?
      have/something/we/can/cold

4 A Would you like some pizza?
   B Yes, _____, please?
      slice/have/I/could/small/a

5 A Excuse me, _____, please?
      a/water/I/glass/could/have/of

6 A Would you like some grapes or some strawberries?
   B _____, please?
      grapes/could/have/I/some

LANGUAGE TIP

Q What's the difference between *Could I have …?* and *Can I have …?*
A The grammar in both is correct.
Could I …? is always appropriate.
Can I …? is a little informal.
Give me … The imperative can be impolite. Use it only in informal situations and with people you know well. (See Unit 9.)

ORDERING DRINKS

It is common to omit *cup* and *glass* when you order drinks.

6 Situation: You work in a coffee shop.

 02.03 Listen to three customers ordering drinks. What would they like? Write their orders.

 # How do you pronounce it?

USING INTONATION TO SOUND POLITE

▶ Intonation is important with requests.
▶ A big fall sounds polite.
▶ Flat intonation can sound rude.

 1 02.04 Listen to these requests. You will hear each one twice.

Listen to the fall on the syllable with stress. One is rude (flat intonation) and one is polite (big fall).

Choose *R* for rude (flat intonation) ➘ or *P* for polite (big fall) ➘.

a Could I have some <u>co</u>ffee, please?
  1 R/P   **2** R/P
b Yes, can I have a <u>sand</u>wich, please?
  1 R/P   **2** R/P
c Can we have something <u>cold</u>, please?
  1 R/P   **2** R/P
d Could I have a <u>small</u> piece, please?
  1 R/P   **2** R/P
e Excuse me, could I have a glass of <u>water</u>, please?
  1 R/P   **2** R/P
f Could I have some <u>grapes</u>, please?
  1 R/P   **2** R/P

2 02.05 Now listen and repeat the request.

Pay special attention to the big fall on *Coke*.

Could …
Could I …
Could I have …
Could I have some …
Could I have some <u>Coke</u> …
Could I have some <u>Coke</u>, please?

3 Now write requests for these food and drink items. Find the syllable where there should be a polite fall.

1 Could _____ , please?
2 _____
3 _____
4 _____
5 _____

 02.06 Now listen and check your answers.

 4 02.06 Listen again and practise making these requests.

Pay special attention to the big fall on the syllables with stress.

The story 3

 02.07* *The flight attendant serves drinks.*

What drinks would these three passengers like?

Listen to the conversations one, two or three times.

Write the drink each passenger chooses.

Are their requests possible? Choose *Yes* or *No* for each one.

Attendant	Would you like a drink with your dinner? I've got some apple juice.
Passenger 1	Yes, please.
Attendant	What would you like to drink with your dinner, sir?
Passenger 2	Have you got any cold beer?
Attendant	Of course … Here you are.
Passenger 3	Could I have some white wine, please?
Attendant	I'm sorry, madam. I haven't got any more white wine. Would you like red instead?

Passenger 1   Yes/No

Passenger 2   Yes/No

Passenger 3   Yes/No

* For an American English version, listen to **11.04**.

 ## Language discovery 2

TALKING ABOUT AVAILABILITY USING *HAVE GOT*

1 Complete the sentences.

  Cover the text of the story 3 conversation.

  Read the sentences.

02.07 Listen again and complete the words.

Then read the text of the story 3 and check your answers.

Flight attendant	I'__ __ / g __ __ / some apple juice.
Passenger 2	H __ __ __ / y __ __ / g __ __ / any cold beer?
Flight attendant	I h __ __ __ __ '__ / g __ __ / any more white wine.

Form

2 Complete the table with the correct form of *have got*.

Grammar summary – *have got*			
Positive			
I/you/ we/they	have *or* 've	got	a drink.
He/she/ it	has *or* 's	got	
Negative			
I/you/we/ they	_____	got	a drink.
He/she/it	_____	got	
Question			
_____	I/you/we/ they	got	a drink?
_____	he/she/it	got	

Question tags				Short answers			
I You We They	've got a drink,	_____	I? we? you? they?	Yes,	I you we they	_____	
He She It	's got a drink,	_____	he? she? it?	Yes,	he she it	_____	
I You We They	haven't got a drink,	_____	I? you? we? they?	No,	I you we they	_____	
He She It	hasn't got a drink,	_____	he? she? it?	No,	he she it	_____	

3 Complete the sentences with the correct parts of *have got*. Use the table to help you.

1 A   What sort of drinks have you got?

    B   I'__ __ / g __ __ / water, juice, beer or wine.

2 A   Could I have chicken, please?

    B   I'm sorry, we __ __ __ __ __' __ / __ __ __ / any more chicken.

3 A   If you're hungry, I'__ __ / g __ __ / a pizza.

    B   H __ __ __ / y __ __ ? Could I have some now, please?

4 A   __ __ __ he __ __ __ any milk for the coffee?

    B   Yes, he __ __ __ __. Here it is.

5 A We __ __ __ __ __'__ / __ __ __ any bread.

B H __ __ __ __'__ / __ __ ? OK, I'll go and buy some.

6 A I __ __ __ __ __'t / __ __ __ chicken but I'__ __ / __ __ __ lamb.

B No, thanks. Can I have a sandwich, instead, please?

7 A They'__ __ / g __ __ / Coke, h __ __ __ __'t / they?

B Yes, I'll ask for some.

8 A Why __ __ __ __'__ he / __ __ __ / any rice?

B I don't know.

TALKING ABOUT AVAILABILITY USING *THERE IS/THERE ARE*

 4 02.08 Listen to these six mini dialogues. Write the food or drink, and choose *Yes, No* or *We don't know*.

1 A What is there to drink?

B There's some beer, if you like.

2 A Is there any bread?

B Yes, it's in the cupboard.

3 A There isn't any cheese!

B Yes, I know. I'll get some later.

4 A There are some biscuits in the tin, aren't there?

B I'm not sure.

5 A Are there any crisps?

B Sorry.

6 A There aren't any grapes.

B Yes, there are. They're in the fridge.

Name of food/drink	Have they got it?
1 _____	Yes/No/We don't know
2 _____	Yes/No/We don't know
3 _____	Yes/No/We don't know
4 _____	Yes/No/We don't know
5 _____	Yes/No/We don't know
6 _____	Yes/No/We don't know

Grammar summary – availability: *there is, there are, some, any*		
With a singular noun e.g. *book*	With an uncountable noun e.g. *water*	With a plural noun e.g. *grapes*
Positive		
There's/There is a ...	There's/There is some …	There are some … (no contraction)
Negative		
There isn't a … .	There isn't any … .	There aren't any …
Question		
Is there a … ?	Is there any … ?	Are there any … ?

Question tag		
There's a …, isn't there? There isn't a …, is there?	There's some …, isn't there? There isn't any …, is there?	There are some …, aren't there? There aren't any …, are there?
Short answers		
Yes, there is.* No, there isn't.	Yes, there is.* No, there isn't.	Yes, there are. * No, there aren't.

* ~~Yes, there's.~~ ✗ Positive contraction at end of sentence is not possible.

Practice

1 Complete these sentences with *some* or *any*.

  1 I've got _____ wine but there isn't _____ beer.

  2 A Is there _____ more pizza?

     B No, but there's _____ bread.

  3 A Are there _____ hamburgers?

     B No, but there are _____ sandwiches.

  4 A Have you got _____ biscuits?

     B No, and there isn't _____ chocolate either.

  5 A Is there _____ soup?

     B Sorry, I haven't got _____ more.

2 Situation: You're at home with a friend. It's time to eat.

  Put this dialogue in the correct order.

  Use your dictionary if necessary.

  a Actually, I don't drink alcohol, so could I have some Coke, fruit juice or something like that instead, please? _____

  b I really don't mind. I like all vegetables. _____

  c What would you like to eat? There's chicken or I've got some beef, too. _*1*_

  d We've got some apple juice in the fridge. Could you get it for me? _____

  e And would you like something to drink? I've got some wine if you'd like some. _____

  f I'd like some chicken, please. _____

  g Of course. Here you are. _____

  h With peas or carrots? _____

The story 4

 02.09 *The passengers have dinner. The flight attendant talks to a passenger.*

Read the sentences and choose *True* or *False*.

1	The chicken isn't good.	True/False
2	More passengers eat beef.	True/False
3	More passengers eat chicken.	True/False
4	The passenger wants to try the beef.	True/False
5	The passenger wants to try the chicken.	True/False

Passenger	This fish isn't very nice at all. What's the chicken like?
Attendant	I think it's very good.
Passenger	Nicer than the beef?
Attendant	I think so, but the beef is more popular. Beef is always the most popular dish on the plane.
Passenger	Could I change this fish then, please? Is it all right if I have a different dinner?
Attendant	Of course. What would you like instead?
Passenger	Can I try the chicken, please, if that's OK?

* For an American English version, listen to **11.05**.

 # Listening and reading 2

Cover the text of the story 4 conversation.

Read the sentences.

 02.09 Listen and try to complete the words.

Then read the text of the story 4 to check your answers.

1 The passenger isn't happy with the fish.
She says, *This fish / i __ __'__ / very nice/ a __ / a __ __.*

2 She wants an opinion about the chicken.
She says *W __ __ __'s / the chicken / l __ __ __ ?*

3 The flight attendant thinks it's very good.
The passenger asks for a comparison with the beef.
She says, *N __ __ __ __ / t __ __ __ / the beef?*

4 The flight attendant thinks *yes.*
She says, *I think / s __.*

5 But the passengers eat more beef.
Beef is m __ __ __ / p __ __ __ __ __ __ than chicken. In fact, beef is t __ __ / m __ __ __ / p __ __ __ __ __ __ dish on the plane.

University Hospitals of Derby and Burton NHS Foundation Trust Library and Knowledge Service

6 a The passenger wants to change the fish.

He says, *C _ _ _ _ / I / change this fish then, please?*

b He wants to have another dinner.

He says, *I _ / i _ / a _ _ / _ _ _ t / i _ / I have a different dinner?*

c He would like to try the chicken.

He says, *C _ _ / I / try the chicken, please, if that's OK?*

💡 Language discovery 3

OPINIONS AND COMPARISONS

Example from the story

The passenger asks for an opinion about the chicken.

She says, *What's the chicken like?*

The attendant thinks the chicken is nicer than the beef, but beef is more popular than chicken. In fact, beef is the most popular dish on the plane.

Form

Grammar summary – comparisons
Comparing two
Short adjectives ➜ adjective + er + than ➜ *nicer than*   Long adjectives ➜ *more* + adjective + *than* ➜ *more popular than*
Comparing three or more
Short adjective ➜ *the* + adjective +*est* ➜ *the nicest*   Long adjectives ➜ *the* + *most* + adjective ➜ *the most popular*

> **COMMON MISTAKE**
>
> *Tea is the most popular drink in Britain.* ✓
> Not, *Tea is the ~~more~~ popular drink in Britain.* ✗
> To compare three or more, say *the most* or *the ...est.*

1 Complete these sentences. Use the table to help you, if necessary.

1 A How big is London?

B Well, it's b _ gg _ _ / t _ _ _ New York.

2 A Which is the t _ _ _ _ _ _ building in the world?

B That's the Burj Khalifa Tower in Dubai, isn't it?

3 Which is m _ _ _ / difficult, understanding English or speaking it?

4 He's t _ _ / m _ _ _ / interesting person I know!

ASKING FOR PERMISSION

Examples from the story

The passenger wants to change the fish, have a different dinner and try the chicken.

He says, *Could I change this fish then, please?*

Is it all right if I have a different dinner?

Can I try the chicken instead?

The flight attendant responds: *Of course.*

2 You are in a friend's house. Ask for permission in these situations.

    1 You want to use the phone.

    2 You want to use the toilet.

    3 You want to smoke.

    4 You want to have some more bread.

    5 You want to watch TV.

SAYING 'YES' AND 'NO' TO REQUESTS

The attendant says: *Of course.*

Another response: *Yes, go ahead.*

Negative responses: *I'm sorry but* + reason.

For example: *I'm sorry but my mother's on the phone at the moment.*

3 Complete these mini dialogues.

    1 A Is it all right if we go later?

       B Yes, o __ / c __ __ __ __ __.

    2 A Can I invite my friend?

       B I'm s __ __ __ __. We've only got three tickets.

    3 A Could I read your magazine?

       B Yes, g __ / a __ __ __ __.

    4 A Is it all right if I borrow your car?

       B I'__ / __ __ __ __ __. I don't think that's possible.

FOOD AND DRINK

The most popular drinks in Britain are tea and coffee. Favourite alcoholic drinks are beer and wine.

Coffee shops are very popular for meeting friends and having a snack, especially a light lunch, such as a sandwich or salad; many offer Wi-Fi.

The traditional English dish ('a roast') is commonly eaten on Sundays at lunchtime, at home or at a pub. This consists of meat cooked in the oven (beef, pork, chicken, etc.) roast potatoes and vegetables with gravy. It is often followed by a traditional dessert (pudding) such as trifle.

Fast food – from the traditional 'fish and chips' to international dishes such as curry, Chinese meals or pizza – is very popular. Most fast-food places offer a takeaway service and many offer home delivery. There are also a large number of restaurants and bars offering international food.

Most restaurants offer at least one vegetarian option and some offer locally sourced and/or organic food.

 Writing

ABOUT YOUR COUNTRY – FOOD AND DRINK

Write answers to the questions.

Use your dictionary to help you.

Write complete sentences if possible.

1 What is the most common drink in your country?
2 What is the most common food? Is it served with rice, potatoes, pasta, etc.?
3 Write about the traditional drinks and dishes in your country.
4 When is the biggest meal of the day – at midday or in the evening?
5 Write about your favourite meal.

Speaking

What would you say?

Situation 1 You are a customer in a coffee shop.

Another customer says to you, *Excuse me, could I have two teas, please?*

You say: _____

Situation 2 In a restaurant

You ask the waiter for chicken. Then your friend says, *Oh the chicken here isn't very nice at all but the beef's wonderful.*

Now you want beef. Talk to the waiter.

You say: _____

Revision

WHAT IS IT IN YOUR LANGUAGE?

Here are some examples of the important points in this unit.

Translate the sentences into your language.

Remember – translate the idea, not the words.

1 **A** Excuse me, could I have some bread, please?
   B Of course, here you are.
2 **A** Beer or wine?
   B I don't mind. I like both.
3 **A** I've got some coffee but I haven't got any milk.
   B There's some milk in the fridge, isn't there?
4 **A** Is it all right if I use your toilet, please?
   B Yes, go ahead.
5 One tea and two coffees, please.

 Writing

---

✉	←REPLY	≪←REPLY ALL	🖉	

1   Dear (your friend's name),

    I'm _____ a _____ with _____ at home next
    _____ .

2   I _____ but I _____ . I _____ tomorrow.

3   _____

4   _____
    _____
    _____

5   _____
    _____

6   Until tomorrow,
    _____

You live in a small flat and you are planning a party. Complete this email to your good friend who lives in the house next door.

1 Greet your friend and say you are planning a party.

2 Write some food and drinks that you have got at home and one thing you haven't got. You decide to buy it tomorrow.

3 There's a small problem – you haven't got any wine glasses. Ask to borrow some from your friend.

4 If lots of your friends decide to come, your flat will be very small. Say this and ask whether you can have the party in your friend's house, if necessary. Compare the size of his/her house and your flat.

5 You decide to call your friend tomorrow and talk about the party.

6 End your message and say goodbye.

 Speaking

Now it's your turn to join the conversation.

🎧 **02.10 Listen again to the story 1 conversation.**
Say the man's words in the spaces.

Test yourself

Which one is right?

Choose the correct sentence, a or b.

1 In a restaurant.
   a Please, please, a Coke.
   b Excuse me, could I have a Coke, please?

2 I'll make you a cup of tea.
   a Is it all right if I have water instead, please?
   b Is it possible I have water in the place of tea?

3 Would you like some white wine or red?
   a Red for me, please.
   b Red to me, please.

4 Fruit juice or lemonade?
   a I don't mind.
   b I'm not mind.

5 **a** I think I go to the supermarket later.
   b I think I'll go to the supermarket later.

6 **a** Could I have some biscuits, please?
   b Could I have any biscuits, please?

7 **a** I haven't got some beer.
   b I haven't got any beer.

8 **a** There isn't any more cake, is there?
   b There isn't any more cake, isn't it?

9 **a** Would you like something for drink?
   b Would you like something to drink?

10 **a** Which test is the more difficult in the book?
   b Which test is the most difficult in the book?

 **Write a dialogue.**

Situation: You are in a restaurant with a friend. It is the end of the meal.

You	Your friend / the waiter
1 Offer your friend tea or coffee.	**2** Your friend wants coffee.

3 You would like coffee too. Call the waiter and order. You'd like some ice cream but it's not on the menu. Ask.

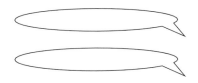

4 The waiter hasn't got any ice cream.

5 He gives you the coffee.

(Ten minutes later . . .)

6 Offer your friend more coffee.

7 Your friend says *no*.

8 Call the waiter and ask for the bill.

(The waiter brings the bill.)

9 Check if it's possible to pay by card.

10 The waiter says *yes*.

SELF-CHECK

I CAN . . .

- ○ . . . respond to offers
- ○ . . . make decisions, using *I'll . . .*
- ○ . . . ask for things, using *Could I have . . . ?*
- ○ . . . order drinks
- ○ . . . talk about availability, using *have got, there is* and *some/any*.
- ○ . . . ask for and give opinions and make comparisons, using *What's . . . like?* and *smaller, more expensive*, etc.
- ○ . . . ask for and give permission using *Is it all right if I . . .?*
- ○ . . . make requests using intonation with a big fall to sound polite.

3 Making conversation

In this unit, you will learn how to:
▶ *talk about everyday activities, using the present simple*
▶ *talk about ability, using* **can**
▶ *express interest, using echo questions.*

VOCABULARY
▶ *countries, nationalities and language*

PRONUNCIATION
▶ *can* **and** *can't;* **intonation: expressing interest with echo questions; stress with**
countries, nationalities and languages

CEFR: *Can understand and use familiar everyday expressions aimed at the satisfaction of needs of a concrete type (A1). Can understand sentences and frequently used expressions related to areas of most immediate relevance and describe family, other people and present or most recent job. Can establish social contact. Can cope with follow-up questions. Can explain what he likes or dislikes (A2).*

The story

03.01* *The conversation on the plane continues …*

Listen to the conversation one, two or three times.

Note ALL the correct answers.

They talk about
- **a** countries
- **b** their families
- **c** nationalities
- **d** their names
- **e** languages.

Woman	Where are you from?
Man	I'm English. And you?
Woman	I'm from England, too.
Man	Oh, really? But your book isn't in English.
Woman	Well, actually, I live in South America, in Uruguay, and so I speak Spanish.
Man	Do you? That's interesting!
Woman	Yes, I like it there. How about you? Do you speak any foreign languages?
Man	I can speak a bit of French.
Woman	Can you?
Man	Yes, I use it in my job sometimes – but I'm not really very good at it.
Woman	Oh, aren't you? I really like languages.

* For an American English version, listen to **11.06**.

 ## Listening and reading

1 Listen and choose.
   Cover the text of the story conversation.
   Read the sentences.

 03.01 Listen and choose *Yes*, *No* or *We don't know*.

Then read the text of the story conversation to check your answers.

1	The woman is English.	Yes/No/We don't know
2	The man's English.	Yes/No/We don't know
3	She speaks Spanish.	Yes/No/We don't know
4	She uses her foreign language in her job.	Yes/No/We don't know
5	She lives in London.	Yes/No/We don't know
6	He lives in London.	Yes/No/We don't know
7	He can speak a little French.	Yes/No/We don't know

8 He uses his foreign language in his job. Yes/No/We don't know

9 Languages are easy for him. Yes/No/We don't know

10 She's interested in languages. Yes/No/We don't know

2 Listen, read and complete.

Cover the text of the story conversation again.

Read the sentences.

🎧 **03.01 Listen and complete the words.**

Then read the text of the story conversation to check your answers.

  a The woman asks, *W _ _ _ _ _ / a _ _ / y _ _ / f _ _ _ _?*

  b The man answers, *I' _ / E _ _ _ _ _ _ _ _.*

  c The woman says *I' _ / f _ _ _ _ / E _ _ _ _ _ _ _ _ , / t _ _.*

3 Asking questions; expressing interest.

🎧 **03.01 Listen to the story again and complete these sentences.**

Then read the text of the story conversation to check your answers.

  a The woman says, *I'm from England.*
  The man is interested. He says, *Oh, r _ _ _ _ _ _?*

  b The woman says, *Actually, I / l _ _ _ _ / in South America, in Uruguay.*
  The man is interested. He says, *D _ / y _ _?*

  c The woman asks about languages.
  She says, *D _ / y _ _ / s _ _ _ _ _ / any / f _ r _ i _ n / l _ n g _ a _ e s?*
  The man answers.
  I / c _ _ _ / s _ _ _ _ _ / a / b _ _ _ / o _ / F _ _ _ _ _ h.
  The woman is interested. She says, *C _ _ _ / y _ _?*

4 Read the text of the story again and complete the sentences.

  1 Asking the same question.

  a The woman asks: *Where are you from?*
  The man doesn't ask, *Where are you from?* He asks, *A _ _ _ / y _ _ _?*

  b The woman says, *I speak Spanish.*
  She doesn't ask the man, *Do you speak Spanish?* She asks, *H _ _ _ / a _ _ _ _ _ / y _ _?*

  2 Making conversation.
  The woman says, *I speak Spanish.*
  Then she says, *A _ _ _ _ _ _ y, I live in South America.*

  3 The man doesn't speak French very well.
  He says, *I speak a bit of French … but I'm not very good / _ _ _ / it.*

> **LANGUAGE TIP**
>
> *And you? How about you?*
> Here, these two questions mean the same.
> You can use both questions with all tenses.
> The structure of the questions is always the same.

Practice

1 Asking about the same topic – *And you? How about you?*

Complete these dialogues.

1 A What's your name?

 B I'm Sam. _____ ?

 A My name's …

2 A I'm cold. _____ ?

 B I'm all right, actually.

3 A Here's the coffee bar. I'd like something cold to drink. _____ ?

 B I think I'll have the same.

2 Making conversation – *actually*

Make mini dialogues. Match 1–5 below with a–e.

1 Terrible weather, isn't it?	**a**	Yes, actually the food here is always good.
2 Are you Japanese?	**b**	I don't mind, actually. I like both.
3 Tea or coffee?	**c**	Yes, I'm from Tokyo, actually.
4 Where is he?	**d**	Yes, it is actually, isn't it?
5 This is really delicious!	**e**	Actually, I'm not sure.

LANGUAGE TIP

Actually

Actually makes the sentence less direct. The British welcome indirectness.

Foreign speakers of English can sometimes use *actually* wrongly:

Situation: A tourist in Europe.

   Actually I am in Paris. ✗ Tomorrow I fly to Madrid.

In some languages *actually* means *now, at the moment*.

In English *actually* is not about time.

Language discovery 1

EVERYDAY ACTIVITIES – PRESENT SIMPLE

Examples from the story

   a The woman says, *I live in South America*.

   b The man says, *I use my French in my job sometimes*.

Meaning

In sentence a) the present simple is for permanent situations.

In sentence b) the present simple is for repeated actions.

Form

Positive				
I You We They	work.		He/she/it	works.

Questions				
Do	I you we they	work?	Does he/she/it	work?

Negative				
I You We They	don't work. (do not)		He/she/it	doesn't work.

Short answers					
	Positive		**Negative**		
Yes,	I you we they	do.	No,	I you we they	don't.
	he/she/it	does.		he/she/it	doesn't.

Question tags					
I You We They	work, don't	I? you? we? they?	I You We They	don't work, do	I? you? we? they?
He She It	works, doesn't	he? she? it?	He She It	doesn't work, does	he? she? it?

1 Complete the sentences about the two passengers.

Use the table to help you, if necessary.

    1 I speak Spanish.   She _____ Spanish.

    2 I live in South America.   She _____ in South America.

    3 I like it there.   She _____ it there.

    4 I use French in my job   He _____ French in his job
       sometimes.   sometimes.

2 Complete the questions and answers about the two passengers. Look at the table and use the information from the story.

Example: Does she speak Spanish? Yes, she does.

1 _____ she live in South America? _____

2 _____ she like it there? _____

3 _____ the man speak Spanish? _____

4 _____ he speak French? _____

5 _____ he live in South America? _____

6 _____ they work together? _____

Now answer the following two questions about you.

7 Do you speak Spanish? _____

8 Do you speak French? _____

ABILITY – *CAN*

Example from the story

The woman asks about languages. He says, *I can speak a bit of French*. She's interested. She says, *Can you?*

Meaning

Here, *can* is for ability.

Form

Positive		
I You He/she/it We They	can	eat fish.

Questions		
Can	I you he/she/it we they	eat fish?

Negative		
I You He/she/it We They	can't	eat fish.

Short answers						
	Positive			**Negative**		
Yes,	I you he/she/it we they		can.	No,	I you he/she/it we they	can't.

Question tags							
I You He/ she/ it We They	can eat fish, can't	I? you? he/she/it? we? they?	I You He/ she/it We They	can't eat fish, can	I? you? he/she/it? we? they?		

Common mistakes – *can*

He can speak French.

NOT ~~*He can to speak French.*~~ ✗

Can you speak English?

NOT ~~*Can you to speak English?*~~ ✗

OR ~~*Do you can speak English?*~~ ✗

 3 **03.02 Listen and complete these questions and short answers.**

   1 The man _____ / _____ French but he _____ / _____ Spanish.

   2 _____ the woman _____ Spanish? Yes, _____ / _____ .

   3 _____ they both _____ English? Yes, they're English.

   4 About you: I _____ / _____ some English.

 How do you pronounce it? (1)

CAN* AND *CAN'T

  ▶ The vowel *a* in *can* has two different pronunciations, one weak / / and one strong / æ /.

  ▶ The vowel *a* in *can't* / a: / is different from the two pronunciations of *a* in *can*.

 1 **03.02 Listen to the sentences again.**

This time pay attention to the pronunciation of *can*. Can you hear three different vowel sounds for the *a*?

Then read 1, 2, 3 to check.

   1 weak *can* /ə/ (*can* is not the most important word in the sentence):

     a The man can speak French.

     b Can the woman speak Spanish?

     c Can they both speak English?

     d I can speak some English.

2 strong *can* / æ / (*can* is the important word):

   a Yes, she can.

3 Negative *can't* / a: / (The negative doesn't change. The vowel is the same as in *car*):

   a He can't speak Spanish.

Q Why is this pronunciation important?

A Because if you say strong *can* instead of weak *can*, sometimes people hear *can't*.

 2 **03.02 Listen again and repeat the sentences.**

Pay special attention to *can/can't*.

 # Language discovery 2

EXPRESSING INTEREST – ECHO QUESTIONS AND *REALLY?*

Examples from the story

1 The woman says, *I'm from England, too.*
The man is interested. He says, *Really?*

2 The woman says, *I live in South America.*
The man is interested. He says, *Oh, do you?*

3 The man says, *I can speak a bit of French.*
The woman is interested. She says, *Oh, can you?*

Form

Echo questions use auxiliary (*do*, *can*, etc.) + subject. Or you can use the response *Really?*, as in Example 1. In Examples 2 and 3, another possible answer is *Oh, really?*

1 Read the sentences and choose *Yes* or *No*.

1 It is always possible to use *Really?*	Yes/No
2 We use echo questions to express interest.	Yes/No
3 If the verb in the first sentence is positive, the echo question is negative.	Yes/No
4 You can use *really* with all tenses. It doesn't change.	Yes/No

 # How do you pronounce it? (2)

INTONATION – EXPRESSING INTEREST, ECHO QUESTIONS

▶ To express interest, intonation is important.

▶ A big fall and a little rise in the voice expresses interest.

▶ A small fall or a flat tone of voice expresses little or no interest.

a   **b**

a very interested   **b** not interested

03.03 Listen to these echo questions.

You will hear each echo question twice: a then b.

One expresses interest (intonation with big fall and small rise) and one is not interested (intonation flat/small fall)

Write *I* for *interested* or *NI* for *not interested*.

Example: 1 a *NI*

1	**a**	Really?	**b**	Really?
2	**a**	Do you?	**b**	Do you?
3	**a**	Can't she?	**b**	Can't she?
4	**a**	Is it?	**b**	Is it?
5	**a**	Does he?	**b**	Does he?
6	**a**	Aren't you?	**b**	Aren't you?

Speaking

EXPRESSING INTEREST WITH ECHO QUESTIONS AND CONTINUING THE CONVERSATION

1 Express your interest.

Read the sentences.

First show your interest by choosing the correct short question from Box 1.

Then choose a sentence from Box 2 to continue the conversation.

Example: His new song is really good. *Is it? What's it called?*

1 I can play the guitar.

2 My brother's new job's very interesting.

3 My father lives in the States.

4 My children don't like ice cream.

5 I'm thirsty.

6 Sue's not here today.

7 I like this cold weather.

8 Jessica can't drive.

9 I don't drink tea.

10 I'm not very well.

Box 1

Are you?	Oh, can you?
Don't you?	Isn't she?
Do you?	Does he?
Can't she?	Aren't you?
Don't they?	Is it?

Box 2

What's the matter?

So, how does she get to work?

What does he do?

I prefer the summer myself.

What sort of music do you play?

Isn't that her, over there?

I have about five cups a day.

Whereabouts?

Would you like something to drink?

It's very popular in my house.

 03.04 **Now listen and check your answers.**

 2 03.04 **Now listen again to Person A in the mini dialogues and respond.**
Remember to show your interest with your intonation.

Very interested   Not very interested

Example: Can you?   Can you?

Ⓥ Vocabulary builder

COUNTRIES, NATIONALITIES AND LANGUAGES

Match these countries, nationalities and languages.
Use your dictionary, if necessary.

> **LANGUAGE TIP**
> All countries, nationalities and languages begin with a capital letter in English.

Country	**Nationality**	**Language**
a Spain	**1** Polish	**A** English
b Japan	**2** Spanish	**B** Spanish
c the United States	**3** Mexican	**C** Polish
d Italy	**4** Portuguese	**D** German
e Portugal	**5** Australian	**E** Chinese
f Egypt	**6** Brazilian	**F** Portuguese
g China	**7** American	**G** Japanese
h Australia	**8** English	**H** Arabic
i Mexico	**9** Italian	**I** French
j England	**10** Egyptian	**J** Italian
k Poland	**11** Japanese	
l Brazil	**12** Chinese	
m Germany	**13** French	
n France	**14** German	

How do you pronounce it?

COUNTRIES – STRESS

 1 **03.05 Where's the stress?**

Read the names of the countries in the box.

Look at the stress patterns below the box. Each syllable has a circle. A large black circle means that the stress is on that syllable, e.g. Norway = ●○

Listen and write each country under the correct stress pattern.

the United States	Italy	Japan	Egypt
China Australia	Mexico	Portugal	Poland
Brazil Germany			

a ●○

Example: *Egypt*

_____

_____

_____

b ○●

_____

_____

_____

c ●○○

_____

_____

_____

d ○●○○

_____

e ○○○○●

_____

LANGUAGES – STRESS

 2 **03.06 Look at the groups of languages. Listen and find the syllable with the stress.**

English	Japanese	Italian	Arabic
Spanish	Chinese		
Polish	Portuguese		
German			

NATIONALITIES AND LANGUAGES – STRESS

3 Checking stress.

Write the name of your country and three more – not those on the list above.

Write the nationality and language for each one. Find the stress on each word.

	Country	Nationality	Language
1	_____	_____	_____
2	_____	_____	_____
3	_____	_____	_____
4	_____	_____	_____

Check your answers in a good dictionary. Here, after the word, you will see the word in phonetics, e.g. *Swedish* **/** ˈswiːdɪʃ/**. A part of this is a mark (ˈ) at the beginning of the syllable with stress.**

> **LANGUAGE TIP**
>
> **Q** In the story (03.01) the woman says, *Where are you from?* Can I say *Where do you come from?*
> **A** Yes, both are correct and common. The meaning is the same.
> **Q** Can I say *Do you speak English?* and *Can you speak English?*
> **A** Yes, both are correct and common.

Speaking and writing

> **TALKING ABOUT YOUR ABILITIES**
>
> The British welcome a modest attitude, especially when speaking. They don't usually say *I can … very well*. However, other people can talk about you and say, e.g., *She can speak Arabic very well*. It is common to talk about yourself in a less positive way than your real ability. For example: *I can speak Italian, but not very well* and *I can cook not too badly*.
>
> When they want to say they can do something very well, the British often describe a situation that tells you their level is good, but without using the words *good* or *very well*. For example:
> **A** *Can you speak French?* **B** *Actually, I'm a French teacher.*
> **A** *Do you cook?* **B** *Oh, me? I'm head chef at the big hotel in town.*
>
> In written English, for example when writing your CV (curriculum vitae), it is common to state your abilities accurately, but without using *very well*. For example:
> *I can speak Korean fluently.*
> ✓ NOT ~~I speak Korean very well.~~ ✗
> *My communication skills are good.* ✓ NOT ~~I communicate very well.~~ ✗

1   03.07 Listen and respond.

Look at the symbols (+)/(−) and the responses.

Listen and repeat the responses.

1	**A** Do you speak Polish?	(−)	**B**	No, not at all.
2	**A** Do you speak Japanese?	(+)	**B**	Yes, but not very well.
3	**A** Can you speak Russian?	(++)	**B**	Yes, not too badly.
4	**A** Do you speak Italian?	(+++)	**B**	Yes, actually it's my native language.

2 03.08 Giving the correct response.

Situation: You can speak two foreign languages.

Read the questions and look at the response symbols (+)(-).

Listen and complete the questions. Then read your response.

1 Can you speak _____ ?   **You** (–) _____ .
2 And do you speak _____ ?   **You** (++)_____ .
3 How about _____ ?   **You** (+)_____ .
4 And what is your native language?   **You** _____ .

3 What can you do? How well? A little? Not too badly?

Write about the following topics.

Use your dictionary to help you, if necessary.

1 Transport – for example, can you ride a bike, drive a car, drive a bus …?
2 In the house – for example, can you cook ...?
3 Sport – for example, swim, ski ...?
4 Music – for example, can you play the piano, sing ...?

4 What would you say?

Situation 1 In the street

Someone speaks to you in a language you can't speak.

You: _____

Situation 2 You are in a language class.

At the end of the class another student takes your dictionary by mistake.

You: _____

Revision

WHAT IS IT IN YOUR LANGUAGE?

Here are some examples of the important points in this unit.

Translate the sentences into your language.

Remember – translate the idea, not the words.

1 Where are you from?
2 I'm from …
3 Oh, really?
4 How about you?
5 **A** Can you speak German?   **B** Yes, but not very well.
6 **A** Do you like it here?   **B** Not very much, actually.
7 **A** He lives in Paris.   **B** Does he? That's interesting.

 # Writing

You apply for a job with an international company. You are writing your CV (curriculum vitae). Write about your abilities and hobbies. Use the present simple and *can*.

Curriculum Vitae

Name _____

Contact details _____

_____

_____

Your computer abilities _____

Your foreign languages _____

Your hobbies _____

 # Speaking

 03.09 Now it's your turn to join the conversation.

Listen again to the story conversation.

Say the woman's words in the spaces.

 # Test yourself

Which one is right?

Choose the correct sentence, a or b.

1 Ability
  a He can swim.
  b He can to swim.

2 a I'm not very good in maths.
  b I'm not very good at maths.

3 Present simple – everyday activities.
  a Do he drive to work?
  b Does he drive to work?

4 Echo questions – making conversation. I'm not an English student.
  a Are you?
  b Aren't you?

5 He lives next door.
  a Does he?
  b Is he?

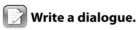 **Write a dialogue.**

Situation: You are at a friend's house. You meet Claudia there. She isn't from your country.

You

1 Ask Claudia where she's from.

Claudia

2 Respond. Ask the same question.

3 Reply.

4 Express interest and make conversation.

5 Ask about languages – which?

6 Respond.

7 Express interest and make conversation.

SELF-CHECK

I CAN . . .
○ . . . talk about everyday activities, using the present simple
○ . . . talk about ability, using *can* and pronouncing *can* and *can't* clearly
○ . . . express interest, using echo questions with the correct intonation.

4 Talking about your daily life

In this unit you will learn how to:
▶ *talk about jobs using the article* a/an
▶ *use prepositions* in, for, to
▶ *ask* Do you like it? *and respond*
▶ *talk about likes and dislikes using verbs + -ing (the gerund).*

VOCABULARY
▶ *jobs and work*

PRONUNCIATION
▶ *stress and weak forms:* do/don't, does/doesn't; *stress for emphasis; intonation in single words/short phrases*

CEFR: *Can introduce himself and others and can ask and answer questions about personal details such as where he lives, people he knows and things he has (A1). Can understand sentences and frequently used expressions related to areas of most immediate relevance and to describe family, other people and present or most recent job. Can cope with follow-up questions. Can explain what he likes or dislikes (A2). Can briefly give reasons and explanations for opinions and plans, and actions (B1).*

The story

 04.01* *The two passengers continue their conversation. They talk about their work …*

Listen to the conversation one, two or three times.

1 What's the man's job?

2 What does the woman do?

Woman	What do you do?
Man	I work in computers. And you? What's your job?
Woman	I'm a teacher.
Man	You're not an English teacher by any chance, are you?
Woman	Yes, I am, actually. I teach in a school in Uruguay.
Man	Really? Whereabouts?
Woman	In a town about 75 miles from the capital. I teach in an International school.
Man	Do you? Do you like your job?
Woman	Yes, I really enjoy teaching and the students are lovely. What about you? What sort of work do you do in computers?
Man	Well, I'm in marketing. I work for a big company, so I travel a lot for my job. In fact, I'm on my way home now from a computer fair in Argentina.
Woman	And do you enjoy working in marketing?
Man	It's OK, but I'm not very keen on all the travelling.

* For an American English version of the story, listen to **11.07**.

Listening and reading

 1 **04.01** **Choose the correct answers.**

Cover the text of the story conversation.

Read the sentences.

Listen and choose the correct answers.

Then read the text of the story conversation to check your answers.

1 The woman

   a lives in London.

   b works in South America.

   c teaches in an International school.

   d doesn't like her job.

2 The man

   a lives in Argentina.

   b is on a business trip.

    c works for a small company.

    d likes his job.

    e really enjoys the travelling.

2 Talking about jobs; likes and dislikes.

Read the sentences.

04.01 **Listen and complete the words.**

Then read the text of the story conversation to check your answers.

    a The woman asks, *What / ___ ___ / you / ___ ___ ?*
       The man answers, *I / w ___ ___ ___ / ___ ___ / computers.*

    b The man asks, *W ___ ___ ___ 's / y ___ ___ ___ / j ___ ___ ?*
       The woman answers, *I' ___ / ___ / teacher.*

    c The woman asks for more information. She says,
       W ___ ___ ___ / s ___ ___ ___ / of / w ___ ___ ___ / do you do in computers?
       The man answers,
       I' ___ / ___ ___ / m ___ ___ ___ ___ ___ ___ ___ ___ g.

    d The man talks about his company.
       He says, *I work / ___ ___ ___ / a big company.*

3 Likes and dislikes.

Complete the sentences.

    a The man asks, *D ___ / y ___ ___ / like / your / ___ ___ ___ ?*
       She answers, *Yes, I / really / e ___ ___ ___ y / t ___ ___ ch ___ ___ g.*

    b She asks, *D ___ / you / e ___ ___ ___ y / w ___ ___ k ___ ___ g / ___ n / marketing?*
       He answers, *___ ___ ' ___ / OK.*

    c He doesn't like the travelling very much. He says,
       I'm n ___ ___ / v ___ ___ ___ / k ___ ___ n / ___ n / all the travelling.

4 Read and complete.

Read the questions.

Read the text of the story conversation again and complete the sentences.

    a The man thinks the woman is an English teacher. He wants to
       check and make conversation.
       He says, *You're / ___ ___ ___ / an English teacher, b ___ / ___ ___ ___ ___ /*
       c ___ ___ ___ ___ ___ ___ , / ___ ___ ___ ___ / you?

    b The woman says she teaches in an International school.
       He asks where. He says *W ___ ___ ___ ___ / ___ ___ ___ ___ ___ s?*

    c The woman talks about her job. Then she asks the man about
       his job.
       She doesn't ask, *How about you?*
       Instead, she asks, *___ ___ ___ ___ about you?*

    d It's the end of the computer fair in Argentina. Where is the man going?

    e He says, *I ___ / f ___ ___ ___ ___ , / I'm / o ___ m ___ / w ___ ___ / h ___ ___ ___ ___ / now / f ___ ___ ___ ___ / a fair in*
       Argentina.

- ▶ The phrase *by any chance* makes a question less direct.
- ▶ *What about you?* and *How about you?* mean the same.
- ▶ *In fact* is very similar to *actually*. (See Unit 3.) *In fact* can be more formal.

Practice

1 Where? and Whereabouts?

Complete these conversations.

Choose a–f from the sentences below.

1 A I live in London.
  B _____ ?

2 A We go to Italy for our holidays.
  B _____ ?

3 A My parents are in Australia.
  B _____ ?

4 A I travel to Cadaques a lot.
  B _____ ?

5 A This is the name of the hotel.
  B _____ ?

6 A Whereabouts do you work?
  B _____ .

LANGUAGE TIP	
Q What's the difference between *where?* and *whereabouts?*	
A The meaning is the same. *Where* is more direct and specific.	
Example: *I can't find my keys? Where are they?*	
Whereabouts is common because it is less direct.	
It is especially common when it is the only word in the question.	
Example: *Paul works in the States. Does he? Whereabouts?*	

a Really? Whereabouts are they?

b Do you? Whereabouts?

c I know what it's called but whereabouts is it?

d In the centre of town, actually.

e That's nice. Whereabouts do you go?

f That's interesting but whereabouts is it?

LANGUAGE TIP

On the way	there back home	No *to* with these words
	to school to work	No *the* with these places
	to the airport	

2 On the way …

Look at sentence e in listening and reading Exercise 4.

Look at the pictures and complete the sentences.

1 Are you on your way to the fair?

No, I'm ___/___/way back.

2 They'___/___/___/ ___ to school.

___'s / on / ___ / ___ / home.

3

He'___ / ___ / ___ / ___ / to work.

4

We'___ / on / ___ / way / ___ / the / ___ .

5

___ / ___ my ___ / there right now.

6

How do you pronounce it?

 DO/DON'T; DOES/DOESN'T

1 Do/don't

▶ The vowel in *do* has two pronunciations, one strong / u: / and one weak / ə/.

▶ The vowel *o* in *don't* / oʊ / is different from the two pronunciations of *o* in *do*.

04.02 Listen to these three sentences. Can you hear three different vowel sounds?

a Do you <u>drive</u>?   weak *do* /ə/ (*do* is not the important word)

b Yes, I <u>do</u>.   strong *do* / u: / (*do* is the important word)

c Oh! I <u>don't</u>.   negative *don't* / oʊ / (the negative doesn't change)

2 *Does/doesn't*

▶ The vowel in *does* has two pronunciations, one strong / ʌ /, one weak / ə/.

▶ The vowel in *doesn't* / ʌ / is the same as in strong *does* / ʌ /

 04.03 Listen to these three sentences. Can you hear two different vowel sounds?

a Does David <u>drive</u>?   weak *does* / ə/ (*does* is not the important word)

b Yes, he <u>does</u>.   strong *does* / ʌ / (*does* is the important word)

c No, David <u>doesn't</u> <u>drive</u>.   negative *doesn't* / ʌ / (the same vowel as strong *does*)

3 *Do/don't; does/doesn't*

 04.04 Listen to the sentences and repeat. The stressed syllables are marked.

Pay special attention to the vowels in *do, don't, does, doesn't*.

1 <u>What</u> do you <u>do</u>?   weak / ə/ strong / u: /

2 <u>Where</u> do you <u>live</u>?   weak / ə/

3 <u>How</u> do you <u>know</u>?   weak / ə/

4 <u>I don't know</u>.   negative / oʊ /

5 <u>Yes</u>, you <u>do</u>.   strong / u: /

6 **A** Does your <u>father</u> like <u>golf</u>?   weak / ə

7 **B** <u>Yes</u>, he <u>does</u>. **C** <u>No</u>, he <u>doesn't</u>.   strong and negative / ʌ /

> **LANGUAGE TIP**
> **Q** Why are these differences important?
> **A** If you know that some words can be very short, with weak vowels, you can understand more when people speak. If you use stress and weak vowels when you speak, people can understand you better.

STRESS FOR EMPHASIS

In the story, the woman asks the man about his job.

She says, *What do you do?*

The man answers. Then he asks, *What's your job?*

Stress (emphasis) is on the important information words in a sentence. For example, A asks: *What's your name?* The important information word is *name*.

B answers and asks the same question. *What's your name?* This time, *name* isn't important –
we know the conversation is about names. This time *your* is important.

4 Where's the stress?

**Read the seven mini dialogues. The person answers a question and then asks the
same question. Find the stressed word in the questions.**

1 I'm <u>fine</u> thanks. How are you?
2 I'm <u>Carol</u>. And you? What's your name?
3 I live in <u>Lon</u>don. Where do you live?
4 My birthday's in <u>April</u>. When's yours?
5 I <u>don't smoke</u>. Do you?
6 I'd like some <u>coffee</u>. Would you like a drink?
7 I <u>live</u> with my <u>parents</u>. Do you live with yours?

 04.05 Now listen and check your answers.

5 Listen and repeat.

 04.05 Listen again and repeat the answers and questions.

Pay special attention to the stress in the questions.

INTONATION AND MEANING – SINGLE WORDS AND SHORT PHRASES

One way to express feelings in English is through intonation.

Example from The story

'It's OK' is positive. 'It's OK' is not very positive.
  ▶ To sound positive, start high and finish low.
  ▶ Flat intonation expresses that you are not very happy or interested.

| positive | = high start | + big fall |
| not very positive | = low start | + small fall |

6 Listen and choose.

 04.06 Listen to the questions and answers.

**For each question, one response is positive and one response is not very
positive.**

Write _P_ for _positive_ or _NP_ for _not very positive_.

▶ _Yeah_ is informal for _Yes._

1 Can you help me?	**5** Is this all right?
a OK	**a** Yes, it's fine.
b OK	**b** Yes, it's fine.
2 How are things?	**6** Do you agree?
a All right.	**a** Of course.
b All right.	**b** Of course.
3 Is that nice?	**7** Do you like it?
a It's not bad.	**a** Yes.
b It's not bad.	**b** Yes.
4 Are you happy about it?	
a Yeah.	
b Yeah.	

7 Listen and repeat.

 04.06 This time listen and repeat the responses. Can you hear the difference? Can you use intonation to sound positive?

Ⓥ Vocabulary builder 1

Jobs
Look at the pictures and the letters.
Write the correct word for each job.
Use your dictionary, if necessary.

1 ITAX VREDIR

2 TAWREI

3 ROTCOD

4 TPSIERECONTI

5 CIMECAHN

6 STEDNIT

7 TACRO

8 OPSH SSTANISAT

9 UROT DUEGI

10 REDSSREAIHR

11 AVRTEL GTAEN

12 EIRSHCA

13 TDUSENT

Language discovery

JOBS WITH THE ARTICLE *A/AN*

Examples from the story

The man asks, *What's your job?*

The woman says, *I'm a teacher.*

Common mistake

She's a teacher. NOT ~~*She's teacher.*~~ ✗

Form

Subject + verb *be*		indefinite article	job
Singular	She's	a	travel agent
	He's	an	actor
Plurals: compare and	He's	a	doctor (+ article *a*)
	They're		doctors (no article)

60

1 What do they do?

Look again at the pictures in the Vocabulary builder. Some people have name labels – for example, the waiter is Dan.

Complete the answers and questions.

Example: *What does Dan do?* He's a waiter.

   1 What does Dan do? _____

   2 What's Pat's job? _____

   3 What does Carl do? _____

   4 What's Kate's job? _____

   5 Now you ask: Jo? _____ . She's a tour guide.

   6 You ask again: Jim? _____ . He's a travel agent.

2 04.07 **Listen and repeat the questions and answers.**

USING PREPOSITIONS – *WORK IN*

Example from the story

The man says, *I'm in marketing.*

3 Correct the mistakes.

Correct A in the conversations. Use the words in the box at the end.

Use your dictionary, if necessary.

Example: David makes planes.

A You're a dentist, aren't you, David?

B No, I'm in engineering, actually.

   1 Jack is a Member of Parliament.

     A Jack works in publishing.

     B No, he's _____ .

   2 Brenda works for Barclays Bank.

     A Brenda's in education.

     B No, she's _____ .

   3 Paul is the director of a language school.

     A Paul works in banking.

     B No, not Paul. He's _____ .

   4 Matt draws pictures for books.

     A Matt works in administration.

     B Are you sure? I think he works _____ .

| publishing | education | banking | engineering | politics |

USING PREPOSITIONS – *WORK FOR*

Example from the story

The man says, *I work for a big company.*

4 Write the words in the correct order.

   1 for/Sue/Amazon/works.
   2 does/for/brother/which/your/company/work?
   3 who/know/she/for/works/do/you?

DO YOU LIKE IT?: QUESTIONS AND RESPONSES

Examples from the story

The woman says: *I really enjoy teaching.*

Then she asks: *Do you enjoy working in marketing?*

The man says: *It's OK but I'm not very keen on all the travelling.*

 5 04.07 Read, listen and repeat.

Read the phrases and look at the symbols.

 04.08 Listen and repeat the phrases.

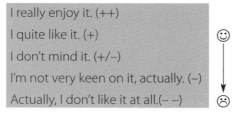

I really enjoy it. (++)
I quite like it. (+)
I don't mind it. (+/–)
I'm not very keen on it, actually. (–)
Actually, I don't like it at all. (– –)

> **LANGUAGE TIP**
>
> To answer only *yes* or *no* to the question *Do you like …?* can sound rude.
> Use one of the phrases above instead.
> ▶ With *actually*, the negative isn't so direct. (This is the other common use
> of the word *actually*.)

6 Listen and respond.

Look at the questions and symbols, for example (++).

04.09 Listen and respond.

Example: You are the woman in the story.

Question: Do you like being a teacher?

(++) You answer: *Yes, I really enjoy it.*

1 Dan, do you enjoy being a waiter?
(+) Yes, _____ .

2 Pat, do you like working in reception?
(–) No, _____ .

3 Carl, how do you like your job?
(++) _____ .

4 Kate, do you enjoy working in a shop?
(+/–) _____ .

5 Jo, what's it like being a tour guide?
(– –) _____ .

6 Do you like working in travel, Jim?
(+) Yes, _____ .

LIKES AND DISLIKES: VERB + *-ING* (GERUND)

Examples from the story

The woman says, *I really enjoy teaching.*

The man says, *I'm not very keen on all the travelling.*

After *enjoy*, *like*, *not mind* and *be keen on* the verb ends in *-ing*. This is the gerund.

enjoy + verb/*ing*	*like* + verb/*ing*
mind + verb/*ing*	be keen on + verb/*ing*

7 Read and find.

Read this interview with a schoolgirl, Sophie.

Find all the verbs + gerunds.

Interviewer	So, tell us about what you like doing and don't like doing, Sophie.
Sophie	Well, I really enjoy going out with my friends at the weekend. I like inviting them home, too. I don't mind doing my homework – I know that's important, but I'm not very keen on helping my mum with the housework.

8 Read and complete.

Complete these mini dialogues using *enjoy*, *like*, *don't mind*, *not keen on*.

Use the verbs in the box.

1 A What sort of thing do you like _____ in the evening?

B Well, actually, I enjoy _____ and I like _____, too.

2 A Jack, can you help us with some housework on Saturday?

B OK. I don't mind _____ but I'm not very keen on _____.

3 A Do you like _____?

B Yes, I really enjoy _____.

4 A That new film is on at the cinema.

B Actually, I'm _____ out tonight. I'm very tired.

5 A I'm sorry but the dentist can't see you for another half an hour.

B That's OK. I _____.

| hoover | cook | go | do | watch TV | make | wait | iron | read |

Ⓥ Vocabulary builder 2

WORK

Match 1–12 with a–l.

First try without a dictionary. Then use your dictionary, if necessary.

1	Hannah works in the house for her family	**a**	She works full-time.
2	Kate is 70.	**b**	She's unemployed.
3	Dawn hasn't got a job.	**c**	She's a colleague.
4	Sue works from 10 until 2 o'clock.	**d**	She does a lot of overtime.
5	Twenty people work for Julie.	**e**	She's a housewife.
6	May works 50 hours a week.	**f**	She's a manager.
7	Denise works from nine to five.	**g**	She works part-time.
8	Moyra is a student doctor at the hospital.	**h**	She works freelance.
9	Chris's office is in her house.	**i**	She's retired.
10	Sheila works in the same office as her sister.	**j**	She works shifts.
11	Lena works on short contracts for different companies.	**k**	She works from home.
12	Lucy goes to university.	**l**	She's a student.

# Writing

1 **Work: How about you?**

Write or prepare to tell a friend about your job/studies. What do you do/study?

Give some extra information about your job/studies.

Use some of the expressions from the Vocabulary builder. How much do you enjoy your job/studies?

> **WORK**
> ▶ In Britain, usual office hours are 9.00 or 9.30 a.m.–5.00 or 5.30 p.m., Monday to Friday, but times vary.
> ▶ Many shops open seven days a week and some supermarkets are open 24 hours a day, only closing from late Sunday afternoon to Monday morning.
> ▶ Using mobile and Internet technology, many people can work from home at least some days. Flexible working hours are possible in some jobs.
> ▶ People usually take a break for lunch at some time between twelve and two o'clock.
> ▶ Four weeks per year is the average holiday plus eight public holidays.
> ▶ The company deducts some taxes from the salary before they pay it.
> ▶ It is not usual to ask people their salary.

2 **Work in your country**

Write or prepare to tell a friend about work in your country. Give information on the points in the Work section.

Use the phrases in the text to help you. Write a minimum of one sentence for each point.

# Speaking

What would you say?

Situation 1 You and John work for the same company. John leaves and goes to work for another company. Someone telephones and asks you, *Can I speak to John, please?*

You say: _____

Situation 2 You work in a shop that is open seven days a week. You work on Saturdays and Wednesdays. It's the end of the day on Saturday. A colleague asks you, *Are you in tomorrow?*

You say: _____

▶ Here *to be in* means *to be here, at work*.

Revision

WHAT IS IT IN YOUR LANGUAGE?

Here are some examples of the important points in this unit.

Translate the sentences into your language.

Remember – translate the idea, not the words.

1 What do you do?
   I'm a …

2 Do you like cooking?
   Yes, I really enjoy it.
   Yes, I quite like it.
   It's OK.
   I'm not very keen on it, actually.
   Actually, I don't like it at all.

3 I don't mind waiting.

4 I'm on my way home.

Writing

You've got a new job. Write an email to your friend Josh.

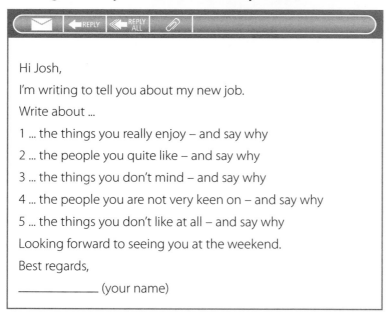

Hi Josh,

I'm writing to tell you about my new job.

Write about …

1 … the things you really enjoy – and say why

2 … the people you quite like – and say why

3 … the things you don't mind – and say why

4 … the people you are not very keen on – and say why

5 … the things you don't like at all – and say why

Looking forward to seeing you at the weekend.

Best regards,

_____ (your name)

Speaking

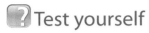 04.10 **Now it's your turn to join the conversation.**

Listen again to the story conversation.

Say the man's words in the spaces.

Test yourself

Which one is right?

Choose the correct sentence, a or b.

1 **a** What work does your brother?
   b What does your brother do?
2 **a** Like you your job?
   b Do you like your job?
3 **a** We're on our way there now.
   b We go to there now.
4 **a** Are you enjoy to travel?
   b Do you enjoy travelling?
5 **a** What sort of company does he work for?
   b For which sort of company he works?
6 **a** We can't use the car but I don't mind to walk.
   b We can't use the car but I don't mind walking.

Choose the correct stress.

7 My brother's a mechanic.
   a What does <u>your</u> brother do?
   b What does your <u>bro</u>ther do?

Write your part of the dialogue.

Situation: You are at a party. You are in the middle of a conversation with a person you don't know.

You	The other person

1 Say what you do.
   Ask his job.

I work in television.

2 Ask for details.

I read the news.

3 You think you know him.

   You think his name is
   David West. Check.

Yes, I am, actually.

4 Ask if he likes working in
   television.

Yes, it's very interesting.
The only thing I'm not too
keen on is working late at
night. What sort of work do
you do exactly?

5 Respond.

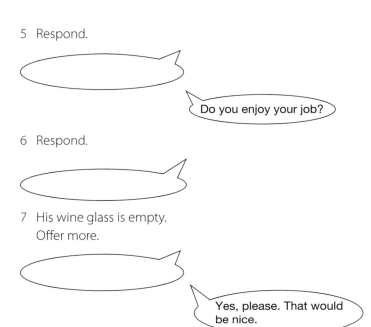

Do you enjoy your job?

6 Respond.

7 His wine glass is empty.
  Offer more.

Yes, please. That would
be nice.

SELF-CHECK

I CAN . . .

⚪	. . . talk about jobs, using *a/an*
⚪	. . . use prepositions *in*, *for*, *to*
⚪	. . . ask *Do you like it?* and respond.
⚪	. . . talk about likes and dislikes, using verb + *-ing*
⚪	. . . use stress for emphasis.

5 Giving explanations

In this unit you will learn how to:
▶ *use possessive pronouns –* mine *etc.*
▶ *use the present progressive for temporary actions in the present*
▶ *choose correctly between present progressive and present simple*
▶ *use the present progressive for future arrangements*
▶ *say why, using* to, so that, because.

VOCABULARY
▶ *first names; the family*

PRONUNCIATION
▶ *extra syllable, 3rd person singular, present simple; weak form of* to

CEFR: *Can introduce himself and others and can ask and answer questions about personal details such as where he lives, people he knows and things he has (A1). Can understand sentences and frequently used expressions related to areas of most immediate relevance. Can use a series of phrases and sentences to describe family and daily routines. Can cope with follow-up questions (A2). Can understand the main points of clear standard input on familiar matters regularly encountered in work and leisure. Can produce simple connected text on topics which are familiar or of personal interest (B2).*

The story 1

 05.01* *The conversation on the plane continues. They exchange names, talk about their families and the reasons for their trips.*

Listen to the conversation one, two or three times.

Choose *Yes* for the things they talk about.

Choose *No* for the things they don't talk about.

They talk about:

a	their names	Yes/No
b	where he lives	Yes/No
c	his family	Yes/No
d	the reason for her trip	Yes/No
e	her mother	Yes/No
f	her father	Yes/No

Woman	What's your name?
Man	Oliver. And yours?
Woman	My name's Tasha. It's short for Natasha, a Russian name. My mother's Russian. So, whereabouts in England do you live, Oliver?
Man	I live in Scotland, actually, in Edinburgh, but I'm staying in London for a couple of weeks, because of my job. And you? Are you on holiday?
Woman	Yes, I'm going to England to see some friends of mine. They live near London.
Man	Oh, right. And your family?
Woman	My father's working in the States at the moment – until next June. He works abroad quite a lot. It's nice because my mother organizes her work so that she can travel with him. Even if they aren't at home, I go to England every year because I need to see other relatives and friends.

** For an American English version, listen to **11.08**.*

Listening and reading

1 Read, listen and choose.

Read the questions.

 05.01 **Listen and choose the right answer.**

1 His name is <u>Oliver/Leo</u>.

2 Her name is <u>Sasha/Tasha</u>.

3 Her name is from <u>Greece/Russia</u>.

4 Her <u>mother/father</u> is from the same country.

5 The man lives in <u>Edinburgh/Glasgow</u>.

6 But for the next <u>two/three</u> weeks his work is in <u>Oxford/London</u>.

7 She's on her way to visit <u>her family/some friends</u>.

8 They live <u>in/near</u> London.

9 Her parents are in <u>South Africa/America</u> for another <u>two years/six months</u>.

10 When her parents aren't in England <u>she goes/doesn't go</u> home.

11 When she goes to England she visits her friends and <u>museums/her family</u>.

2 Read, listen and complete.

Read the sentences.

 05.01 Listen and complete the words.

Then read the text of the story conversation to check your answers.

  1 The woman asks the man his name.

    He says, *Oliver.* Then he asks the same question *A __ __ / y __ __ __ __* ?

  2 a Oliver has work in London for two weeks.

      He says, *I' __ / s __ __ __ __ __ __ / in London for a couple of weeks.*

    b He says why.

      B __ __ __ __ __ __ / o __ / my job.

  3 Oliver asks Tasha, *Are you on holiday?*

    She says, *Yes, / I' __ / g __ __ __ __ __ / t __ / England / t __ / see some friends / o __ / m __ __ __*

  4 Tasha's parents aren't in England now.

    She says, *My / f __ __ __ __ __ 's / w __ __ __ __ __ g / in the States at the moment.*

  5 Tasha's mother likes travelling with her father but she works.

    Tasha says, *My mother organizes her work s __ / t __ __ t / s __ __ / c __ __ travel with him.*

  6 Why does Tasha go to England every year?

    She says, *B __ __ __ __ __ e / I / n __ __ __ / t __ / see other relatives and friends.*

3 Read and complete.

Read the sentences.

Read the text of the story conversation again and complete the words.

  1 Tasha is the short name. Natasha is the long name.

    Tasha is s __ __ __ t / f __ __ Natasha.

  2 Tasha says, *My mother's Russian.* Then she starts a new topic.

    She says, *__ __ / whereabouts in England do you live, Oliver?*

  3 Tasha asks, *Whereabouts in England do you live, Oliver?*

    Oliver doesn't live in England; he lives in Scotland.

    He says, *I live in Scotland /, a __ __ __ __ __ __ __.*

  4 Oliver's going to London. How long for? Two weeks.

    He says, *f __ __ / a / c __ __ __ __ e / o __ / weeks.*

5 Is Tasha working? No, she's __ __ holiday.

6 Tasha says, *I'm going to England to see some friends. They live near London.*
Oliver responds with another question.
He says, *O __, / r __ __ __ t. And your family?*

7 Tasha's father works in other countries. He works a __ __ __ __ __ .

8 Does Tasha's father work in other countries all the time?
Not all the time but q __ __ __ e / __ / l __ __ of the time.

9 Tasha goes to England when her parents are there and when her parents aren't there.
She goes to England e __ __ __ / i __ her parents aren't there.

10 How often does Tasha go to England? E __ __ __ __ / y __ __ r.

4 Make sentences.

Practise the expressions in Exercise 3.

Choose one from each column, A, B, C, D, to make five sentences.

A	B	C	D
'Uni' is	on	a couple	weekend.
The baby spends	short	the time	of months.
She phones home	with us for	every	university.
My brother is staying	from uni	holiday to	Italy.
They're going	a lot of	for	asleep.

Language discovery 1

 NAMES

 **First names**

▶ In Britain, it is common to have one first name, one middle name and one family name.

Example:

First	*Middle*	*Family name or surname*
Victoria	Ann	Smith

▶ Some people have more than one middle name. It is not common to use your middle name(s).

▶ First names and middle names often come from other members of the family.

▶ It is very common to shorten first names, e.g. *Victoria* → *Vicky*.

▶ If a first name has a short form, it can be more formal to use the long form. e.g. *Michael* can be more formal than *Mike*.

▶ When we write a name, we usually start with the first name, e.g. *Emily Gardener*. *Emily* is the first name; *Gardener* is the family name. On official papers and documents, the family name usually comes first.

▶ At work it is very common to use first names.

▶ You can give your child the names you like. There is no official list.

Example from the story

Tasha is short for Natasha.

1 Match the names.

Look at the following names.

Match the short and long names.

Girls		Boys	
1	Abi _____	1	Ollie _____
2	Beth _____	2	Chris _____
3	Ellie _____	3	Nick _____
4	Sam _____	4	Dom _____
5	Kate _____	5	Sam _____
6	Ros _____	6	Josh _____
7	Chris _____	7	Mike _____
8	Mel _____	8	Finn _____
9	Jess _____	9	Tom _____
10	Becky _____	10	Matt _____

Girls		Boys	
Jessica	Christine	Nicholas	Samuel
Abigail	Rosalyn	Michael	Matthew
Bethany	Eleanor	Dominic	Thomas
Melanie	K/Catherine	Finley	Christopher
Samantha	Rebecca	Oliver	Joshua

2 Names for men and women.

As you can see, some short names are the same for both men and women.

How many examples can you find in the lists?

3 Asking someone about their name.

Put these words in the right order:

for/name/what/your/'s/short?

4 About you: first names.

Write answers to these questions or prepare to tell a friend.

Is your first name short for another name?

Does another member of the family have the same name?

Where does your name come from?

Is it common or unusual in your country?

What does your first name mean?

USING *SO, ...* TO START A NEW TOPIC

Example from the story

Tasha: *My mother's Russian. So, whereabouts in England do you live, Oliver?*

▶ We can use *so* to change the topic.

▶ In the example, Tasha talks about her mother.

▶ Then she asks Oliver where he lives. *So* starts the new topic.

▶ *So* is not essential but it introduces a change of topic.

5   Using 'So, ...' in a conversation.

Situation: John and Sophie live in Miami. They have a party. Two guests have a conversation.

Read the conversation. The topic changes three times.

Choose where to say *So*.

Jo	My name's Jo, and yours?
Sam	Sam.
Jo	Where do you come from Sam?
Sam	I'm from New York. I work in a bookshop there.
Jo	Do you like it?
Sam	Yes, I really enjoy it, actually. I love books. Do you know this town well?
Jo	Quite well. I come for a holiday from time to time. How about you? Where do you go on holiday?
Sam	I like going to Europe for my holidays – I love London and I know Paris and Rome and a few other places. How do you know John and Sophie?
Jo	John's my brother.
Sam	Oh, right.

CORRECTING PEOPLE USING *ACTUALLY*

Example from the story

Tasha: *So, whereabouts in England do you live, Oliver?*

Oliver doesn't live in England. He lives in Scotland.

He says: *I live in Scotland, actually.*

He doesn't say the wrong information, *I don't live in England*. This can sound rude.

He says *I live in Scotland, actually*. He says the correct information + *actually*.

▶ With *actually* the correction is less direct.

▶ *Actually* goes at the beginning or the end of the correction: *Actually, I live in Scotland* or *I live in Scotland, actually*.

6 Read the short dialogues and correct the mistakes.

Example: A Good morning, Jo. **B** My name's Sam, actually.
(Your name's Sam.)

1 A So, what's it like working for Sony?

B _____
(You work for Panasonic.)

2 A Excuse me … here's your bag.

B _____
(The bag isn't yours.)

3 A Would you like some wine?

B _____
(You don't drink alcohol.)

4 A Please take me home.

B _____
(You can't drive.)

5 A So, whereabouts in France are you from?

B _____
(You're from Italy.)

6 A Peter's really nice, isn't he?

B _____
(You don't know Peter.)

7 A Sue?

B _____
(You're Sue's mother.)

8 A Lovely, isn't it?

B _____
(You're not very keen on it.)

9 A What sort of work does your husband do?

B _____
(You're not married.)

7 05.02 **Listen and say the responses.**

USING ABROAD

Example from the story

Tasha's father works abroad.

Abroad has no preposition and no article (*the*). It isn't correct to say:

He works ~~in the~~ abroad. ✗

He goes ~~to~~ abroad for his holiday. ✗

8 **Complete these answers with *abroad* and information about Oliver and Tasha from the audio.**

1 Is Tasha's mother in England?

No, _____ .

2 Does Tasha live in England?

No, she _____ .

3 Oliver _____ a lot for his job.

4 Tasha's father _____ quite a lot.

5 What sort of holidays do you like?

I enjoy (travel) _____ .

How do you pronounce it?

'HE', 'SHE', 'IT' AND 'WHO?' FORMS OF PRESENT SIMPLE

Example from the story

My mother organizes her work.

1 **05.03 Listen to the sentence on the audio and choose a or b.**

Remember, a syllable is part of a word with a vowel sound.

The verb *organize* has three syllables – *or-gan-ize***.**

The word *organizes* has:

a three

b four syllables?

▶ Some verbs add an extra syllable / ɪz / with *he* and *she*, *it* and *who?*

2 **05.04 Listen and repeat these verbs.**

close	fin-ish	re-lax	watch	dance
clos-es	fin-ish-es	re-lax-es	watch-es	danc-es

3 My wife and I.

Situation: Kate and Joey are married. Joey has a shop and his wife works in a supermarket. Who does what in their house?

Read Joey's sentences.

Complete the verbs and write the number of syllables for each verb where you see brackets ( ). All the verbs here change.

Practise the extra syllable. Read the verbs aloud as you write.

   Example: 1 I close (1) my shop at 6.00 but Kate's
   supermarket closes (2) at 9.00.

   2 I finish ( ) work early but she _____ ( ) late.

   3 At home I wash ( ) the dishes and she _____
   ( ) the clothes.

   4 I fix ( ) the car and she _____ ( ) things in the
   house.

   5 I relax ( ) in the bath but she _____ ( ) with a
   book.

   6 I watch ( ) sport on TV but Kate _____ ( ) news
   programmes.

   7 I dance ( ) a bit but my wife _____ ( ) well.

   8 I use ( ) soap but my wife _____ ( ) shower gel.

   9 I change ( ) the baby in the morning and Kate
   _____ ( ) her at night.

   10 I sneeze ( ) when I'm ill but she _____ ( ) every
   morning.

   11 I organize ( ) the money and she _____ ( ) the
   holidays.

   12 I kiss ( ) my wife and my wife _____ ( ) me.

 05.05 **Listen and check your answers.**

4 Listen and repeat.

 05.05 **Listen again and repeat.**

Pay special attention to the extra syllable for *she***.**

78

ASKING *WHO?* – PRONUNCIATION OF 3RD-PERSON SINGULAR -*ES*

5 Who does these things in the story *My wife and I*? Kate or Joey?

Complete the questions with one word only.

    1 Who _____ the dishes?   Joey.

    2 Who _____ work at 9.00?   Kate does.

    3 Who _____ sport on TV?   Joey does.

    4 Who _____ things?   They both do.

▶ When *who* is the subject of the verb, there is no *does*. Use *who* + verb with *s* or *es*.

    Q When do we add an extra syllable for *he*, *she*, *it* and question *who*?

    A When it's difficult to say the *s* without adding an extra vowel sound. An extra vowel sound = extra syllable. (It's the same reason why we add -*es* for plural nouns, as we saw in Unit 3.)

PRESENT SIMPLE 3RD-PERSON SINGULAR: PRONUNCIATION AND SPELLING SUMMARY

For *he*, *she*, *it* and *who*, add an extra syllable to verbs ending in:

-se	-ce	-ge	-ze	-ss	-sh	-tch	-x
close use organize	dance	change	sneeze	kiss	wash finish	watch	relax fix
				Here, the spelling changes, too. Add *es*.			

6 Look and decide.

Look at the verbs.

Which ones change with *he***,** *she***,** *it* **and question** *who***?**

touch	cross	read	think	want	drink	mix	pass
	manage		pronounce	wish			

Vocabulary builder

THE FAMILY: CLOSE RELATIVES

Who's who in this family?

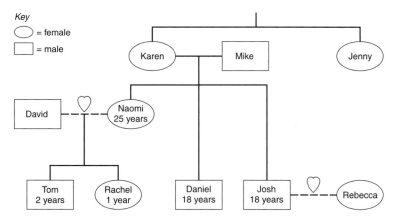

Key

◯ = female

▢ = male

Karen   Mike   Jenny

David ----♡---- Naomi 25 years

Tom 2 years   Rachel 1 year   Daniel 18 years   Josh 18 years ----♡---- Rebecca

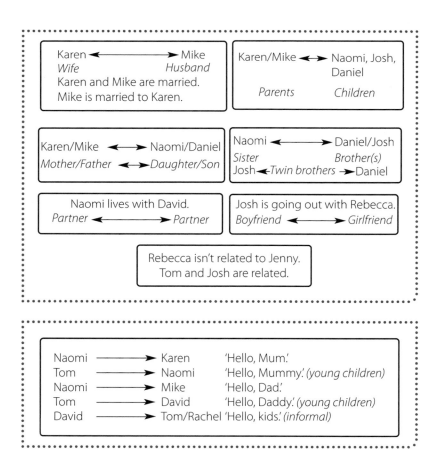

Karen ⟷ Mike
Wife   *Husband*
Karen and Mike are married.
Mike is married to Karen.

Karen/Mike ⟷ Naomi, Josh, Daniel
Parents   *Children*

Karen/Mike ⟷ Naomi/Daniel
Mother/Father ⟷ *Daughter/Son*

Naomi ⟷ Daniel/Josh
Sister   *Brother(s)*
Josh ← *Twin brothers* → Daniel

Naomi lives with David.
Partner ⟷ *Partner*

Josh is going out with Rebecca.
Boyfriend ⟷ *Girlfriend*

Rebecca isn't related to Jenny.
Tom and Josh are related.

Naomi → Karen   'Hello, Mum.'
Tom → Naomi   'Hello, Mummy.' *(young children)*
Naomi → Mike   'Hello, Dad.'
Tom → David   'Hello, Daddy.' *(young children)*
David → Tom/Rachel 'Hello, kids.' *(informal)*

1 Read and complete.

Look at the family diagram and the vocabulary in the boxes.

Now complete these sentences with the vocabulary from the diagram and boxes.

Use your dictionary, if necessary.

1 🔊 **Mike:** Could I speak to Karen, please? It's her _____ here.

2 🔊 This is Karen, Josh's mother. Is my _____ there, please?

3 I'm Naomi, Daniel's sister. Is my _____ here, please?

4 **A:** Who's David? **B:** Naomi's _____ .

5 **A:** Josh, are you _____ / _____ Mike? **B:** Yes, he's my dad.

6 **Mike:** Naomi's a lovely _____ .

7 **Mike:** I'm married to Karen now. Sue's my first _____ .

8 **Naomi:** Daniel's my _____ .

9 Josh is Daniel's _____ / _____ . They look exactly alike.

10 Josh is in love with his _____ . He wants to marry her. He asks her, *Will you marry me?*

11 When David goes to work, little Tom says, *Bye, bye, _____ .*

12 **A:** Naomi, is Daniel a _____ of yours? **B:** Yes, he's my brother.

13 We always give our _____ flowers on Mother's Day.

14 🔊 It's Daniel here, Naomi's brother. Can I leave a message for my _____ , please?

15 **a** Naomi and David have got two _____ .

   b When Naomi takes them out, she says, *Come on, _____ ! We're going out.*

16 🔊 **Daniel:** I need to talk to Mum. **Naomi:** Mum isn't here but _____ is. Shall I get him?

17 Tom is in a shop. He can't find Naomi. He says, *Where's my _____ ?*

18 Naomi and Josh are _____ and _____ .

19 **A:** Who's Karen _____ / _____?
   B: Mike.

20 **A:** Who's Rebecca _____ / _____ / _____ ?
   B: Her _____'s name's Josh.

> ### LANGUAGE TIP
> We say *Come on, kids!* (informal) or *Come on, children!* but with a singular, we use the name, e.g. *Come on, David!*
> We say *Married to …* and *related to …* (not *married/ related with …*).

POSSESSIVE *'S* – CONTRACTION OF 'IS' AND 'HAS'

A sentence can have more than one possessive *'s*.

Look at the examples.

1

Who's	Karen?	Mike's	wife.
is		*possessive* 's	
		NOT ~~The wife of Mike.~~ ✗	

2

Karen's	daughter's	name's	Naomi.
possessive 's	*possessive* 's	is	

NOT ~~The name of the daughter of Karen is Naomi.~~ ✗

3

What's	David's	son's	name?
is	*possessive* 's	*possessive* 's	

NOT ~~What is the name of the son of David?~~ ✗

4

Who's	Jack?	A friend of	Daniel's.
is			*possessive* 's

NOT ~~A friend of Daniel.~~ ✗

▶ Add *'s* to the name in the phrase *A friend/cousin/neighbour/colleague of* + name + *'s*.

2 Complete the words in these sentences about the family in the Vocabulary builder.

1 **A** Who's Josh?   **B** M_____' __ / s_____.
2 **A** Who' Mike?   **B** K_____' __ / h_____.
3 Daniel' __ / m_____' __ / n_____' __ / Karen.
4 Josh' __ / f_____'s / n _____' __ / Mike.
5 Mike' __ / d_____' __ / n _____' __ Naomi.
6 **A** What' __ / K_____ n' __ / d _____' __ / n_____?   **B** Naomi.
7 **A** Who' __ Daniel?   **B** A f_____ / o __ / J _____' __.

3 Write about you and your family.

Choose the right information to make a paragraph about you and your family.

Use your dictionary, if necessary.

Example: I'm ⎰ married.
⎱ ~~not married.~~

My husband's
wife's
partner's   name's Mary/John.
girlfriend's
boyfriend's

I've got one
two   children.
three

OR

I haven't got any children.

About you   **About your partner**

My name's _____ .   My ⎧ husband's

My family and friends   ⎪ wife's name's _____ .

  call me _____ .   ⎨ partner's

I'm ⎧ married   ⎪ girlfriend's

    ⎩ not married   ⎩ boyfriend's

I've got a   partner.

           girlfriend.

           boyfriend.

OR

I haven't got a partner/girlfriend/boyfriend.

About your brothers and sisters

I've got one brother.   His name's _____ .

      two brothers.   Their names are _____ and _____ .

      three brothers. Their names are _____ , _____ and _____ .

      four, etc.   Their names are _____ , _____ and _____ .

      brothers.

I've got one sister.   Her name's _____

      two sisters.   Their names are _____ and _____ .

      three sisters.   Their names are _____ , _____ and _____ .

      four, etc. sisters. Their names are _____ , _____ and _____ .

OR

I haven't got any brothers or sisters. I'm an only child.

About your parents

Both my parents are alive. They live in _____ .

Both my parents are alive but they aren't together. My mother lives in _____
and my father lives in _____ .

My mother's alive but my father's dead. She lives in _____ .

My father's alive but my mother's dead. He lives in _____ .

Both my parents are dead.

About your children

I've got one child, a son. His name's _____ .

I've got one child, a daughter. Her name's _____ .

I've got two, three, four, etc. children. Their names are _____ , _____ and _____ .

 # Language discovery 2

POSSESSIVE PRONOUNS – *MINE* ETC.

Examples from the story

1 The woman asks the man his name.

He says, *Oliver.* Then he asks the same question.

He says, *And yours?*

2 Why is Tasha going to England?

She says, *To see some friends of mine.*

▶ *They're friends of mine* is more common than *they're my friends*.

1 Use the possessive pronouns in the box to complete the table.

Subject	Possessive adjective	Possessive pronoun
I	my	_____
he	his	_____
she	her	_____
you	your	_____
we	our	_____
they	their	_____

ours   mine   theirs   his   yours   hers

2 Complete the sentences with the correct possessive pronoun.

  1 A My birthday's in April. When's _____? **B** In November.

  2 We're seeing friends of _____ for dinner tomorrow.

  3 A Does David know Jack? **B** Yes, Jack's a friend of _____ .

  4 That isn't their car. _____ is blue.

  5 A Is Jo a classmate of _____? **B** Yes, we're in the same English class.

  6 The family is going on holiday.

    a Which bag is yours?   That big one's _____

    b And John's?   The red one's _____

    c Where's Mary's?   _____ is this black one.

    d How about Kay's and Mike's?   _____ are in the car.

    e And we can take _____ .   Come on, let's go.

💡 Language discovery 3

PRESENT PROGRESSIVE – TEMPORARY ACTIONS

Example from the story

Tasha's parents aren't in England now.

She says, *My father's (father is) working in the States until June.*

The name of the tense is the present progressive.

Meaning

1 Choose the right answers, a, b or c.

  1 In this example from the story, the present progressive is for:

  a the past.

  b the present.

  c the future.

  2 The action is:

  a permanent.

  b temporary.

Form

2 Choose the right answers, a or b.

  1 In this example from the story, the verb has:

  a one word.

  b two words.

  2 The present of *be* <u>is/isn't</u> part of this tense.

▶ Here the present progressive is for a temporary action in the present.

3 Complete the table.

Use the correct part of the verb *be*.

Contractions are in brackets.

Positive		Negative	
I __ __ (__'m)		I __ __ not (__'__) not	
He __ __ She __ __ It('__)	working.	He __ __ not She('__) not OR She __ __ n't It('__) not OR It __ __ n't	working.
You __ __ __ We __ __ __ They ('__ __)		You __ __ __ not We('__ __) not They('__ __) not OR They __ __ __ n't	

Questions		Question tags – to make conversation Echo questions – to express interest	
		Positive	**Negative**
__ __ I		__ __ I?	aren't I?
__ __ he __ __ she __ __ it	working?	__ __ he? __ __ she? __ __ it?	__ __ n't he? __ __ n't she? __ __ n't it?
__ __ __ you __ __ __ we __ __ __ they		__ __ __ you? __ __ __ we? __ __ __ they?	__ __ __ n't you? __ __ __ n't we? __ __ __ n't they?

4 Answer *Yes* or *No* to these questions.

  1 The main verb is always with *-ing*.

  2 To make questions, you use auxiliary *do*.

  3 To ask a question, you change the word order.

  4 In questions, the verb *be* is before the person.

  5 The negative can have two forms.

  6 The *I* form of the negative question tag is irregular.

5 What's happening at home?

Situation: Mark arrives home. He's talking to his brother, Dave. They've got one sister, Sharon, and a brother, Jamie.

Complete the conversation. Use the correct parts of the present progressive and appropriate verbs.

Mark	Where's Dad?	
Dave	He'_____ / _____ the car. This water's for him.	
Mark	And Mum?	
Dave	She's in the kitchen – _____ a cake for your birthday.	
Mark	What'_____ Jamie _____?	
Dave	_____ TV in his room.	
Mark	_____ / _____?	
	_____ Sharon _____ her homework?	
Dave	Of course she _____'_____ . She's upstairs with some friends. They'_____ / I_____ / to music.	
Mark	They a _____'t / I_____ / _____ my new CD, a _____ / they?	
Mark goes to Sharon's room.		
Mark	Sharon, what / _____ / you / I _____ / t _____?	
Sharon	Your new CD. It's great! I'_____ really _____ it!	
Mark	A _____ / y_____? Now come on. Give it back to me.	
Sharon	Sorry! Here you are.	

Q In the conversation, what's the difference between these two answers?

Mark What's Jamie doing?

| **a** | **Dave** | He's watching TV. |
| **b** | **Dave** | Watching TV. |

A Both are correct and common – **a** is always appropriate;
b is more informal.

Q In the story, why is it: *My father's living in the States until June*? (present progressive)

Can I also say, *My father lives in the States*? (present simple)

A This is a very important point. The grammar in both sentences is correct, but they mean different things.

With the present progressive (*My father's living*), the situation is temporary.

With the present simple (*My father lives*), the speaker thinks the situation is permanent. So, *My father lives in the States until June* is wrong.

LANGUAGE TIP

Q **Situation:** It's 3.00. Where's Sharon?
A Is it correct to say, *She's sleeping*?
This answer is not wrong but it's not common. *She's asleep* is more common. It's the same with questions and the negative.
Is she asleep? is more common than *Is she sleeping?*
She isn't asleep is more common than *She isn't sleeping.*

PRESENT SIMPLE OR PRESENT PROGRESSIVE?

6 Choose the correct verb form.

Choose present simple for permanent situations.

Choose present progressive for temporary situations.

1. Your teacher's ill, so today I teach/I'm teaching your class.
2. Are you in a hotel? No, I stay/I'm staying with friends.
3. My son lives/is living with me until his new flat is ready.
4. Now, come on Joseph, you are/you're being very naughty today. Stop that and sit down. Usually you are/you're being a very good boy.
5. Normally, I work/I'm working hard but this month I don't/I'm not. It's very quiet.
6. Does your daughter live/Is your daughter living at home? Yes, she's only 14.

PRESENT PROGRESSIVE – PERSONAL FUTURE ARRANGEMENTS

Example from the story

Oliver is on a plane on his way to London.

He says, *I'm staying in London for a couple of weeks.*

Meaning

7 **Answer these questions. For 1, 2 and 3, find the right answer. For 4, answer *Yes* or *No*.**

   1 Here, this tense is for an action in the:

     a Past   **b** Present   **c** Future

   2 The decision to stay in London is:

     a In the **past** **b** In the **present** **c** In the future

   3 The arrangement is <u>personal/part of a timetable</u>?

   4 **a** The plan is for Oliver to spend two weeks in London.   Yes/No

     b The action to arrange the time in London is in the past.   Yes/No

▶ Here the present progressive is for personal future arrangements.

8 **Complete this conversation between two friends.**

> **A**   What _____ / you _____ this evening?
>
> **B**   I'_____ / _____ to the cinema with Don. Would you like to come with us?
>
> **A**   No, thanks, Jim'_____ / _____ in a minute. We'_____ / _____ out for a drink.
>
> **B**   Which pub _____ / you / _____ / _____?
>
> **A**   The one by the river.

> **LANGUAGE TIP**
>
> **Example:** *I'm going to the cinema this evening.*
> **Q** Can I also say, *I go to the cinema this evening?*
> **A** No. *I'm going to the cinema this evening* is a personal future arrangement. The present progressive is the only correct tense.
> (The present simple is used for the future, but only to talk about a one-off action that is part of a timetable, schedule or itinerary – see Unit 8.)

Practice

1 Present or future meaning?

Read the sentences. They are all in the present progressive.

Which sentences refer to an action in the present?

Which sentences refer to a personal future arrangement?

Choose *present* or *future* for each sentence.

   1 I'm doing it right now!

   2 I'm leaving soon.

   3 Is he arriving on Friday?

   4 I'm busy talking on the phone at the moment.

   5 I'm seeing him in the morning.

   6 The telephone's ringing – can someone please answer it?

7 I'm having dinner with him tomorrow evening.

8 They're having a holiday at the end of the contract.

9 You're not meeting John after work, are you?

10 A Mummy, I can't sleep.

  B I'm coming in a minute, darling.

2 Future arrangements.

Read the mini dialogue about arrangements for next weekend.

Find the personal future arrangements.

> **A**　　　　　So, what are you doing next weekend?
> **B**　　　　　Well, on Saturday morning I'm visiting a friend. Then,
> 　　　　　　　in the evening we're having dinner in the new pizza
> 　　　　　　　restaurant. On Sunday my parents are coming for the
> 　　　　　　　day.

3 Find the mistakes.

There are five mistakes with the verbs in this mini dialogue. Write the correct dialogue.

  A Do you come to class tomorrow?

  B No, I won't.

  A Why you can't come?

  B Because tomorrow comes my mother from Germany. I go to the airport to meet her.

4 What are you doing next weekend? Write or prepare to tell a friend.

Write a minimum of three things about your arrangements for next weekend.

Language discovery 4

 ANSWERS TO 'WHY ...?': *TO, SO THAT, BECAUSE*

Examples from the story

Tasha says, *I'm going to England to see some friends.*

Then Tasha says, *My mother organizes her work so that she can travel with my father.*

Why does Tasha go to England every year?
She says, *because I need to see other relatives and friends.*

Why is Oliver staying in London for two weeks?
Because of his job.

Summary – saying why

A Why is Tasha travelling to England?	
To	
B Because she wants to/likes to/needs to	visit friends and family.
So (that) she can	
A Why is Oliver staying in London?	
B Because of his job	(*because of* + noun)

Complete the answers.

Why is Tasha travelling to England?

Write *because, because of* or *so (that) she can*.

    a _____ buy new books for her job.

    b _____ her friends and relatives.

    c _____ it's her country.

    d _____ have a holiday.

COMMON MISTAKE

Saying why

Example from the story:

Tasha says, *I'm going to England to see some friends.*

This is the infinitive of purpose. In other words, it answers the question *Why?* or *What for?*

NOT: ~~I'm going to England for to see some friends.~~ ✗

NOT: ~~I'm going to England for seeing some friends.~~ ✗

How do you pronounce it?

 SAYING WHY: USING AN INFINITIVE OF PURPOSE: *TO* + VERB

Look at the words with stress in this phrase: … *to see some friends.*

The pronunciation of *to* is weak / tə/. The important word in the phrase 'to see' is *see*.

1 Complete sentences 1–8 with an expression from the box.

Example: We go to France *to buy nice wine.*

    1 I'm phoning _____ .

    2 I go to the coffee bar _____ .

    3 I need some change _____ .

    4 I'm going to the kitchen _____ .

    5 You call 999 _____ .

    6 I swim _____ .

    7 She's in Italy _____ .

    8 I'd like to go to London _____ .

> to relax and keep fit
>
> to learn Italian
>
> to make a phone call
>
> to have some tea
>
> to tell you about the party
>
> to get an ambulance ~~to buy nice wine~~
>
> to visit the museums
>
> to talk to my friends and have a snack

 05.06 Listen and check your answers.

 2 05.06 Listen to the sentences again and repeat them.

Pay special attention to weak form *to* / tə/. The stress is on the verb after *to*.

3 Read the questionnaire and choose the right answers for you.

Then read your answers aloud. Remember the weak pronunciation of *to* in infinitives of purpose.

Why are you learning English?
- ☐ Because I like it. It's a hobby.
- ☐ Because I need it for my job.
- ☐ Because I need it for my studies.
- ☐ Because I want to visit England.
- ☐ So I can travel independently.
- ☐ So I can understand and talk to my colleagues and/or visitors.
- ☐ So I can get a better job.
- ☐ To pass exams.
- ☐ Because I want to understand the words of songs in English.
- ☐ Because I like to watch films in English.
- ☐ To help my children with their English studies.
- ☐ Because there is an English-speaking person in my family.

What are your main reasons? _____

_____

_____

_____

Why are you using this *Complete English as a Foreign Language* book?
- ☐ To improve and practise my English in general.
- ☐ To learn how to communicate better in English.
- ☐ To understand speakers of English when they talk.
- ☐ To improve my pronunciation.
- ☐ To improve my vocabulary.

☐ To improve my grammar.

☐ To find out more about British life and customs.

☐ Because I can't go to classes.

☐ Because I study on my own.

What are your main reasons? _____

_____

_____

_____

Speaking

What would you say?

Situation 1 You are next in a queue in a shop. The shop assistant asks *Who's next?*
The person behind you says, *Me.*

You: _____

Situation 2 The phone rings. Your friend answers it. You're in your room. Your friend calls
you and says, *It's for you.*

You: _____

Revision

WHAT IS IT IN YOUR LANGUAGE?

Here are some examples of the important points in this unit.

Translate the sentences into your language.

Remember – translate the idea, not the words.

1 Here's my car. Where's yours?

2 Maria's a friend of mine.

3 I'm studying English because of my job.

4 I listen to the CD to improve my pronunciation.

5 I'm working tomorrow.

6 A Where's Pat? **B** She's having a bath.

7 I don't work so that I can be with my children.

Writing

You're on holiday. Write a email to your friend Charlie. For each space choose the correct verb from the box.

Use the present simple, the present progressive or the infinitive of purpose.

> write   relax   visit   have   take (x2)   stay   go (x2)
> meet   sunbathe   live

Hi Charlie

We **1** _____ a great time on holiday in Malta.

We **2** _____ in a lovely hotel, opposite the beach.

I **3** _____ to you from my room – it's very comfortable.

Every morning we **4** _____ for a swim, then
we **5** _____ by the pool and **6** _____.

Tomorrow we **7** _____ the boat to a little island near here.

A friend of ours **8** _____ there for a year.

We **9** _____ him for lunch and then he **10** _____ us on a
tour round the island **11** _____ the beauty spots.

Don't forget we 12 _____ to the theatre on the 20th. I've got
the tickets.

See you when we get back,

_____ (your name).

Speaking

05.07 Now it's your turn to join the conversation.

Listen again to the story conversation.

Say Tasha's words in the spaces.

? Test yourself

Which one is right?

Choose the correct sentence, a or b.

1 Where's Sue?
- **a** She's in holidays.
- **b** She's on holiday.

2 a Do you go out this evening?
- **b** Are you going out this evening?

3 I go to the cinema a lot:
- **a** because of I like new films.
- **b** because I like new films.

4 I'm working hard:
- **a** so as to can travel abroad.
- **b** so that I can travel abroad.

5 Why are you calling David?
- **a** To invite him to the party.
- **b** For to invite him to the party.

6 We go there:
- **a** all the weekends.
- **b** every weekend.

7 I like playing tennis:
- **a** even if it's raining.
- **b** if even it's raining.

8 a I don't wait any more. I leave right now.
- **b** I'm not waiting any more. I'm leaving right now.

9 a Susan is the girlfriend of Paul and Paul's a friend of me.
- **b** Susan is Paul's girlfriend and Paul's a friend of mine.

10 a She's a friend of Peter.
- **b** She's a friend of Peter's.

For 11 and 12 choose the appropriate answer.

11 You live at number 2, don't you?
- **a** No.
- **b** Actually, my house is number 3.

12 I'm a friend of your brother's.
- **a** Oh, right.
- **b** Yes.

Write a dialogue.

Situation: You are in a new English class in England. You meet another student. She is not the same nationality as you.

You   **Gloria**

1 Say your name and ask her name.

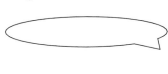

2

I'm Gloria.

3 Ask why she's studying English.

4 says it's because of her job, and asks you the same question.

5 Answer the question. (work/tourism)

Ask about her arrangements for after the class.

6 She answers library/
homework.

7 Answer lunch/cafeteria/
friends.

She asks you the same
question.

SELF-CHECK

I CAN . . .

○ . . . use possessive pronouns – *mine* etc.

○ . . . use the present progressive for temporary actions in the present

○ . . . choose correctly between present progressive and present simple

○ . . . use the present progressive for future arrangements

○ . . . say why, using *to*, *so that*, *because*

○ . . . use infinitives of purpose, with weak *to*.

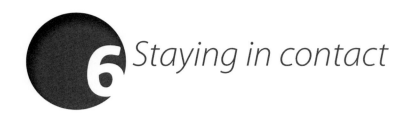

6 Staying in contact

In this unit you will learn how to:
▶ *talk about future plans, using* going to
▶ *talk about making arrangements: possibilities, suggestions and offers*
▶ *use phone language.*

VOCABULARY
▶ *numbers, family names*

PRONUNCIATION
▶ *using stress to correct mistakes*

CEFR: *Can handle numbers, quantities, cost and time. Can ask people for things and give people things (A1). Can understand sentences and frequently used expressions related to areas of most immediate relevance. Can make and respond to invitations, suggestions and apologies. Can make arrangements to meet, decide where to go and what to do (A2). Can understand the main points of clear standard input on familiar matters regularly encountered in work and leisure (B1).*

The story

 06.01 * *Tasha and Oliver continue their conversation. They exchange personal details and plan future contact.*

Listen to the conversation one, two or three times.

Read the sentences below and decide *Yes* or *No*.

    1 Oliver would like to see Tasha again.

    2 Tasha would like to see Oliver again.

    3 He gives her his contact details.

    4 She gives him her contact details.

    5 They arrange a meeting.

    6 They arrange to make a phone call.

    7 They're arriving in London soon.

Oliver	As I'm working in London for two weeks, we could … we could meet for a drink one evening, if you like.
Tasha	Yes, that would be nice.
Oliver	Shall I give you my number? I'll give you both my mobile and my office numbers – then you can phone me and we can arrange something.
Tasha	OK. Just a minute. Where's my phone?
Tasha opens her bag and gets her phone.	
Tasha	OK, what's your family name?
Oliver	Rees.
Tasha	Is that R double E, C, E?
Oliver	No, it's R, double E, S, actually, and my mobile number is 0769 1894304.
Tasha	0769 1 …?
Oliver	894 … 304 and the phone number of the London office is 020 7402 3277.
Tasha	020 7402 …?
Oliver	3277. You can get me on extension 159, I think it is. Yes, 159. Or you could email me. My email address is orees (O, R, double E, S) @ starmail.com.
Tasha	OK. When we land, I'll send you a text and then you'll have my number. I can give you the landline number of my friend's house now, if you like.
Oliver	Why not? Then I can call you.

Tasha	My other name's Harrison, by the way. Tasha Harrison.
Oliver	Harrison, 'H', Tasha Harrison. And your friend's number is …?
Tasha	020 8549 6682.
Oliver	020 8949 …
Tasha	Actually, it's 020 8549 6682 … Yes, that's it.
Oliver	When would you like me to call, during the day or in the evening?
Tasha	I don't mind. I'm going to visit relatives and do other things but I'm going to spend time at home with my friends, too. So, any time's all right with me, really. I'm on holiday!
Oliver	Right then, I'll phone you sometime next week, Tasha, if that's OK.
Tasha	Yes, I'll look forward to it.
Oliver	Oh, look, the 'Fasten your seat belts' sign is on. We're landing in a minute.

* For an American English version, listen to **11.09**.

Listening and reading

LANGUAGE TIP
▶ For @ in an email address, we say *at*.
▶ For the *dot* or *full stop* in an email or Internet address, we say *dot*.
▶ For example, for *@starmail.com* we say *at starmail dot com*.

1 06.01 **Listen and answer the questions.**

Cover the text of the story.

Read the questions.

For 1 and 5 listen and choose the correct answers.

For 2, 3 and 4 complete the information where possible.

1 Oliver talks about
   a dinner
   b a drink ⎫ next week.
   c the cinema ⎭

2 Oliver's details
   a his family name
   b the name of his hotel
   c his mobile phone number
   d his office phone number
   e his email address

3 Tasha's details
   a her family name
   b her friend's name
   c her friend's address
   d her friend's phone number
   e her email address

4 Tasha's plans for her holiday
(three activities)

    a _____

    b _____

    c _____

5 Who's phoning who and when?

    a Oliver's phoning Tasha

    b Tasha's phoning Oliver

    c next weekend

    d next week

    e in the day

    f in the evening

2 Listen, read and complete.

Read the sentences.

06.01 Listen again and complete the words.

Then read the text of the story to check your answers.

1 **a** Oliver would like to see Tasha again.
He suggests a drink. He says, *We c __ __ __ d meet for a drink.*

   b Tasha responds. *Yes, t __ __ t / w __ __ __ d / be / n __ __ e.*

2 **a** Oliver talks about possible contact. He offers to give Tasha his phone numbers.
He says, *S __ __ __ __ __ / __ / give you my number?*

   b Then he says, *I' __ __ / give you both my mobile and office numbers – then you / __ __ __ __ /*
phone me and we / __ __ __ __ / arrange something.

3 Oliver also talks about email.
He says, *Or you / __ __ __ __ __ / email me.*

4 **a** Tasha also talks about possible contact.
She decides to send Oliver a text so that he has her number.
She says, *I' __ __ / s __ __ __ __ / y __ __ / a text.*

   b Tasha also wants to give Oliver her friend's number.
She says, *I / __ __ __ __ / give you the landline number of my friend's house now if you like.*

5 **a** Oliver offers to phone Tasha next week.
He says, *I' __ __ / phone you some time next week.*

   b Tasha feels positive about it.
She says, *I' __ __ / l __ __ k / f __ __ w __ __ d / t __ / i __*

6 Oliver asks Tasha for a time.
He says, *When w __ __ __ __ / you / l __ __ __ / m __ / t __ / call?*

7 Tasha talks about her plans for her holiday.
She says, *I' __ / g __ __ __ __ / t __ / v __ __ __ t / relatives and do other things but I'm / g*
__ __ __ __ / t __ / s __ __ __ __ / time at home with my friends, too.

CONTACT INFORMATION

3 Read and complete.

06.01 **Read the text of the story again and complete the words.**

1 Oliver would like to meet Tasha for a drink. Does he say exactly when?
No. He says, *We could meet o __ __ / e __ __ __ __ __ __ g.*

2 a Oliver checks whether it is all right with Tasha. He says,
We could meet for a drink …, i __ / y __ __ / l __ __ __.

  b Later he checks that a phone call is all right.
He says, *i __ / t __ __ __ 's / __ __.*

3 Is the meeting fixed? No.
Oliver says, *You can phone me … and we can a __ __ __ __ __ __ / s __ __ __ __ __ __ __ __ g.*

4 020 7402 3277 isn't Oliver's direct number. His direct number is e __ __ __ __ __ __ __ n
159.

5 Oliver gives Tasha his contact details and she gives him her friend's landline
number t __ __.

6 Tasha needs time to find her phone. She says *J __ __ __ / a minute.*

7 Does he need Tasha's family name? Yes. Has he got it? No. Tasha gives him this
information. She says *My other name's Harrison, b __ / t __ __ / w __ __.*

8 a Does Tasha choose day or evening for the phone call?
No. She says, *I / d __ __ __' __ / m __ __ d.*

  b Oliver can phone in the day and he can phone in the evening.
He can phone a __ __ / t __ __ __.

9 Tasha accepts Oliver's suggestion. Oliver starts his promise to call her next week with
the phrase, *R __ __ __ __ __ / t __ __ n.*

10 Which day is Oliver calling Tasha? We don't know exactly. He says,
S __ __ __ t __ __ __ / next week.

11a This is a 'fasten your seatbelts' s __ __ __.
Is it __ __? Yes. Why? Because they're arriving
soon.

  b Planes take off and l __ __ __.

12 Verb *get*.
  a Why does Tasha open her bag? – to <u>get</u> her phone.
  b Oliver says, *You can <u>get</u> me on extension 159.*
    Which one means *contact*, which one means *take*?

Vocabulary builder 1

NUMBERS 1–10

1 Write the number for each word. Use your dictionary, if necessary.

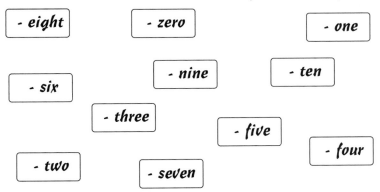

- eight   - zero   - one

- six   - nine   - ten

- three   - five   - four

- two   - seven

2 Practise numbers 1–10.

Practise saying the numbers backwards as fast as possible: ten, nine, etc.

Practise counting in twos.

What are the even numbers? Two, four, etc.

What are the odd numbers? One, three, etc.

PHONE NUMBERS

3 06.02 Listen and choose.

Read the sentences.

Listen to the phone numbers and choose a or b.

1 For *0* they say:
  a zero
  b O (the name of the letter).

2 When two numbers are the same, for example *77*, they say:
  a two sevens
  b double seven

3 For *8549* they say:
  a eight – five – four – nine
  b 85 (eighty-five), 49 (forty-nine).

Oliver	… and the phone number of the office is 020 7402 3277.
Tasha	And your friend's number is …?
Oliver	020 8549 6682.

 # Practice

SOMETIME AND *ANYTIME*

Example from the story

I'll phone you sometime next week.

▶ Here *sometime* means:

   a you are promising a phone call.

   b The time of the call isn't fixed.

Another use of *sometime*: *I've got an appointment sometime next week.*

Meaning: The appointment is fixed for next week but I don't know/remember when exactly.

With *Phone me anytime*, you are saying you are available <u>all the time</u>.

▶ *Anytime* means:

   a the time isn't fixed.

   b The person can choose the time.

For example, *You can call me anytime tomorrow.*

The person can call at 9, 10 or 11, etc. – when they like.

1 Complete these sentences with *some time* or *any time*.

   1 When's John coming back from Australia?

   _____ tomorrow, I think.

   2 When can I use the laptop?

   _____ you like.

   3 When can we visit him in hospital?

   _____ between 10 a.m. and 9 p.m.

   4 When's your appointment at the dentist's?

   _____ next Wednesday.

BY THE WAY

We know that indirect language is very common in English. *By the way* is another example.

Example from the story

Oliver wants to add Tasha to his contacts. He needs her family name. Before he asks, she gives him the extra information. She says, *My other name's Harrison, by the way.*

With *by the way* the sentence or question is:

   ▶ correct

   ▶ communicative

   ▶ indirect.

Without *by the way* the sentence or question is:

   ▶ correct

   ▶ communicative

   ▶ direct

Q When do I use *by the way*?

A To make the question or information indirect.

OR

To introduce a new topic in an indirect way.

By the way can go at the beginning or the end of the question or sentence.

2 What would you say in these situations?

Example: Your colleague's talking to you about her husband. You want to know her husband's job. Ask her.

By the way, what does your husband do? OR *What does your husband do, by the way?*

1 You're talking to a friend. You can't remember her boyfriend's name.

2 Your colleague's baby is very ill. He is in hospital. You're talking to your colleague. Ask about the baby.

3 You buy a new computer. You're at work, talking to your colleagues. Tell them.

4 You're at a friend's house. Your friend is having a party tomorrow. You would like your new girlfriend to come to the party. Ask your friend.

5 Your friend Mary is thinking about a trip to England. You want to know her decision.

6 Your friend promises to give you the phone number of a new friend. It's a week later. Ask for the number.

7 You invite a new friend to dinner. You want to cook fish. You're talking to the friend on the phone. Check that he likes fish.

8 A colleague is having a meeting with a new client. You join the meeting. Say hello and introduce yourself.

How do you pronounce it? (1)

USING STRESS TO CORRECT MISTAKES

In English we often use stress to correct mistakes.

How do you correct, for example, a wrong phone number in your language? Some languages use extra words. For example, 'No, it's not 3, it's 2.'

Example from the story

1 06.03 Listen and repeat.

Listen to this example from the story.

Oliver	And your friend's number is …?
Tasha	020 8549 6682.
Oliver	020 8949 …
Tasha	Actually, it's 020 8549 6682.

▶ To correct a person, we stress the correct number(s).

Listen again and repeat the last line.

2 **Read and find the differences.**

Read the four mini dialogues.

Find the different number in B – the number(s) where there is a mistake.

1 **A** Is that 8954 6210?
   B Sorry, this is 8954 3210.

2 **A** I'm calling 01223 55 31 13.
   B Sorry, you've got the wrong number. This is 01223 55 31 31.

3 **A** Hello, Anna's Coffee Shop?
   B I'm trying to get 8749 4168.
   A Sorry, this is 4178.

4 **A** Hello! Vicky?
   B Sorry, there's no one called Vicky here.
   A Isn't that 01932 214218?
   B No, I'm afraid not. This is 01532 214218.

 3 06.04 **Listen and correct.**

Now listen to the four mini dialogues again and repeat the last lines, using stress to correct the mistakes.

4 **Read and correct.**

Where are the 'mistakes' in the mini dialogues? Some of the 'mistakes' are only a different opinion.

Find the 'corrections', the syllable(s) with stress in B.

1 **A** I'd like to meet your girlfriend.
   B Julie? She's my sister.

2 **A** The meeting's on Thursday.
   B I think it's on Wednesday.

3 **A** He's a good singer.
   B He's a fantastic singer.

4 **A** We need some sandwiches.
   B We need lots of sandwiches.

5 **A** The dictionary's not on the desk.
   B No, it's under the desk, on the floor.

6 **A** I can phone you tomorrow.
   B No, it's my turn, I'll call you.

5 06.05 **Listen and correct.**

Now, listen to the dialogues and correct the mistakes, using stress.

Language discovery 1

 TALKING ABOUT FUTURE PLANS, USING *GOING TO*

Example from the story

Tasha talks about her holiday plans.

She says, *I'm going to visit relatives and do other things but I'm going to spend time at home with my friends, too.*

Meaning

Here, *going to* is for future plans.

Form

The form is the verb *go* in present progressive + *to* + verb.

1 Make mini dialogues.

Match sentences 1–9 with the correct sentence or question a–i.

1 A _____
   B Because he's not at home.

2 A _____
   B After the news.

3 A _____
   B Oh, is he? Who to?

4 A _____
   B Is he? I hope he passes.

5 A _____
   B Are you? That's nice.

6 A _____
   B Oh, just a sandwich, I think.

7 A _____
   B Yes, I think they are.

8 A _____
   B I can, if you like.

9 A _____
   B Aren't you? Why not?

> **a** I'm going to visit my parents next week.
> **b** Are your friends going to buy that house?
> **c** He's going to take his driving test next year.
> **d** We aren't going to invite them.
> **e** What are you going to have for lunch?
> **f** Why aren't you going to call his landline?
> **g** Who's going to make some tea?
> **h** When are you going to put the TV off?
> **i** He's going to get married.

MAKING ARRANGEMENTS: POSSIBILITIES, SUGGESTIONS AND OFFERS

Examples from the story

We could meet for a drink one evening.

You can get me on extension 159.

I'll phone you sometime next week.

Shall I give you my number?

When would you like me to call you?

▶ Here, *can, could, I'll, shall I?* and *would you like me to?* are all similar in meaning.

Meaning and form

Situation: Your friend is ill, in hospital. You want to visit him/her. You are talking to his/her partner.

Summary – possibilities, suggestions, offers	
I can I could I'll	go to the hospital tomorrow.
Shall I Would you like me to	go to the hospital tomorrow?

▶ All these expressions are correct and appropriate.

▶ *Could* is a little less direct than the others.

▶ *Shall I?* and *Would you like me to?* are questions. Here, *I can, I could* and *I'll* aren't questions but they need a response.

▶ To say *yes*, you can use an echo question. (Echo questions are explained in Unit 2.)

▶ *Can you? Could you?* and *Would you?* are echo questions for the expressions given.

▶ The offer and the echo question can have different verbs.

Examples: 1 A I'll do that for you.

  B Can you?

2 A I could ask him.

  B Would you?

Q Can I say *It's possible for me to (go to the hospital tomorrow)* for offers?

A The grammar is correct.

  ▶ Students of English often say *It's possible, Is it possible? It isn't possible.* It is more common to say *I can, I could, I'll, shall I?* or *Would you like me to?* for offers.

2 Read and answer.

Situation: Debbie is my neighbour. She's got four young children. I arrive at her house.

Read the conversation and answer the three questions.

Me	Hi, Debbie. Isn't it cold today? How are you?
Debbie	Not very well at all, actually, and it's nearly time for school.
Me	I can take the children to school for you if you like.
Debbie	Really? Are you sure?
Me	Yes, of course.
Debbie	That's very kind of you. I feel really terrible!
Me	Right, now you just go and sit down and I'll make you a cup of tea. Shall I call the doctor?
Debbie	Could you? Thanks.
Me	Where can I find the number?
Debbie	In the little book by the phone. Could you ask for an appointment as soon as possible, please?
Me	No problem. How about dinner this evening? Would you like me to cook for you all? The children could eat at my house.
Debbie	Thanks for the offer, but it's all right. My husband doesn't mind cooking, actually.

  1 Choose a or b. Debbie is:
     a fine.
     b not very well.
  2 I offer to do four things for her. Note them down.
  3 For each of my offers, does Debbie say *Yes* or *No*?
     ▶ *Really? Are you sure?* It is common to check an offer of help before you say *yes*.
     ▶ *Not very well at all, actually* is more common than *I'm ill*.

3 Read and complete.

Read the sentences. Find the exact words in the dialogue with Debbie.

Complete the dialogue.

  1 I offer to take the children to school.   Debbie says *Yes*.
     I say _____ .   She says _____ .
  2 I offer to make a cup of tea.
     I say _____ .

3 I offer to call the doctor.
   I say _____ .

Debbie says *Yes.*
She says _____ .

4 I need help to find the number.
   I ask _____ .

5 I offer to cook dinner.
   I say _____ .

6 I suggest the children eat at
   my house.
   I say _____ .

Debbie says *No.*

She says _____ .

 4 **06.06 Listen and repeat.**

Now listen to the dialogue with Debbie. The long sentences are divided into short phrases. The short phrases are repeated to build the longer sentences.

Pause the audio in the gaps, and repeat what you hear. Pay special attention to your intonation.

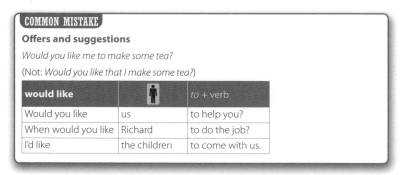

COMMON MISTAKE

Offers and suggestions

Would you like me to make some tea?

(Not: *Would you like that I make some tea?*)

would like	👤	*to* + verb
Would you like	us	to help you?
When would you like	Richard	to do the job?
I'd like	the children	to come with us.

5 Read and complete.

Situation: You are on the phone to your friend. Your friend is bored.

Read the conversation and complete with the correct phrases. Several options are possible.

I can   I could   We could   Shall I
Would you   I'll   Shall we
Would you like me to   Could you

Your friend	I'm bored.
You	_____ **1** go to the cinema(?)
Your friend	That's a good idea. _____ **2** go to the ABC(?) They've got nine screens there.
You	Why not? I've got the car tonight. _____ **3** pick you up on the way(?)
Your friend	_____ ? **4** Great! Thanks!
Your friend	Do you know what time the films start there?
You	I've got no idea. _____ **5** call and ask(?)
Your friend	Don't worry, I think it's usually about eight o'clock.
You	Fine. _____ **6** get to your house around seven(?) Is that OK?
Your friend	Yes, an hour is plenty of time to get there, decide which film to see and buy the tickets.
You	See you later, then. Bye.
Your friend	Bye!

6 **Do they mean *yes* or *no*?**

Now look at these responses from the dialogue.

For each response, decide: do they mean *yes* or *no*?

Suggestions/offers	**Responses**
1 We could go to the cinema.	That's a good idea.
2 Shall we go to the ABC?	Why not?
3 Shall I pick you up on the way?	Can you? *or* Could you? *or* Would you?
4 I'll call and ask (the times).	Don't worry.

Summary – saying *Yes* and *No* to offers and suggestions	
Saying *Yes* That's very kind of you. (Yes,) That's a good idea. (Yes,) Why not? (Yes,) That would be nice. OK. Could you? Can you? Would you?	Saying *No* Thanks (for the offer), but it's all right. Don't worry ...

You can see from these expressions that:

▶ It is very common to say *yes* without using the word *yes*.

▶ It is very common to say *no* without using the word *no*.

These are more examples of indirect language.

Vocabulary builder 2

FIRST NAMES AND FAMILY NAMES

> **FAMILY NAMES (OR SURNAMES)**
>
> Q How do I answer the question, *What's your name?*
>
> A In an informal situation, give your first name. In a formal situation, give your first name and then your family name(s). In official situations give your family name.
>
> Nowadays, at work most people are informal – they use first names.
>
> When a woman gets married, she very often changes her family name and takes her husband's name – for example, Lily Dickens marries Jack Green and her new name is Lily Green or Mrs Green. Some women keep their family name. Others keep their family name and add their husband's (e.g. Lily Dickens-Green).
>
> Here are some of the most common family names in Britain: Smith, Jones, Taylor, Williams, Brown, Davies, Evans, Wilson, Thomas, Roberts, Johnson, Lewis, Walker, Robinson, Wood, Thompson, White, Watson, Jackson, Wright, Green, Harris, Cooper, Hughes, Lee and Martin.
>
> Some family names are male first names + *s*. For example, First name: Edward; family name: Edwards.

1 Which name is it, the first name or family name?

Look at the two lists. They are the same except for the *s* at the end of the family name.

 06.07 Listen to eight mini dialogues – one for each pair of names in the lists.

Choose the first name or the family name.

First names	Family names
1 William	Williams
2 Daniel	Daniels
3 Peter	Peters
4 Richard	Richards
5 Steven	Stevens
6 Hugh	Hughes
7 Matthew	Matthews
8 Edward	Edwards

Listen again and check your answers.

## Writing

Names in your country.

Write your answers or prepare to tell a friend.

How many names do people usually have in your country?

_____

Which names do people use more at work, first names or family names?

_____

What happens to a woman's name when she gets married?

_____

What are the most common family names in your country?

_____

In your language have you got special words or names for people who are special to you? Give some examples.

_____

Do you have special titles for older people?

_____

Phone services

1 **06.08 Listen and complete.**

Read the information.

Listen and complete the numbers for Britain.

International phone calls:

The international code for Britain is: _____

Special services:

Emergency – fire

        police

        ambulance   } _____ This number is free.

Directory enquiries:

national: _____

international: _____

Listen again and check your answers.

2 **What are these numbers in your country?**

Complete the phone number information for your country.

PHONE NUMBERS

▶ Most landline codes in the UK begin with 01. See the map.

▶ London has two landline codes – 0207 for Inner London and 0208 for Outer London.

▶ Mobile numbers begin with 07 and have 11 numbers.

▶ Some big companies have numbers beginning 08.

▶ Phone calls to 0800 numbers are free.

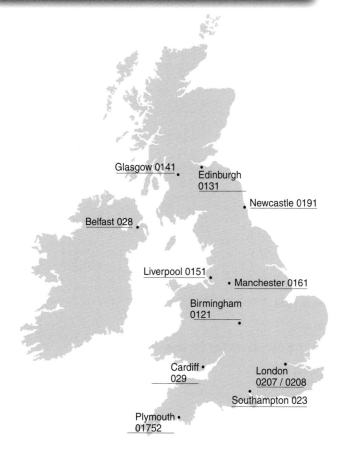

Glasgow 0141
Edinburgh 0131
Newcastle 0191
Belfast 028
Liverpool 0151
Manchester 0161
Birmingham 0121
Cardiff 029
London 0207 / 0208
Southampton 023
Plymouth 01752

 ## Language discovery 2

USING PHONE LANGUAGE

1 06.09 What do these phone sounds mean?

Read the sentences a–e.

Listen and match sounds 1–5 with sentences a–e.

a It's engaged. Try again later.

b Oh dear! It's out of order.

c That means you've got a line. You can dial now.

d Wrong number? Dial it again.

e It's ringing. Someone'll answer it in a minute.

> **LANGUAGE TIP**
>
> On the phone we say:
> *This is ...* (Not: *I am ...*)
> *Is that ...?* (Not: *Are you ...?*)
>
> *John speaking.*
> *It's John speaking.*
> *It's John here.* } (Not: *I am John.*)
> *John here.*
> *Speaking.* } (Not: *Yes, I am X.*)

 2 **06.10** **Listen to and read the two mini dialogues.**

> *Ring ring ...*
> **Rachel**   6537. Hello?
> **Richard**   Can I speak to Rachel,
>   please?
> **Rachel**   Speaking.
> *Ring ring ...*
> **Rachel**   Hello?
> **Mac**   This is Mac. Is that Rachel?
> **Rachel**   Yes, it's me.

3 **Complete these two dialogues with the phrases from the mini dialogues in Exercise 2.**

1

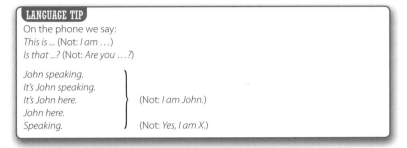

Hi, _____ Tom. _____ Andrea?

Hello, Tom. No, _____ Vicky. Hang on a minute and I'll call her. Andrea, _____ Tom on the phone for you.

Tom   Vicky

2

Hello. Is David there, please?

Peter   David

How do you pronounce it? (2)

SPELLING

1 06.11 Listen and complete.

Situation: I teach a class of people who want to be English teachers. Here is my register (list of students). Some names are missing. The spelling of some names is wrong.

Listen and write or correct the family names.

CLASS REGISTER

1 Lesley _____

2 Denise Varnish

3 Matt Hanant

4 Anne _____

5 Simon _____

6 John Pierson

7 Joan _____

8 Liz Thomson-Smith

2 What's the question?

The answer is S – M – I – T – H.

The question is: _____ ?

Speaking and listening

It is easy to confuse some letters, for example *s* and *f* or *p* and *b*, especially on the phone. To make the difference, we say, for example, *F for Foxtrot* or *S for Sierra*. Some people use other common words or names for this, for example *A for apple*.

THE INTERNATIONAL PHONETIC ALPHABET (IPA)

Look at this example:

Receptionist	What name is it, please?
Caller	Eva Rach.
Receptionist	Is that R – A – T for Tango?
Caller	No, it's R – A – C for Charlie – H.

Here the speakers are using the IPA (International Phonetic Alphabet, also sometimes called the NATO Alphabet) to make sure it is clear which letter they are saying.

1 06.12 **Listen and repeat the letters and words.**

A – Alpha	N – November
B – Bravo	O – Oscar
C – Charlie	P – Papa
D – Delta	Q – Quebec
E – Echo	R – Romeo
F – Foxtrot	S – Sierra
G – Golf	T – Tango
H – Hotel	U – Uniform
I – India	V – Victor
J – Juliet	W – Whisky
K – Kilo	X – X-ray
L – Lima	Y – Yankee
M – Mike	Z – Zulu

2 Spell aloud this Japanese family name using the IPA:
S A K O T A.

WHICH LETTER IS IT?

Example from the class register exercise

A My name's Farnish.

B Is that with an *F* or a *V*?

A With an *F*.

3 06.13 **Listen and choose.**

Look at the pairs of names.

Listen and choose the correct spelling, a or b.

1 a	Hallis	**b**	Harris
2 a	Fraser	**b**	Frazer
3 a	Stephens	**b**	Stevens
4 a	Simms	**b**	Sims
5 a	Stupps	**b**	Stubbs
6 a	Initial F	**b**	Initial S

SPELLING VOWELS

Many learners of English have problems with the names of English vowels (*a, e, i, o, u*). Here's some practice.

4 06.14 **Listen and complete the spelling of these surnames.**

   1 P __ P __ R
   2 S N __ __ T H __
   3 S M __ __ T __ N
   4 T __ Y L __ R
   5 S H __ R __ D __ N
   6 R __ __ D __ R
   7 S __ M __ __ L S

Listen again and check your answers.

5 **Spelling your name aloud and giving your contact details**

   Practise spelling your names and address aloud – clarify difficult letters.

   Practise saying the numbers aloud.

First name _____

Middle name(s) _____

Family name(s) _____

Phone number (home) _____

Email address _____

Address _____

Passport number _____

6 **What would you say?**

Situation 1 You phone a friend in England from your country. You get a wrong number.

You: _____

Situation 2 You are on the phone. The mobile signal is very bad. You can't hear the other person.

You: _____

Revision

WHAT IS IT IN YOUR LANGUAGE?

Here are some examples of the important points in this unit.

Translate the sentences into your language.

Remember – translate the idea, not the words.

   1 **a** We could go out for a pizza tonight.
      b That's a good idea!
   2 **a** I'll book the restaurant for tomorrow.
      b I'll look forward to it.
   3 **a** Shall I make some coffee?
      b Yes, please.

4 a Can I help you?

  b It's very kind of you, thank you, but it's all right.

5 By the way, how's your mother today – is she better?

6 I'm going to buy a car tomorrow.

Writing

You and your friend Jo get a new flat. Write a Facebook entry about your future plans, using *going to* – e.g. *We're going to paint the kitchen yellow*.

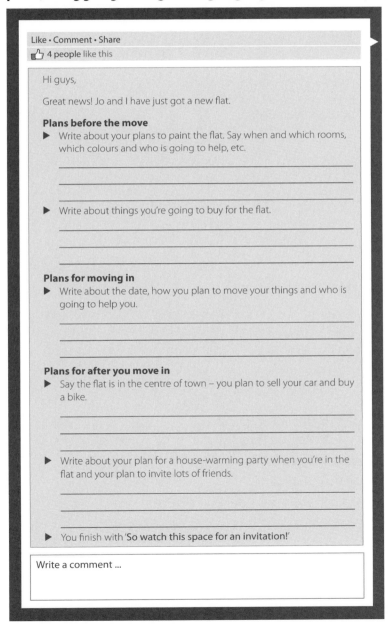

Like • Comment • Share

👍 **4 people** like this

Hi guys,

Great news! Jo and I have just got a new flat.

Plans before the move
▶ Write about your plans to paint the flat. Say when and which rooms, which colours and who is going to help, etc.

_____

_____

_____

▶ Write about things you're going to buy for the flat.

_____

_____

_____

Plans for moving in
▶ Write about the date, how you plan to move your things and who is going to help you.

_____

_____

_____

Plans for after you move in
▶ Say the flat is in the centre of town – you plan to sell your car and buy a bike.

_____

_____

_____

▶ Write about your plan for a house-warming party when you're in the flat and your plan to invite lots of friends.

_____

_____

_____

▶ You finish with 'So watch this space for an invitation!'

Write a comment ...

Speaking

06.15 Now it's your turn to join the conversation.

Listen again to the story conversation.

Say Oliver's words in the spaces.

Test yourself

Read and choose.

Which one is right? Choose a or b.

1 Three plus five is:
   a nine.
   b eight.

2 Surname, family name and other name mean:
   a the same.
   b something different.

3 You ask someone to wait. You say:
   a A moment.
   b Just a minute, please.

4 Beer or wine?
   a I don't mind.
   b It is not matter.

5 I can't speak to Peter. His number is:
   a occupied.
   b engaged.

6 I can't use the machine. It's:
   a out of operation.
   b out of order.

7 On the phone:
   a Here speaks Rodica.   **b** This is Rodica.
   a Is that Peter?   **b** Are you Peter?

8 **a** Please, it is possible I speak with Jenny?
   b Could I speak to Jenny, please?

9 Your phone number is in my:
   a contacts.
   b agenda.

10 The shop is open 24 hours a day. You can go shopping:
   a all the times.
   b at any time.

11 a Would you like that I go with you?

    b Would you like me to go with you?

12 Shall I ask him?

    a Yes, you shall.

    b Yes, please.

13 Shall we go out for a drink after work?

    a Sorry, I go out with my wife to a family dinner.

    b Sorry, I'm going out with my wife to a family dinner.

14 a Why he is going to sell the house?

    b Why is he going to sell the house?

Which one is better? Choose a or b.

15 Would you like me to translate that for you? I speak Japanese.

    a Yes, I would.

    b Thanks.

16 Shall I do that?

    a No.

    b I'm all right, thanks.

Which ones are right?

17 I'll do that for you, shall I?

    a Can you? Thanks.

    b Could you? Thanks.

    c Would you? Thanks.

 Write a dialogue.

Situation: You are on the phone to your friend.

You	**Your friend**
1 Suggest a Chinese meal and a DVD at his house. 	 *What can we do this evening?*
3 You offer to get the food and DVD on the way. 	**2** Respond *Yes*. 
	4 Respond *Yes*. Ask him/her to get Chinese chicken with rice. 
5 Respond *Yes* and offer to get some beer.	**6** Respond *No*. Say you've got some.
7 You ask what type of film he'd like to see.	**8** Say you have no preference.

SELF-CHECK

I CAN . . .

○ . . . talk about future plans, using going to

○ . . . talk about making arrangements: possibilities, suggestions and offers

○ . . . use phone language

○ . . . use stress to correct mistakes.

7 Travelling and handling money

In this unit you will learn how to:

▶ *Invite people to do things, using* **If you would like to …**
▶ *Suggest doing something together, using* **Let's …,** *and respond*
▶ *Ask people to do things, using* **Can you …?, Could you …?** *and* **Would you mind …?** *and respond*
▶ *Ask for help, using indirect questions.*

VOCABULARY

▶ *numbers, luggage and travel, prepositions, money*

PRONUNCIATION

▶ *linking words; understanding numbers*

CEFR: *Can handle numbers, quantities, cost and time. Can ask people for things and give people things (A1). Can understand sentences and frequently used expressions related to areas of most immediate relevance. Can make and respond to invitations, suggestions and apologies. Can ask about things and make simple transactions in shops (A2). Can understand the main points of clear standard input on familiar matters regularly encountered in work and leisure (B1).*

The story 1

 07.01 *The plane is arriving in London at Heathrow Airport.*

Situation: *The pilot of the plane talks to all the passengers. He makes an announcement.*

Listen to his announcement one, two or three times

Choose ALL the things he talks about.

The captain talks about
    a seat belts
    b passports
    c the time
    d the arrival time
    e the temperature
    f the weather.

Pilot	Good morning, ladies and gentlemen. This is your captain speaking again. In a few moments, we will begin our descent into London's Heathrow Airport. Please return to your seats and fasten your seatbelts. If you would like to adjust your watches, the time in London is now 6.50 in the morning and the temperature on the ground is –2 degrees centigrade. Our estimated time of arrival is 7.15. That's a quarter past seven on the ground in London. The forecast for today is cold … but bright.

* For an American English version, listen to **11.10**.

Listening and reading

 1 **07.01 Listen and choose.**

Read the questions.

Listen and choose a or b.

  1 The time in London is now:
    a six fifteen (6.15).
    b six fifty (6.50).
  2 The temperature is:
    a 2 degrees Centigrade.
    b –2 degrees Centigrade.
  3 They're landing at:
    a seven fifteen (7.15).
    b seven fifty (7.50).

LANGUAGE TIP

British weather reports and forecasts sometimes give the temperature in both centigrade (Celsius) and Fahrenheit. Note: 0 °C = 32 °F.

2 Read and complete.

Read the sentences.

Read the text of the pilot's announcement in the story and complete the words.

1 The pilot wants to talk to all the people on the plane.
  He says, *Good morning, l _ _ _ _ _ s / and g _ _ _ l e _ _ n.*

2 Does he say, *I am your captain*? No, he uses telephone language. He says, *T _ _ _ _ / _ _ / your captain.*

3 We don't call the pilot *Pilot Smith*, we say *C _ _ _ _ _ _ Smith.*

4 The pilot invites the passengers to change the time on their watches. He says *I _ / y _ _ / w _ _ _ _ _ / l _ k _ / t _ / adjust your watches, the time in London is . . .*

5 Does the pilot know the exact time they are arriving in London? No, he says, *Our e _ _ _ _ _ _ _ _ d / time / o _ / a _ r _ _ _ _ l / is 7.15.*

6 What television programme is immediately after the news? Usually it's the weather f _ _ _ _ _ _ _ where they talk about the weather for the rest of today, tomorrow, etc.

How do you pronounce it?

 PRONOUNCING GROUPS OF WORDS – LINKING WORDS

▶ When we speak, we often join a word to the next word.

▶ This happens when one word ends with a consonant and the next word starts with a vowel.

▶ Two examples from the story are *ladies and*, *this is*.

▶ Sometimes the last letter isn't a consonant. It's the last sound that's important – for example, in the phrase *time in London*, the last sound in *time* is /m/.

 07.02 Read, listen and repeat.

Read the phrases. They are from the story.

Listen to these phrases and repeat them.

Pay special attention to the linking words marked.

> ladies‿and gentlemen
>
> This‿is your captain speaking‿again.
>
> in‿a few moments
>
> The time‿in London‿is now 6.50.
>
> That's‿a quarter past seven‿on the ground‿in London.

Ⓥ Vocabulary builder 1

NUMBERS TO 100

1 Complete the table with these numbers.

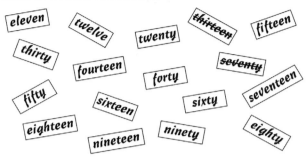

1 one	**11** _____		
2 two	**12** _____	**20** _____	
3 three	**13** thirteen	**30** _____	
4 four	**14** _____	**40** _____	
5 five	**15** _____	**50** _____	
6 six	**16** _____	**60** _____	
7 seven	**17** _____	**70** seventy	
8 eight	**18** _____	**80** _____	
9 nine	**19** _____	**90** _____	**100** a hundred

2 Write these numbers in figures.

ninety-nine _____	twelve _____	forty-three _____	thirty-one _____
eleven _____	seventy-six _____	eighty-five _____	twenty-two _____
sixty-four _____	fifty-seven _____	seventeen _____	a hundred _____

3 Write these numbers in words.

18 _____	59 _____	13 _____
93 _____	15 _____	21 _____
86 _____	16 _____	45 _____
19 _____	37 _____	12 _____
14 _____	68 _____	100 _____

> **LANGUAGE TIP**
> **Maths in words**
>
> | | + | − | x | ÷ | = |
> |---|---|---|---|---|---|
> | | and | take away | times | divided by | is |
> | more formal/ technical | plus | minus | multiplied by | | equals |

Example:

Q How do you say 2 + 7 in English?

A There are two ways:

   g Two and seven are nine.

   h Two plus seven equals nine (more formal/technical).

 4 Now try some mental maths. Say these sums aloud when you do them.

Example: Eleven and five and seventeen and forty-two is _____ . You say, *Eleven and five is sixteen, and seventeen is thirty-four, and forty-two is seventy-six.*

   1 Nine and six and twenty-three and eighteen is _____ .

   2 Four and twelve and two and fourteen is _____ .

 5 Say these numbers aloud as quickly as possible.

   a Say the even numbers up to 20 – two, four, six, etc.

   b Say the odd numbers up to 20 – one, three, five, etc.

   c Count in fives up to 50. Five, ten, etc.

   d Count in threes up to 36. Three, six, etc.

   e Can you say the eight times table in English?

     One eight is eight

     Two eights are sixteen

     Three eights are …

6 Write the sums in figures.

Use the numbers and signs in the box to help you.

   a Twenty plus ten equals thirty. 20 _____ 30.

   b Twelve minus one is eleven. _____

   c Four multiplied by six equals twenty-four. _____

   d Twenty-seven divided by three is nine. _____

4	12	30	11	3	10	27	6	1	24	9	20
		+		–		×		÷		=	

Language discovery 1

 INVITING PEOPLE TO DO THINGS

Example from the story

The pilot invites the passengers to change the times on their watches.

He says, *If you would like to adjust your watches …*

▶ We use *if you would like to* for two situations:

   1 to invite people

   2 to ask and tell people to do things in a polite, indirect way.

For example:

1 *We're having a small dinner party on Saturday. If you would like to join us …* Meaning: *I'm inviting you to the dinner party.*

2 *If you would like to take a seat for a moment …* Meaning: *Please sit down and wait.*

▸ When you are asking someone to do something, it is common not to finish the sentence.

For example:

Situation: At the reception of a small hotel.

Receptionist: *If you would just like to follow me, please …* (He/she doesn't say *I can show you to your room* – the meaning is clear from the situation. She doesn't need to finish the sentence.)

▸ This expression is particularly common in formal and new situations.

1 Where can you hear these 'invitations'?

Read the 'invitations' 1–10.

Match each invitation with one of the places in the pictures. You can use each place more than once.

1 If you would like to come back for your watch sometime later this afternoon … around 4 …

2 If you would like to sit there, Kevin, next to my husband …

3 I've got your son here. I'm afraid he's not very well, so if you would like to come and pick him up …

4 I'm sorry but Mr Smith isn't here this afternoon. If you would like to give me your name and number …

5 If you would like to come with me to the cash desk …

6 If you would like to go through to the waiting room …

7 If you would like to go in, the manager can see you now …

8 If you would like to just open your mouth and say *aah*… oh yes …

9 If you would all like to come to the table …

10 If everybody would like to be quiet now, please …

Q What are the possible responses to these invitations? Is it OK to say *Yes*?

A *Yes* alone isn't appropriate.

Look at these responses.

1 You can say,   *Thank you.*
                            Yes, that's fine.
                            Yes, of course.
                            Yes, I'll + verb.

2 You say nothing and 'do' the action.

3 If you are following someone, you can say, *After you*.

2 Read and match.

Match each sentence with an appropriate response, a–e, in the box.

1 In a shop:

    A If you would like to come back for your watch sometime later this afternoon … around 4 …

    B _____

2 In a school:

    A I've got your son here. I'm afraid he's not very well, so if you would like to come and pick him up …

    B _____

3 In an office:

    A I'm sorry but Mr Smith isn't here this afternoon. If you would like to give me your name and telephone number …

    B _____

4 In a shop:

    A If you would like to come with me to the cash desk …

    B _____

5 In an office:

    A If you would like to go in, the manager can see you now.

    B _____

a **Thank you.**

b **Yes, I'll be there as soon as I can.**

c **Yes, of course, it's Ford, and my mobile is ...**

d **Yes, that's fine.**

e **After you.**

The story 2

07.03* *Our story continues. Oliver and Tasha get off the plane.*

1 Listen and put the conversation in order.

In the story 2, the conversation between Oliver and Tasha is in six parts, a–f. The six parts are in the wrong order.

Look at pictures 1–6. The pictures are in the correct order.

Listen and write the correct letter, a–f, for each picture.

a

Oliver	Well, it's been really nice talking to you, Tasha.
Tasha	Yes, and thanks for the help with the luggage.
Oliver	I'll be in touch next week, then.
Tasha	Yes, bye.
Oliver	Bye.

b

| Oliver | Wow, this suitcase is a bit heavy – is that it now? |
| Tasha | The suitcase, the small bag and my handbag – yes, that's everything. |

c

Oliver	Now, it's this way. You haven't got anything to declare, have you?
Tasha	No, nothing.
Oliver	We can go through the green channel, then. Over there.

d

| Immigration officer | Thank you, madam. Sir, your passport, please. Thank you. |

e

Oliver	Do you need a trolley?
Tasha	That would be a good idea – I've got quite a lot of luggage.
Oliver	They're just over here. Now, let's find the rest of the luggage.

f

Tasha	Would you mind waiting for just a minute, Oliver?
Oliver	Of course not. The suitcases aren't here yet, anyway.
Tasha	Could you look after my trolley? Oh, and can you take my coat, please?
Oliver	Sure, go ahead.

Tasha asks for help at the information desk.

Airport employee	Can I help you?
Tasha	Yes, could you tell me where the ladies' is, please?
Airport employee	Of course, madam. Just over there. Can you see the sign?

* For an American English version, listen to **11.11**.

2 Choose the correct sign for each picture 1–6.

INFORMATION DESK   CUSTOMS   ARRIVALS

PASSPORT CONTROL   TROLLEYS

BAGGAGE RECLAIM 5

3 Where are the people?

Read the sentences and mini dialogues A–F.

Choose the correct letter A–F for each of the pictures 1–6.

A Could you open your bag for me, please?
Yes, of course.

B Hello, Rachel, it's lovely to see you again. How are you?

C Excuse me, I'm from this flight but my suitcase isn't here.

D Have you got a visa?
Yes, it's on the next page.

E I think we need two, don't you? One isn't enough for all this luggage.

F How can I help you, sir?
Where can I change some money, please?

4 Read and choose a or b.

Read the sentences.

Read the text of the story 2 conversation again and choose a or b.

1 Tasha has got:
  a one piece of luggage.
  b two pieces of luggage.

2 They go to the:
  a green channel at customs.
  b red channel at customs.

3 Tasha needs to:
  a change some money.
  b go to the toilet.

5 Read and complete.

Read the sentences.

Read the text of the story 2 conversation again and complete the words.

1 They get the trolley. Oliver suggests they find their suitcases.
He says, *Now, I __ __ ' __ / find the rest of the luggage.*

2 a Tasha asks Oliver to wait for her. She says,
W __ __ __ __ / you / m __ __ __ __ / w __ __ __ __ __ g / for just a minute?

7 Travelling and handling money   133

b Oliver responds, *Of / c _ _ _ _ _ e / n _ t.*

   c Tasha asks Oliver to look after her trolley and take her coat.

   She says, *C _ _ _ _ _ / y _ _ / look after my trolley? Oh, and / c _ _ / y _ _ / take my coat, p _ _ _ _ _ ?*

   d Oliver responds, *S _ _ _ / g _ / a _ _ _ d.*

3 **a** The person at the information desk offers Tasha help.

   She says, *C _ _ / l / h _ _ _ _ / y _ _ ?*

   b Tasha asks for help to find the ladies' toilets.

   She asks, *C _ _ _ _ _ / y _ _ / t _ _ _ _ / m _ / where the ladies' / _ _ /, please?*

> ### LANGUAGE TIP
> *The ladies'* is the short expression for *the ladies' toilets.*
> *The men's* or *gents'* are short expressions for *the (gentle)men's toilets.*
> We say *the ladies'/men's is over there.* (Not: *are*)
> The words *ladies'* and *gents'* are for public toilets only.

6 **Find the words and phrases.**

Read the sentences.

Read the text of the story 2 conversation again. Find and complete the words and phrases.

1 Oliver has only got one suitcase but Tasha's got q _ _ _ _ / a / l _ _ / of / l _ _ g _ _ e.

2 Are the suitcases on the way? *Yes.*

   Are the suitcases there? *No, not y _ _ .*

3 Tasha asks Oliver to wait. To wait isn't a problem because the suitcases aren't there.

   Oliver says, *The suitcases aren't here yet, a _ _ w _ _ .*

4 How can you ask, *Is that all (your luggage?)* in two other ways?

   Is that _ _ ? or *Is that e _ _ _ _ _ t _ _ _ g?*

5 When you take someone somewhere, you can say, *It's t _ _ _ / w _ _ .*

6 **a** Oliver checks Tasha hasn't got anything to declare. He says, *You / h _ _ _ _ _ ' _ / got / a _ _ th _ _ _ _ / to declare, / h _ _ _ _ / y _ _ ?*

   b Has Tasha got anything to declare? *No, n _ _ _ _ _ _ g.*

7 Oliver is happy about meeting Tasha on the plane. He says, *I _ ' _ / b _ _ n / r _ _ _ _ _ y / n _ _ e / t _ _ k _ _ g / t _ / you, Tasha.*

8 Tasha thanks Oliver f _ _ his help with her suitcase.

9 He says he'll contact her next week. He says, *I ' _ _ / b _ / i _ / t _ _ _ _ _ / next week.*

10 Verb *get*: in part **e** Oliver says, *I'll go and get one* (trolley).

   Here, *get* means:

   a buy.

   b bring one here.

Vocabulary builder 2

LUGGAGE AND BAGGAGE

Q What are the differences between *suitcase*, *luggage* and *baggage*?

A Answer:

Meaning

1 This is a suitcase.

2 This is luggage.

3 This is baggage.

Form

  ▸ *Suitcase* is countable – *one suitcase* (two syllables), *two suitcases* (three syllables).

  ▸ *Luggage* and *baggage* are uncountable/mass words.

Example: Our suitcases and bags are in the car.
             OR
             Our luggage is in the car.

  ▸ The unit word for *luggage* is *piece*. For example, an airport employee might say: *How many pieces of luggage have you got?*

  ▸ We often say *case* for *suitcase*. *Suitcase* is more formal.

1 Complete the sentences with *(suit)case(s)*, *luggage*, *pieces of luggage* or *baggage*.

  1 People take guitars, boxes and all sorts of _____ on planes.

  2 Passengers can take one small piece of hand _____ on to the plane with them.

  3 On this flight you can take two _____ of _____ .

  4 Let's go, kids! Are your _____ in the car?

USING THE CORRECT PREPOSITIONS

In English, prepositions are very important. Always pay special attention to the correct preposition in a phrase.

2 Choose the correct preposition from the box to complete the sentences.

for   on   with   to   at   in

1 Thank you _____ a lovely evening!

2 Just a minute. I'm talking _____ my sister.

3 Bye! Don't forget to stay _____ touch.

3 Choose the correct preposition.

Choose one preposition from the box for each group of phrases.

You will need to use some prepositions for more than one group.

on   to   by   at   in

1 _____	**2** _____	**3** _____
… car multiplied … divided …	… the end of the day … any time We arrive … one o'clock. Look … the example.	… Rome … the morning … a shop
4 _____	**5** _____	**6** _____
… the ground … this flight … the plane … Channel 4	Next … Paul I'm talking … my sister Listen … the conversation Pay attention … your pronunciation.	… your country … the shower … ten minutes … the spaces
7 _____	**8** _____	**9** _____
… Sunday evenings … TV I'm not keen … it. … the next page	She walks … school Please go … the information desk. We're on our way … the park.	… Unit 3 … figures … a few moments

Language discovery 2

 SUGGESTING DOING SOMETHING TOGETHER, USING *LET'S* …

Example from the story

Oliver and Tasha get a trolley. Oliver suggests they find their suitcases.

He says, *Now, let's find the rest of the luggage.*

Meaning

Who is making a suggestion? Oliver.

Does the suggestion include Oliver? Yes.

▶ Use *let's* when the suggestion includes you.

Form

Let's + verb:

▶ The negative is *let's not* + verb.

▶ The short answer is, *Yes, let's.*

▶ The question tag is *Let's (go), shall we?*

Let's – summary of responses	
☺ Positive responses are	Yes, let's!
	OK/All right.
	Yes, why not?
	That's a good idea.
	Yes, why don't we?
☹ Possible negative responses are	No, let's not.
	Do you really want to?
	I'm not too sure.
	Perhaps not .
	Actually, I'm not too keen.

1 Write suggestions and responses.

Situation: You live with Chris, a friend of yours.

Write suggestions and responses for these situations.

1 It's very hot. You and Chris are sitting in the garden, talking. You're thirsty.

You _____

Chris _____ ☺

2 You both have a friend, Hilary. Hilary is ill. Suggest you both go and visit her this afternoon.

You _____ ?

Chris _____ ☹

3 Chris puts the TV on. There's a football match on. You don't like football and there's a good film on Channel 5.

You _____ the football. Why don't we watch the film on Channel 5 instead?

Chris _____ ☺

4 You are talking about a holiday. Suggest Mexico.

You _____ Mexico.

Chris _____ ☹

Chris suggests inviting Sam (another friend), too.

Chris _____

You _____ ☹

5 You are going to a party tonight. You're very tired. You don't want to go.

You _____ to the party. _____ stay here instead.

Chris Shall we have a Chinese takeaway?

You _____ ☺

Q What's the difference between *We could .../We can ...* (see Unit 6) and *Let's ...*?

A Here are two examples:

Situation: You're with a friend, talking about this evening.

    a We could go to the cinema.

    b Let's go to the cinema.

▶ In **a** *We could* …, the cinema is a possibility.

▶ In **b** *Let's* …, you would like to go to the cinema and you would like the other person to go, too.

▶ *We could* is less direct.

ASKING PEOPLE TO DO THINGS, USING *CAN YOU...? COULD YOU...? WOULD YOU MIND...?*

Examples from the story

    1 Tasha asks Oliver to wait for her. She says, *Would you mind waiting for just a minute?* Oliver responds, *Of course not.*

    2 Tasha asks Oliver to look after her trolley and take her coat.
       She says, *Could you look after my trolley? Oh, and can you take my coat, please?*
       Oliver responds, *Sure, go ahead.*

▶ A response isn't always necessary. The person can 'do' the action without a response.

Grammar summary – asking someone to do something		
Request	**Responses – it's OK**	**Responses – it isn't OK**
Can you + *verb* …?	Sure	
Could you + *verb* …?	Of course	I'm afraid I can't
	Of course I can/could	I'm sorry but I can't
	Yes, that's no problem	I'm sorry but + *reason*
Would you mind	Of course not	
+ *verb*/ing?	Not at all	

▶ It is very common to say *please* when you ask someone to do something.

▶ Answers *Yes, I can*, *Yes, I could*, *No, I can't*, *No, I wouldn't*, etc. alone are not usually appropriate.

▶ *Would you mind?* means *Is it a problem for you to …?*

    If it is not a problem, the response is negative: *No, of course not.*

▶ When you say *no*, it is common to give a reason.

Example: *Could you cook the dinner tomorrow, please?*
            I'm sorry, I can't. I'm going out to dinner with Julie.

▶ *Could* is less direct than *can*.

▶ *Would you mind ...?* can be more formal than *Can you?/Could you?*

Grammar summary – asking someone NOT to do something	
	☺ **Positive response**
	Oh! I'm sorry.
Would you mind not + *verb* + -ing?	☹ **Negative responses**
	Is it really a problem? (*indirect*)
	What's the problem? (*very direct!*)

# Practice 1

1 Write requests and choose responses.

Read the situations.

Complete the requests.

Choose an appropriate response from the box, where necessary.

1 Someone speaks to you in English but you don't understand. Ask them to say it again.
   You Ca _____ , please?

2 You are eating with friends. You would like some water. The bottle is at the other end of the table.
   You Co _____ ?
   Your friend _____ .

3 Your child asks for help with his/her English homework.
   Your child Mum/Dad, ca _____ ?
   You _____ .

4 You are a tourist and you've got a camera. You want a photo with your friends. You ask another tourist.
   You W _____ ?
   The tourist _____ .

5 The telephone rings. You are just going in the shower. Ask the person to call you back in ten minutes.
   You Ca _____ ?
   The caller _____ .

6 A friend is staying in your house. She smokes in the kitchen.
   You really don't like it. Ask her not to.
   You W _____ ?
   Your friend _____ .

7 Someone tells you a new word in English. You want to write it but you don't know the spelling.
   You Co _____ ?
   The other person _____ .

Responses

Of course. What is it?

I'm sorry but I'm going out right now and it's urgent.

Oh, sorry!

Not at all – what do I do?

Yes, it's T – H – A … etc.

Yes, here you are.

2 **07.04 Understanding official announcements.**

Situation: On a plane or at an airport.

Read the flight attendants' requests and invitations (a–g).

Listen to the announcements 1–7. Just try to understand the message – it is not necessary to understand all the words. You will hear each one twice.

Match the requests and the announcements.

a Could you please go back to your seat, sir? We're landing soon.

b I'm sorry, could you please sit down again, madam? The plane is still moving.

c Could you put those bags in the overhead compartments, please?

d Could you please hurry, sir? The aircraft is ready to leave.

e Could you please stay in your seat, sir, and fasten your seatbelt? It's a little bumpy ahead.

f If you wouldn't mind filling this in, madam … You'll need it at passport control.

g If you would like to report to the special desk, sir, when you get off the plane …

> **LANGUAGE TIP**
>
> In hotels, restaurants, airports, shops, etc., the staff say *sir* to a man and *madam* to a woman. Clients and customers don't use *sir* or *madam* with staff.
>
> If we use the family name, we say *Mr* or *Mrs* or *Ms* + family name.

Language discovery 3

 ASKING FOR HELP – INDIRECT QUESTIONS

Examples from the story

The person at the information desk offers Tasha help.

She says, *Can I help you?*

Tasha asks for help to find the toilets.

She says, *Could you tell me where the ladies' is, please?*

Direct question	Where's the ladies', please?
Indirect question	Could you tell me where the ladies' is, please?

Meaning and form

▶ Both *Could you …* and *Can you …* are grammatically correct.

▶ *Could you …* is very common because it is indirect.

▶ Use *Could you tell me …*
   Can you show me …   } to ask for help.
   Would you mind explaining …

▶ In these expressions, *asking for help* and *asking someone to do something* are the same.

Common mistake – word order in indirect questions

Can you tell me how much this is, please? ✓

(subject + verb ✓)

(NOT: *Can you tell me how much is this, please?*) ✗

(verb + subject ✗)

▶ Word order is important with indirect questions.

Q Where is the question form in indirect questions?

A At the beginning.

Can you …
Could you … } is the question. (verb + subject)
Would you mind …

▶ The question is at the beginning.

▶ The second part of the sentence is not a question. For this reason there is no question form here.

Indirect questions – verb *be*			
Indirect question phrase	**question words**	**subject**	**verb**
Can you tell me	where		
Could you tell me	how much	it	is?
Would you mind telling me	when		
	who		

Complete the indirect questions.

Here are six direct questions asking for help.

Ask the questions in a polite (indirect) way.

Start with *Excuse me, …*

    1 Where's the coffee bar?
      Excuse me, ca ⎯⎯⎯⎯⎯⎯⎯⎯⎯⎯⎯⎯ ?

    2 Where are the toilets?'
      Excuse me, co ⎯⎯⎯⎯⎯⎯⎯⎯⎯⎯⎯⎯ ?

    3 How much is this?
      Excuse me, co ⎯⎯⎯⎯⎯⎯⎯⎯⎯⎯⎯⎯ ?

    4 How much are these?
      Excuse me, w ⎯⎯⎯⎯⎯⎯⎯⎯⎯⎯⎯⎯ ?

    5 How much is this magazine?
      Excuse me, ca ⎯⎯⎯⎯⎯⎯⎯⎯⎯⎯⎯⎯ ?

    6 How much are these crisps?
      Excuse me, co ⎯⎯⎯⎯⎯⎯⎯⎯⎯⎯⎯⎯ ?

LANGUAGE TIP

Money (sterling)
- ▶ The currency (unit of money) in Britain is the pound (£).
- ▶ The sign £ goes in front of the number, for example £15. (Not: 15£).
- ▶ There are 100 pence (we often say *p*) in £1.
- ▶ The coins are: 1p, 2p, 5p, 10p, 20p, 50p, £1, £2.
- ▶ The notes are: £5, £10, £20, £50.

Q How do we say, for example, *£3.20*?

A We can say, *Three pounds, twenty pence* (more formal)

OR *Three pounds, twenty* ⎫
  (less formal).
OR *Three pounds, twenty p* ⎭

Writing

ABOUT YOUR COUNTRY: MONEY

Read the questions.

Either write your answers or prepare to tell a friend.

1 What is the currency in your country?

_____

2 What are the coins?

_____

3 What are the notes?

_____

4 How do you write it?

_____

5 How do you say it?

_____

The story 3

07.05* *Our story continues. Oliver is in a shop in the airport.*

Oliver	Excuse me, do you sell *Marketing Week*?
Assistant	Yes, sir, they're here.
Oliver	And a packet of mints – have you got Polos?
The assistant gets a packet of Polos.	
Assistant	£4.45 please, sir.
Oliver	Sorry, I haven't got any change. Is £20.00 all right?
Assistant	Yes, no problem. Fifteen pounds, 55p change.
Oliver	Thanks.

* For an American English version, listen to **11.12**.

 1 07.05 Listen and answer.

Read the questions.

Listen and choose the correct answers.

1 Oliver buys <u>one/two/three/four</u> things.

2 Oliver's got the right money. <u>Yes/No</u>

2 Listen and choose.

Read the sentences.

 07.05 Listen again and choose the correct answer.

1 Oliver buys:
  a a newspaper.
  b a magazine.

2 He buys:
  a a Mars bar too.
  b a packet of Polos too.
  c a packet of crisps too.
  d a bar of chocolate too.

3 The total price is:
  a £5.45.
  b £4.55.
  c £4.45.

4 Oliver gives the man:
  a £5.
  b £10.
  c £20.

5 The change is:

  a £15.45.

  b £15.05.

  c £5.55.

  d £15.55.

6 The change is:

  a right.

  b wrong.

Vocabulary builder 3

SNACKS

1 Label the pictures.

  Choose one expression from Box 1 and one word from Box 2.

  Use your dictionary, if necessary.

  Example: a packet of polos

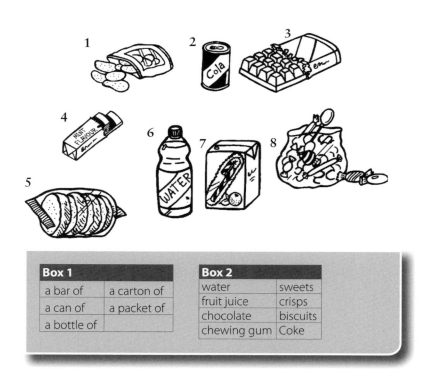

Box 1	
a bar of	a carton of
a can of	a packet of
a bottle of	

Box 2	
water	sweets
fruit juice	crisps
chocolate	biscuits
chewing gum	Coke

07.06 Listen and check your answers.

> **SNACKS**
> ▶ Snacks are very common in Britain.
> ▶ Sweet things are very popular, especially sweets and chocolate, for example Polos (mint sweets) and Mars bars.
> ▶ It is common to have biscuits and cakes, especially with tea and coffee.
> ▶ Savoury snacks, for example crisps and nuts, are also popular.
> ▶ All the snacks in Exercise 1 are very common.
> ▶ People eat snacks at any time of the day.
> ▶ At work, a snack with tea and coffee is very usual.
> ▶ For people interested in healthy eating, shops often have fruit, yoghurts and cereal bars as healthier snacks.
> ▶ In the summer, ice cream is a popular snack.

2 About you: snacks

Write answers to the questions or prepare to tell a friend.

1 What do people eat and drink between meals in your country?

2 Write two lists:

   a snacks you like.

   b snacks you don't like.

How do you pronounce it?

 UNDERSTANDING NUMBERS

07.07 Is it 13 or 30?

Look at the stress pattern.

13 thir<u>teen</u>		30 <u>thir</u>ty	
14 four<u>teen</u>		40 <u>for</u>ty	
15 fif<u>teen</u>		50 <u>fif</u>ty	
16 six<u>teen</u>		60 <u>six</u>ty, etc.	

Can you hear the difference?

Listen and choose the correct picture, a or b.

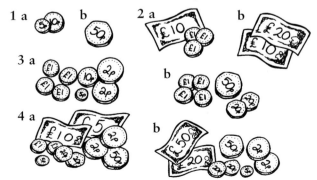

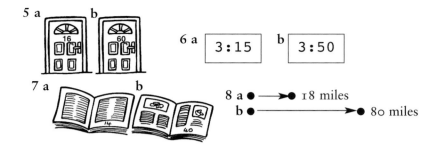

5 a b

6 a 3:15   b 3:50

7 a b

8 a ●——→● 18 miles
   b ●——————→● 80 miles

1 **A** Excuse me, how much is this, please?
   B 50p.
2 **A** How much does this cost, please?
   B £13.
   A Sorry, is that £13 or £30?
   B £13, sir.
3 **A** Do you know how much this is, please?
   B £4.90.
4 **A** Excuse me, could you tell me how much this costs, please?
   B Of course. That's £17.99.
   A Is that one, seven or seven 'O'?
   B One seven, seventeen.
5 **A** Where do you live?
   B At number 60.
6 **A** At what time?
   B At 3.15.
7 **A** Where is it?
   B On page 40.
8 **A** How far is it to the town?
   B 18 miles.

Practice 2

1 **Asking the price.**

   Read 1–4 of the transcript of audio track 07.07.

   Copy the four questions to ask the price.

   Choose *direct* or *indirect* for each one.

   1 _____? Direct/Indirect
   2 _____? Direct/Indirect
   3 _____? Direct/Indirect
   4 _____? Direct/Indirect

2 07.07 Listen again and repeat the questions and answers.

> **COMMON MISTAKE**
>
> **Indirect questions**
> ▶ The word order in indirect questions is always the same.
>   The question is at the beginning and the rest is normal word order – subject first,
>   then verb.
>   *Excuse me, could you tell me how much this costs, please?*
>   (Not: *Excuse me, could you tell me how much does this cost, please?*)
> ▶ Use *if* with *yes/no* indirect questions.
>   Direct question: *Does this shop open on Sundays?*
>   Indirect question: *Do you know if this shop opens on Sundays?*

3 Asking for help – indirect questions.

Which one is correct? Choose a or b.

1 Excuse me, do you know how much _____, please?
  a are these   **b** these are
2 Could you tell me _____, please?
  a where the coffee bar is   **b** where is the coffee bar
3 Do you know when _____?
  a starts the film   **b** the film starts
4 Excuse me, can you tell me _____?
  a where this train goes   **b** where does this train go
5 Do you know what _____?
  a does he do   **b** he does
6 Excuse me, can you tell me _____ to the town centre, please?
  a how far is it   **b** how far it is
7 Could you tell me _____ there?
  a how do I get   **b** how to get
8 Do you know when _____?
  a he is arriving   **b** is he arriving
9 Can you tell me what _____ in English?
  a is this   **b** this is
10 Can you tell me _____ to London?
  a does this train go   **b** if this train goes
11 Could you tell me _____ the right bus for the
   airport, please?
  a if this is   **b** is this

Choose a, b, or c.

12 Do you know _____?*
  a what means this word
  b what this word means
  c what does mean this word

*This one's difficult for very many learners of English – have you got it right?

Speaking

What would you say?

1 You buy something in a shop.
The person gives you the wrong change.

_____

2 You are at baggage reclaim at the airport. Your suitcase doesn't come.

_____

Revision

WHAT IS IT IN YOUR LANGUAGE?

Here are some examples of the important points in this unit.

Translate the sentences into your language.

Remember – translate the idea, not the words.

1 You arrive at a restaurant. The person working there says, _If you would like to follow me … (I'll show you to your table)._

2 A What shall we do today?
   B Let's go to my brother's.
   A Fine, why not?

3 A Shall we walk there?
   B I'm not too keen on that idea. Let's go by car.

4 A Can I help you?'
   B Yes, could you tell me where the coffee bar is, please?

5 A I'm sorry I can't go tomorrow. Would you mind changing the meeting to Wednesday?
   B Of course not – that's no problem.

6 At the end of a conversation you say, _It's been nice talking to you._

7 Do you need a trolley? I'll go and get one.

Writing

1 Write these sentences in the correct order and find the preposition.

Example: me/at/and/come/see/o'clock/three/_preposition_
      Come and see me at three o'clock.

1 morning/we/on/the/London/tour/could/a/go/of/_preposition_
2 car/go/let's/_preposition_
3 are/talking/who/you/_preposition_?
4 it/be/to/is/TV/going/_preposition_?
5 brother/stand/your/next/_preposition_
6 passengers/there/this/many/are/plane/how/_preposition_?

7 of/they/have/the/don't/dinner/end/the/flight/together/*preposition*?

8 ♪ Bye! you/minutes/see/I'll/five/*preposition*

9 mind/would/signing/page 2/you/please/*preposition*?

10 time/can/mind/change/any/you/your/*preposition*.

2 Making polite requests.

Look at the example from Exercise 1 – *Come and see me at three o'clock*.

Come is the imperative. In English, using the imperative can seem very direct and abrupt (there is more on this in Unit 9).

It is more common to ask people to do things in a polite/indirect way.

Which request phrase is suitable in each situation?

> **Would you mind ....?   Can you ....?   Could you ...?**

Talking to a friend _____

Asking an office colleague for help _____

Asking a hotel receptionist for help _____

Now read the imperative sentences. They are all very direct and abrupt. Decide which person you are talking to and write the request in a polite/indirect way.

1 Turn the TV off!

2 Show me how to use the new photocopier!

3 Pass me the bread!

4 Sign here, sir!

5 Don't use your mobile in here, madam!

6 I'm in a meeting. Take a message for me!

7 Take a seat for a moment!

8 Lend me £20!

9 Lend me your stapler!

10 Call a taxi for me!

LANGUAGE TIP

In the story, Tasha uses all three expressions when she asks Oliver, *Would you mind waiting for just a minute?*, *Could you look after my trolley?* and *Can you take my coat?* There are two reasons for this.

1   Their relationship is changing – they are getting more friendly.

2   When we ask a person to do more than one thing, we often mix the phrases.

Please is very common in English. You can use it with all three phrases.

 Speaking

🎧 07.08 **Now it's your turn to join the conversation.**

**Look at the text. It's the complete conversation from The story 2,
when Oliver and Tasha get off the plane. Notice the linking in Oliver's words.**

Listen and read Tasha's words in the spaces.

Find and note where there is linking between Tasha's words.

Immigration officer	Thank you, madam. Sir, your passport, please. Thank you.
Oliver	Do you need a trolley?
Tasha	That would be a good idea – I've got quite a lot of luggage.
Oliver	They're just over here. Now, let's find the rest of the luggage.
Tasha	Would you mind waiting for just a minute, Oliver?
Oliver	Of course not. The suitcases aren't here yet, anyway.
Tasha	Could you look after my trolley? Oh, and can you take my coat, please?
Oliver	Sure, go ahead.

Tasha asks for help at the information desk.

Airport employee	Can I help you?
Tasha	Yes, could you tell me where the ladies' is, please?
Airport employee	Of course, madam. Just over there. Can you see the sign?
Oliver	Wow, this suitcase is a bit heavy – is that it now?
Tasha	The suitcase, the small bag and my handbag – yes that's everything.
Oliver	Now, it's this way. You haven't got anything to declare, have you?
Tasha	No, nothing.
Oliver	We can go through the green channel, then. Over there.
Oliver	Well, it's been really nice talking to you, Tasha.
Tasha	Yes and thanks for the help with the luggage.
Oliver	I'll be in touch next week, then.
Tasha	Yes, bye.
Oliver	Bye.

? Test yourself

Which one is right?

Choose a or b.

1 Thirty-five and twenty-nine are:
   a forty-six.
   b sixty-four.

2 If you would like to go in now, madam …
   a Yes, I would.
   b Thank you.

3 **a** Would you mind to wait, please?
   b Would you mind waiting, please?

4 **a** I'm hungry. Let's have something to eat!
   b I'm hungry. Let's to have something to eat!

5 Could you help me, please?
   a Yes. What do you want?
   b Of course. What would you like me to do?

6 Excuse me, can you tell me where the station is, please?
   a Yes, I can.
   b Yes, it's just over there.

7 **a** I'll get a trolley for the luggages.
   b I'll get a trolley for the luggage.

8 The information desk? It's:
   a in this way.
   b this way.

9 **a** Bye, I'll see you tomorrow.
   b Bye, I see you tomorrow.

10 Would you mind coming back later? (You can go back later.)
   a Yes.
   b Sure, it's no problem.

11 **a** Can you tell me where are the taxis, please?
   b Can you tell me where the taxis are, please?

12 £24.75. This is:
   a pounds twenty four, seventy-five.
   b twenty-four pounds, seventy-five.

Write a dialogue.

Situation: Eva is an au pair with the Lewis family. (She works in the family, helping with the children and the house.) It's the morning and Barbara, Lewis and Eva are talking about the day.

Barbara	Eva/child

1 Barbara asks Eva to take the children to school. She's working this morning.

2 Eva says *yes*.

Would you like me to go to the supermarket on the way back?

3 Barbara says *yes* and asks Eva to buy bread, milk and cartons of fruit juice.

4 Eva responds. She asks if Barbara needs more things from the shop.

5 Barbara says *no* and asks Eva to take the children to the park after school.

She also asks her to work on Saturday evening.

6 Eva says she can take the children to the park but she can't work on Saturday evening. She's going to a party.

7 It's the afternoon. Eva is in the park with the children. One of the children sees an ice-cream van and suggests they all have an ice cream.

SELF-CHECK

I CAN . . .
○ . . . invite people to do things, using *If you would like to . . .*
○ . . . suggest doing something together, using *Let's . . .*, and respond
○ . . . ask people to do things using *Can you? Could you?* and *Would you mind . . . ?* and respond
○ . . . ask for help, using indirect questions
○ . . . link words together so that my English sounds natural.

8 *Using public transport*

In this unit you will learn how to:
▶ *use prepositions at the end of questions*
▶ *ask for and give instructions*
▶ *ask for help*
▶ *ask for and understand travel information*
▶ *ask for and give the time*
▶ *use the present simple for timetables and itineraries.*

VOCABULARY
▶ *public transport; the time*

PRONUNCIATION
▶ *stress in place names*

CEFR: *Can handle numbers, quantities, cost and time. Can follow short, simple written directions (A1). Can understand sentences and frequently used expressions related to areas of most immediate relevance. Can find specific, predictable information in simple everyday material such as timetables. Can get simple information about travel, use of public transport, give directions and buy tickets. Can ask for and give directions referring to a map or plan (A2). Can deal with most situations likely to arise while travelling (B1).*

The story 1

 08.01* *Oliver is at the information desk at the airport. He needs to get to the centre of London.*

Listen to the conversation one, two or three times.

1 Read the question and choose the correct answer.

How is Oliver going to the centre? By train, by bus or by taxi?

2 Choose ALL the correct answers.

The man says Oliver can go by bus, or by:

a coach.

b taxi.

c Underground.

d train.

Airport employee	Can I help you?
Oliver	Yes, could you tell me how to get to the centre of town, please?
Airport employee	You can go by bus, by train or by Underground, sir. Which part of London are you going to?
Oliver	I need to get to Victoria Station.
Airport employee	Then you can take the A1 Airbus. It goes all the way to Victoria.
Oliver	The A1, right. And where do I get the bus from?
Airport employee	Just over there, sir. You see the sign that says, 'Airbus'? You follow that sign.
Oliver	Oh, I see! Do you know when the next bus leaves?
Airport employee	In ten minutes, sir – at 8.05.
Oliver	And how long does it take to get there?
Airport employee	I'm not sure – the best thing to do is ask the driver.
Oliver	Many thanks for your help.

* For an American English version, listen to **11.13**.

Listening and reading 1

 1   08.01 Listen and choose the right answer.

Cover the text of the story 1.

Answer the questions. There is only one correct answer to each question.

1 Where exactly in London is Oliver going?

    a Waterloo Station

    b Paddington Station

    c Victoria Station

    d Euston Station

2 What's the name of the bus?

   a London bus

   b Airbus

   c Central bus

   d Express bus

3 Which of the following statements is correct?

   a It's a long walk to the bus.

   b The bus is very near.

   c The bus goes from the train station.

   d The bus is downstairs.

4 The next bus leaves:

   a in an hour.

   b in half an hour.

   c in two minutes' time.

   d in ten minutes' time.

5 When does the bus arrive in London?

   a we don't know

   b in one hour

   c in half an hour

   d in ten minutes

2 Read and complete the words.

Read the sentences.

08.01 Listen again and try to complete the words.

Then read the story to help you, if necessary.

1 a Oliver doesn't know how to get to the centre of town. He asks for help. He says,
C _ _ _ _ _ / you / t _ _ _ _ / me / h _ _ / t _ / g _ _ _ / t _ / the centre of town, please?

   b There are three possibilities. The man says, *You / c _ _ / g _ / b _ / bus, / b _ / train or
b _ / Underground.*

2 a The man asks where exactly in London Oliver is going. He says, *Which part of London /
a _ _ / y _ _ / g _ _ _ _ g / t _ ?*

   b Oliver answers, *I / n _ _ _ _ / t _ / g _ _ / t _ Victoria Station.*

3 a The man suggests the Airbus.
He says, *Y _ _ / c _ _ _ / t _ _ _ _ / the A1 Airbus.*

4 a Oliver doesn't know where the buses are. He asks, *Where / d _ / I / g _ _ / t _ _ /
b _ _ / f _ _ _ _ ?*

   b The man gives Oliver instructions.
Y _ _ / f _ II _ _ _ / the sign that says 'Airbus'.

5 Is it necessary to change?
No, the A1 bus goes *a _ _ / t _ _ _ / w _ _ / to Victoria Station.*

6 Oliver wants to know the time the journey takes. He asks,
H _ _ / I _ _ _ _ / d _ _ _ _ / it / t _ _ _ _ / t _ / g _ _ / there?

How do you pronounce it?

LONDON'S MAIN STATIONS – STRESS

Example from the story

The man asks Oliver: *Which part of London are you going to?*

Oliver answers: *I need to get to Victoria.*

Cover the text of audio 08.02.

 08.02 **Listen and repeat the names.**

Read the transcript. Listen again and find the stress for each one.

1 Victoria
2 Paddington
3 Marylebone
4 King's Cross
5 St Pancras
6 Euston
7 Liverpool Street
8 Waterloo

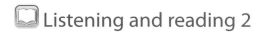

📖 Listening and reading 2

1 **True or false?**
Read the sentences.
Look at the information and map about the London Underground.
Choose *True* or *False*.

Can you correct the *False* sentences?

1 London has eleven Underground lines.		True/False
2 There are ninety-five Underground stations.		True/False
3 Each line has a number.		True/False
4 There is only one fare.		True/False
5 It costs the same all day at the weekend.		True/False
6 You can use Oyster cards and Travelcards on London buses and trains.		True/False
7 It doesn't cost much to use public transport in Britain.		True/False

- ▶ There are just over 249 miles/400 km of Tube tunnel under London's streets, with 11 Underground lines and 270 stations.
- ▶ London Underground carries more than 1 billion passengers (1,229 million) a year.
- ▶ 225,000 passengers a day use Waterloo Station.
- ▶ Each line has a name and a colour. For example, the District Line is green and the Circle Line is yellow. London is divided into six fare zones. Central London is Zone 1.
- ▶ The fare you pay depends on the number of zones you travel in. The cheapest way to travel in London is with an Oyster card. You can also buy a one-day Travelcard. Both the Oyster card and the Travelcard are valid on the Underground, the trains and the buses in London. The Travelcard is valid only after 9.30 in the morning Friday, but all day Saturdays, Sundays and public holidays. Family tickets are also available.
- ▶ Public transport is quite expensive in Britain.

 2 **08.03 Famous places in London – where's the stress?**

You are on a tourist bus in Central London.

Look at the bus route with twelve famous places.

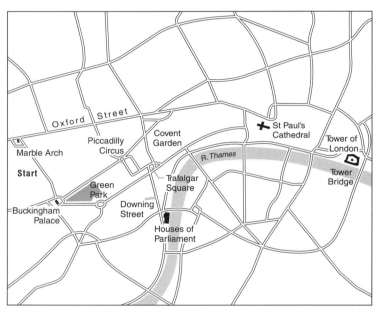

Listen to the announcement.

Read the transcript. Listen again and find the syllable with stress for each place, 1–12.

He's getting off the bus and she's getting on the bus.

Good morning, ladies and gentlemen. Welcome to the Tour of London bus. If you would like to look at your maps for a moment, I can tell you a little bit about our route. This bus stops at the following famous places:

1 Marble Arch
2 Oxford Street
3 Piccadilly Circus
4 Green Park
5 Buckingham Palace
6 Trafalgar Square
7 Downing Street
8 The Houses of Parliament
9 The London Eye
10 St Paul's Cathedral
11 Tower Bridge
12 The Tower of London

Passengers are reminded that you can get on or off the bus at any one of these stops. We hope you enjoy your tour with us this morning.

▶ The stress is at the beginning on two names, <u>Ox</u>ford Street and <u>Dow</u>ning Street.
▶ For most place names the stress is on the second word, such as *Park*, *Palace*, *Square*, *Road*, *Bridge*: London <u>Bridge</u>, Kensington <u>Pa</u>lace.
▶ *Street* is different – the stress is on the first word.

3 08.03 Listen and repeat.

Listen again and repeat the names of these famous places.

 How do you pronounce it?

STRESS ON PLACE NAMES – ADDRESSES

▶ English has lots of words for *Road* or *Street*.

 1 08.04 Listen and repeat.

Listen and repeat these street names. You will hear each one twice.

Find the syllable with stress.

Park Road	High Street	Eton Avenue
Buckingham Gardens	Tudor Drive	Moor Close
West Hill	Elm Crescent	Rose Walk
River Lane	Church Grove	Esher Place
Orchard Way	Maple Court	Nova Mews

2 Find the abbreviation.

When we write an address, we often use an abbreviation – a short form – of the word that means *road*.

Find the abbreviation for the following full words. Example: *1C.*

Full word	**Abbreviation**
1 Road	**a** Ave.
2 Gardens	**b** Dr.
3 Lane	**c** Rd
4 Street	**d** Cl.
5 Drive	**e** St
6 Crescent	**f** Gdns
7 Grove	**g** Pl.
8 Court	**h** Ct
9 Avenue	**I** La.
10 Close	**j** Gr.
11 Walk	**k** Wk
12 Place	**I** Cres.

> **LANGUAGE TIP**
> When we say or write an address, the number is first, before the name of the street – for example *2 Park Road, 57 Eton Avenue.*

Language discovery 1

PREPOSITIONS AT THE END OF QUESTIONS

Examples from the story

1 The man asks Oliver exactly where in London he's going.

He says:

(Question) *Which part of London are you going to?* (preposition!)

Oliver answers:

(Positive) *I'm going to Victoria.*

2 Oliver doesn't know where the buses are.

He asks, *Where do I get the bus from?* (preposition!)

(Possible answer) *You get the bus from the bus stop outside the terminal.*

▶ The grammar is correct with the preposition at the end.

Complete these mini dialogues with the correct question from the list, a–l.

1 **A** _____ ?

   B My brother – I call him every week.

2 **A** _____ ?

   B This picture. Isn't it attractive?

3 **A** _____ ?

   B My girlfriend. It's her birthday today.

4 **A** _____ ?

   B My boyfriend. I miss him.

5 **A** _____ ?

   B My keys. Do you know where they are?

6 **A** There's an urgent email for you.

   B _____ ?

7 **A** I like reading.

   B _____ ?

8 **A** She's married.

   B _____ ?

9 **A** I'm going to that new restaurant this evening.

   B _____ ?

10 **A** **Taxi driver:** _____ ?

   B The station, please.

11 **A** We could go and see that new film this weekend.

   B _____ ?

12 **A** I'd like to book a Eurostar ticket to Paris, please.

   B _____ ?

a Do you know who it's from?
b Oh, is she? Who to?
c They're nice flowers. Who are they for?
d Who are you talking to?
e Of course, sir. When for?
f Are you really? Who are you going with?
g What are you looking at?
h What's it about?
i Do you? What sort of books are you interested in?
j What are you looking for?
k Who are you writing to?
l Where to, madam?

V Vocabulary builder

PUBLIC TRANSPORT VEHICLES

1 Choose the correct words.

Write the names of these vehicles. Choose words from Box 1.

Where do they go from? Choose the place from Box 2 and match it to the picture.

Use your dictionary, if necessary.

Box 1		Box 2	
taxi	train	station	coach station
Underground (train)	bus	bus stop	taxi rank
coach			platform

GETTING AROUND ON PUBLIC TRANSPORT

 2 08.05 Read, listen and complete.

Read the mini dialogues and look at the words in the box.

Listen and complete the dialogues with the correct word(s) from the box.

1 A I don't know the Underground.
Could you give me a _____ , please?
B Of course. Here you are.

162

2 **A** Excuse me, do you know the time of the next train, please?

   B I'm not sure. There's a _____ over there, on the wall.

3 **A** Excuse me, how much is a _____ to London?

   B Is that a _____?

   A No, a _____ , please. I'm coming back this evening.

4 **A** I want to buy a ticket but the _____ is closed.

   B You can get one at the _____ over there.

5 **A** Which _____ does the train go from, please?

   B Number five, right at the end, over there.

6 **A** What's the _____ to the town centre, please?

   B £1.70.

7 **A** Which _____ is Victoria in?

   B One, I think. It's in the centre, isn't it?

8 **A** Which _____ is Heathrow on?

   B The blue one, but I don't know the name of it.

9 **A** Are you going to Edinburgh during your stay?

   B I'd like to but it takes nearly five hours.

   A That's a long _____ .

10 **A** Is this a _____ train?

   B No, I'm afraid it stops at all stations.

11 **A** Is this a _____ train?

   B No, sorry, change at the next stop.

12 **A** I'm not sure which platform to go to.

   B Let's listen to the _____ .

13 **A** We're going on an _____ to Cambridge tomorrow.

   B Oh, are you? What time does your coach leave?

14 **A** *In a taxi.* The fare is £8.80. How much _____ shall I give him?

   B If you give him £10.00, that's fine.

| direct platform journey ticket machine timetable |
| fare line ticket excursion fast announcements tip |
| zone single return map ticket office |

3 Label the pictures.

Now label the pictures, using words from the box in Exercise 2.

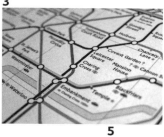

COMMON MISTAKE

~~This is a long travel.~~ ✗

This is a long journey. ✓

Q What's the difference between *travel* and *journey*?

A *Journey* is usually a countable noun.

▶ *Journey* is the time and/or distance from A to B.

For example: *It's a long journey from England to North America.*

▶ *Travel* can be:
  ▷ a verb
  ▷ an uncountable noun.

▶ *Travel* is general movement.

For example:

a I travel a lot for my job.

b Foreign travel is good for a person's education.

4 Travel or journey?

Complete with *journey* or *travel*.

1 It's a long _____ to get here.

2 He's a _____ agent.

3 Foreign _____ helps people understand other cultures.

4 How long does the _____ take?

TRIPS

5 Read and choose.

**Choose the correct phrase from the box to complete the sentences.
Use your dictionary, if necessary.**

> **change your ticket   get on   book a ticket   go on the excursion
> find out about times and prices   get off   cancel the trip**

You would like to go on an excursion.

1 First you _____ .

2 Then you _____ .

3 If something happens and you can't go, you can either

    a _____ or **b** _____ .

4 On the day of the trip you **a** _____ the coach. When you get there, you

    b _____ the coach and have a good time!

Language discovery 2

ASKING FOR INSTRUCTIONS, GIVING INSTRUCTIONS

Examples from the story

Asking for instructions

The man at the information desk says, *Can I help you?* Oliver says, *Yes, could you tell me how to get to the centre of town, please?*

The man says *You can take the A1 Airbus.*

Oliver asks, *Where do I get the bus from?*

Giving instructions

The man answers, *You follow the sign that says 'Airbus'.*

Answer these questions about instructions.

Examples: Where do I get the bus from? You follow the sign …

Meaning and form

1 Choose a, b or c.

   1 In the two examples, *get* and *follow* are:

     a in the past.

     b in the present.

     c in the future.

   2 The tense is:

     a present simple.

     b present progressive.

     c future simple.

▶ We can use the present simple to ask for and give instructions.

2 Read and decide.

Read the seven questions.

How many are correct?

Direct questions
How do I get to the town centre?
How can I get to the town centre?
How could I get to the town centre?

Indirect questions
Can you tell me how to get to the town centre?
Could you tell me how I get to the town centre?
Do you know how I can get to the town centre?
Do you know how I could get to the town centre?

Q What are the differences?

A All the questions are appropriate in most situations.

   ▶ The indirect questions are very common.

   ▶ *Could* is the most indirect.

Summary – instructions						
1 Asking for instructions						
Direct questions						
How	do can could	I get to the town centre?				
Indirect questions						
Can	you	tell show	me	how	I I can	get to the
Could		explain	to me		I could to	town centre?
Do you know how I		can could		get to the town centre?		
2 Giving instructions – present simple						
You go … You follow … You take …						
3 For more than one possibility						
You can + *verb* (without *to*) + or + *verb* (without *to*)						
For example: *You can walk or go by bus.*						

3 Put the words in the right order to complete the question.

1 Excuse me, _____ the station from here, please?

to/how/I/do/get

2 Excuse me, _____ a ticket for tomorrow?

can/where/I/book

3 Excuse me, _____ excursions to Oxford?

out/I/how/find/about/could

4 Can you show me _____ a ticket from this machine, please?

to/how/buy

5 Could you tell me _____ the coach station, please?

to/get/I/how

6 Do you know _____ this door, please?

how/open/can/I

7 Do you know _____ my return ticket, please?

change/I/could/how

Example from the story

Oliver asks, *Where do I go to get the bus?*

The man says, *You follow the sign that says 'Airbus'.*

▶ To give instructions, use the present simple.

4 Complete the instructions.

Situation: You want to make a trip from London to Paris on the Eurostar train. You ask a friend for instructions.

Complete your friend's instructions. Choose the correct verb phrases from the box below the text.

Look at the pictures for help.

It's not necessary to understand all the words. Just try to get the general idea.

She's going down the escalator.

He's going up the escalator.

He's going through the door.

When you get to St Pancras Station, (1) _____ the signs to 'Eurostar'.
(2) _____ the escalator and (3) _____ your ticket from the ticket office.
Then (4) _____ ticket check and security control. After that (5) _____
in the departure lounge. When you hear the announcement to board the train
(6) _____ the right escalator or travelator for your part of the Eurostar platform
and (7) _____ the train, (8) _____ your luggage in the special luggage
racks and (9) _____ your seat. If you need refreshments during the journey – tea,
coffee, something to eat, (10) _____ the buffet car.

> **you go to   you put   you go up   you wait   you go down**
> **you look for   you get on   you go through   you follow**
> **you collect**

ASKING FOR HELP

5 Correct these questions if necessary. Some of the verbs are wrong.

  1 Where I sign?
  2 Can you tell me what do I write in this card?
  3 Where pay I, please?
  4 Can you tell me where I go now, please?
  5 How do I get a taxi?
  6 How I open this door?
  7 Do I write this in English or my language?
  8 I give a tip or not?

6 Now match the questions 1–8 with the possible answers a–h.

  a If you could just wait over there, please, sir.
  b At the bottom, just here.
  c At the cash desk over there, please.
  d Yes, people usually give about 10 per cent.
  e 'Happy birthday' is fine.
  f I can call one for you, madam.
  g They open automatically when the train stops.
  h Either – it doesn't matter.

AN INVITATION TO DINNER: *WHAT DO I SAY? WHAT DO I DO?*

7 Read and choose.

  Situation: Your English colleague invites you to his house for dinner.

  You don't know about British customs and habits.

  You ask a friend to help you.

  Look at the questions a–l.

  Read the dialogue: the answers are given but the questions are missing.

Choose the correct question for each answer.

The first one is completed as an example.

a What do I say if she offers me more food and I don't want it?

b What do I do if they speak very fast and I don't understand?

c Do I shake hands when I arrive?

d Do I take a present? And if so, what sort of present do I take?

e I don't know his wife's name? What do I call her? Do I call her *madam*?

f What do I say if I want to use the bathroom?

g What do I say when I want to leave?

h The invitation is for seven o'clock. What time do I arrive?

i ~~What do I wear?~~

j Do I do anything the next day?

k What do I do and say when I leave?

l What time do I leave?

1 **You** What *do* I wear?
Your friend Informal clothes are fine.

2 **You** _____ ?
Your friend A box of chocolates or flowers is the most common type of present. Lots of visitors like to give a little present from their country. That's fine, too.

3 **You** _____ ?
Your friend Punctuality's quite important here, so it's best to get there within about ten minutes of the time, but not before the time.

4 **You** _____ ?
Your friend Yes, the usual thing is to shake hands and say, *Pleased to meet you* or *How do you do?* when you meet his wife. *How do you do?* is more formal than *Pleased to meet you.*

5 **You** _____ ?
Your friend No, we only use that word in shops and places like that. If you call her *Mrs Parker* to start with, she'll tell you her first name, I'm sure.

6 **You** _____ ?
Your friend You just ask them to speak more slowly.

7 **You** _____ ?
Your friend You say, *No thanks. I'm fine.*

8 **You** _____ ?
Your friend You just say, *Is it all right if I use the toilet?*

9 **You** _____ ?
Your friend You can say, *It's getting late. I'd better go now.*

10 **You** _____ ?
Your friend Between ten and eleven o'clock is normal.

11 **You** _____ ?
Your friend You shake hands again and say, *Thank you for inviting me – it was a lovely evening.*

12 You _____ ?

> **Your friend** You can say *thank you* again to your colleague at work if you like but it's not necessary to write a letter. Some people write a short note or card. This is a formal thank you.

Meaning and form

8 **Read and choose.**

Answer these questions about the verbs in questions a–l in Exercise 7. Choose a, b or c.

1 In the exercise, the dinner is:

  a in the past.

  b in the present.

  c in the future.

2 The tense in the questions is:

  a present simple.

  b present progressive.

  c future simple.

> **LANGUAGE TIP**
>
> We use the present simple to ask for and give instructions or information about a system. In the exercise above, you are asking for information about the cultural systems of invitations – in other words, the habits and customs.
>
> **Q** What's the difference between, for example, *What shall I wear?* (Unit 7) and *What do I wear?*
>
> **A** *What shall I* (+ verb) …? asks for a suggestion.
>
> *What do I* (+ verb) …? asks for information about a system. In other words, *What is the right thing to do/ say/wear, etc. in this situation?*

 ABOUT YOUR COUNTRY: INVITATIONS

Read the questions.

Either write your answers or prepare to tell a friend.

Situation: A colleague invites me to dinner.

Answer my questions about customs and habits in your country.

1 In England, it's common to invite someone to the house. Which is more common in your country, an invitation to the house or to a restaurant?

2 What do I wear?

3 Do I take a present? If so, what sort of present do I take?

4 The invitation is for seven o'clock. Is that a usual time here for a dinner invitation? What time do I arrive?

5 What do I do when I arrive? Do I shake hands with him, with his wife?

6 I don't know his wife's name. What do I call her?

7 What time do I leave?

8 Do I do or say anything the next day?

The story 2

 08.06* *Our story continues. Oliver is walking towards the A1 Airbus. A man talks to him.*

1 Listen and choose.

Read the question.

Listen to the conversation and choose the correct answer.

What's the time?

a 8.00

b 7.55

c 7.52

d 5.28

Man	Excuse me, can you tell me the time, please?
Oliver	Yes, it's five to eight.
Man	Many thanks.

* For an American English version, listen to **11.14**.

2 08.06 Listen again and complete.

Cover the text of the story 2.

Read the questions.

Listen and complete the words.

1 The man asks Oliver the time. He says, Excuse me, *c __ __/y __ __/t __ __ __/m __/*
t __ __/t __ __ __/, please?

2 Oliver answers,
Yes, i __'__/f __ __ __ /t __/e __ __ __t.

3 The man thanks Oliver. He says, *M __ __ __/t __ __ __ __ __.*

Language discovery 3

ASKING FOR AND UNDERSTANDING TRAVEL INFORMATION

Understanding the time

1 Read 1–6 and draw the hands for these watches.

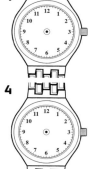

1 Eleven o'clock
2 Half past three
3 A quarter past four

4 A quarter to six
5 Ten to nine
6 Twenty-five past ten

> **TIMETABLES**
>
> *Can you give me times of the trains to . . ., please?*
> ▶ There are two ways to say the time. The previous exercise is the usual way in spoken English.
> ▶ When we want to be very specific, for example, for a timetable:
>   ▷ *we use the 24-hour clock*
>   ▷ *we say the exact number of minutes past the hour, even if it's more than 30. For example, 8.43 is eight forty-three and 11.56 is eleven fifty-six.*
>   ▷ *We say O like the name of the letter for timetables.*

2 08.07 Listen and write the times.

Times of the trains to go   To come back

1 _____   1 _____
2 _____   2 _____
3 _____   3 _____
4 _____   4 _____

Understanding frequency – how often do the trains go?

3 Read and match.

Read the expressions in Boxes 1 and 2.

Read the timetables (a, b, c).

For each timetable, choose one phrase from Box 1 (1, 2, 3) and one phrase from Box 2 (A, B, C).

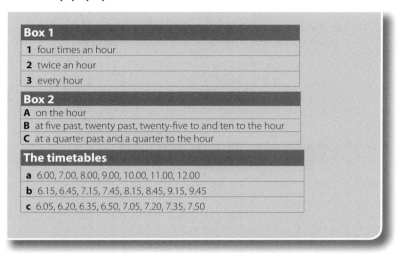

Box 1
1 four times an hour
2 twice an hour
3 every hour

Box 2
A on the hour
B at five past, twenty past, twenty-five to and ten to the hour
C at a quarter past and a quarter to the hour

The timetables
a 6.00, 7.00, 8.00, 9.00, 10.00, 11.00, 12.00
b 6.15, 6.45, 7.15, 7.45, 8.15, 8.45, 9.15, 9.45
c 6.05, 6.20, 6.35, 6.50, 7.05, 7.20, 7.35, 7.50

How long from now?

In the story 1, Oliver asks, *When does the bus leave?*

The employee answers, *In ten minutes(' time) at 8.05.*

In ten minutes (' time)

4 Make four mini dialogues.

Match the questions 1–4 with the correct response, a–d.

1 When's the next train?

2 When's my mummy coming?

3 When do they get to Australia?

4 When are you going back to your country?

a In a week('s time). They're in Hong Kong at the moment.

b In two minutes('time). Come on, let's run!

c In six months('time), at the end of my course.

d In a few minutes('time). She's on her way.

How long does it take?

In the story 1, Oliver wants to know the time the journey takes. He asks, *How long does it take to get there?*

▶ To talk about length of time for an activity we use the verb *take*.

▶ *It takes* (impersonal subject *it* + verb *take*) + verb with *to*.

It takes	my daughter	a long time	to get ready.
Or with the pronouns *me, you, him, her, us, them*…			
It takes	her	a long time	to get ready.

5 Complete these mini dialogues (1–4) with sentences a–d.

1 How long does it take to get there?

a No, only a few minutes. It's easy.

2 Does it take a long time to do that?

b I know. Mine's the same.

3 It doesn't take long to walk there.

c About ten minutes. It's not far.

4 It takes my daughter a long time to get ready in the mornings.

d No, it's very near.

▶ To talk about a specific person with the expression *it takes*, we say *it takes* + person + verb with *to*.

Example:

A How long does it take you to get to work?

B It usually takes me about 50 minutes.

OR you can give a short answer: *About 50 minutes.*

 6 How long does it take you?

Write some things about you, or prepare to tell a friend.

How long does it take you to have breakfast?

How long does it take you to get ready in the morning?

Does it take you a long time to get to work/school? Is it far?

How long does it take your best friend to get to your house from his/her house?

How long does it take you to get to the nearest supermarket from your house?

Does it take you long?

7 Write questions for these answers.

1 _____ ?
I don't eat much in the mornings, really – about ten minutes, I suppose.

2 _____ ?
No time at all – I work from home.

3 _____ ?
I can walk there in about five minutes – I go shopping there most days.

4 _____ ?
School starts at 8.45 and they leave at 8.15, so it's about a half-hour walk.

ASKING AND GIVING THE TIME

8 08.08 Listen and decide.

Look at the digital clocks.

Listen to the six mini dialogues asking and giving the time.

For each clock, write the correct numbers 1–6. There is more than one answer for each clock.

a	**b**	**c**
12.58		13.00		13.04

Expressions for asking the time

9 08.08 Listen and complete.

There are five different expressions for asking the time.

Listen again and, this time, complete the questions.

1 Dad, / _____ ' ___ / _____ time?
2 Excuse me, c _____ / _____ / _____ / _____ / _____ /time, please?
3 John, / _____ / _____ / _____ / _____ time?
4 Could/ _____ / _____ / _____ what/ _____ / _____ / _____ , please?
5 Excuse me,/ _____ / _____ / _____ / _____ / _____ /time/ _____ / _____ ,
please?
6 _____ /you/ _____ / _____ /the time/ _____ , Sharon?

> **LANGUAGE TIP**
> There are lots of ways of asking this simple question in English. Look at the summary.
> All the questions are correct, appropriate and common in most situations.
> The questions in the first group are the most direct.
> When you ask someone you don't know, start with *Excuse me* ...
> *Could you tell me* } *what time it is?* can be formal.
> *Do you know*

Summary – asking the time			
What's Have you got Do you know		the time (please)?	
Could you Can you	tell me	the time (please)?	
	tell me what	the time	is (please)?
		time	it is (please)?
Do you know	what	the time	is (please)?
		time	it is (please)?

THE PRESENT SIMPLE FOR TIMETABLES AND ITINERARIES

 10 08.09 **Listen and complete.**

Situation: You are in London. You want to go to Cambridge for the day. You want to leave London between 9.00 and 10.00 a.m. You phone National Rail Enquiries for some information.

Cover the text of the audio.

Look at the timetable (*d = departs = leaves; a = arrives = gets there*).

Listen and complete the timetable.

London King's Cross	d	08:24	08:45			10:00	10:25
Cambridge	a	09:28	09:42			11:09	11:16

Information officer	National Rail Enquiries – Can I help you?
Man	Yes, I'd like some information about the times of trains from London to Cambridge, please.
Information officer	Which day are you thinking of travelling?
Man	It's for tomorrow.
Information officer	And what time of day would you like to travel?
Man	We'd like to leave London between nine and ten in the morning.
Information officer	Right. There's one that **leaves** at exactly nine o'clock.
Man	What time does that get to Cambridge?
Information Officer	The nine o'clock **gets** in at twelve minutes past ten. Then there's the nine twenty-four, which **arrives** at ten sixteen, and also a nine fifty-four, which **gets** to Cambridge at ten forty-six.
Man	Let me just repeat that to make sure I've got it right. There are three trains. The nine o'clock **arrives** at twelve minutes past ten, the nine twenty-four **gets** there at sixteen minutes past ten and the nine fifty-four **arrives** in Cambridge at ten forty-six.
Information Officer	That's correct.
Man	Thank you very much.
Both	Goodbye.

Meaning and form

11 Choose a, b or c.

Answer these questions about meaning and form of the verbs in bold in the text of audio 08.09.

1 The journey to Cambridge is:
   a in the past.
   b in the present.
   c in the future.

2 The tense of the verbs is:
   a present simple.
   b present progressive.
   c future simple.

Q Tomorrow is in the future. Why are these verbs in the present simple?

A Because we are talking about a timetable.
   ▸ When we talk about an organized future activity and it is part of a timetable or schedule, we use the present simple.

   Let's look at another example.

Situation: Monica is going on a business trip to Scotland next week. Her secretary, Angie, is telling her the itinerary.

Angie	**You leave** on the 10.30 flight on Monday and **you arrive** in Edinburgh at 11.10. **You have** a lunch meeting with Mr Jones at 12.30 and then at 3.30 **you take** the train to Glasgow.

All these verbs are in the present simple because they are Monica's itinerary or schedule.

Now look at the next part of the conversation.

Monica	Where **am I staying** in Glasgow?
Angie	I've got you a room at the King's Hotel. **You're staying** there for two nights.

Q Why are these verbs in the present progressive?

A These are personal future arrangements (see Unit 5).

Summary
To talk about fixed future events we use:
Present progressive when it's a personal future arrangement.
Present simple when it's part of a timetable or organized schedule.

▸ Sometimes both the present simple and present progressive are correct. The focus is a little different.

For example: *I go home next week* – more factual, more focus on the schedule.

I'm going home next week – more personal.

12 Choose a, b or c.

Answer these questions about *I'm going home next week* and *I go home next week*.

   1 In both sentences, the decision is:
      a in the past?
      b in the present?
      c in the future?

   2 In both sentences, actions to organize the trip home are:
      a in the past?
      b in the present?
      c in the future?

1 Write the verbs in the correct tense.

Situation: Simon is at a travel agent's, collecting his tickets for a short trip to Italy.
The assistant talks about his itinerary.

> **Travel agent**   Here are the tickets for your trip to Italy. You (fly) _____ (1) to Naples with
> Alitalia on the 12th of next month. The flight (leave) _____ (2) Heathrow at
> lo.15. When you get to Naples a coach (pick you up) _____ (3) from the airport
> and they (drive)_____ (4) you direct to your hotel. The next morning the
> coach (take) _____ (5) you on an excursion to the ruins of Pompeii. In the
> afternoon you (get) _____ (6) the Eurostar train to Rome.
>
> **Simon**   What (happen) _____ (7) when we arrive in Rome? How (get) _____
> (8) to the hotel?
>
> **Travel agent**   A bilingual guide (meet) _____ (9) the train and (take) _____ (10) you on a
> city tour. They (show) _____ (11)
> you all the important sights such as the Colloseum and the Vatican and then the
> coach (leave) _____ (12) you at your hotel. On the Sunday you (be) _____
> (13) free in Rome and you (come) _____ (14) back to London on the evening
> flight.
>
> **Simon**   What time (get) _____ (15) back?
>
> **Travel agent**   I think it's twenty-past nine. Just let me check – yes, nine twenty-five.
>
> **Simon**   That all sounds wonderful. I'm looking forward to it.

Q In the mini dialogue, are the verbs in B in the present simple?

Can you tell me how I get to Waterloo, please?

Go to Oxford Street and take the Bakerloo Line.

A No. These verbs are in the imperative (verb without *to*).
- ▶ People who work in transport often use the imperative to give instructions.
- ▶ Here the imperative is impersonal and short.

(For more information and practice on the imperative, see Unit 9.)

2 Practise some travel questions.

There are a lot of different questions in this unit. How many can you use now?

Read the questions.

Choose the correct question (a–j) for each answer (1–10). The first one is done as an example.

    a Could you tell me how to get to London from here, please?
    b How often do the trains run to Waterloo?
    c When's the next coach to Glasgow, please?
    d How long does it take to get to Cambridge from London?
    e Is this the right train for Birmingham?
    f Which platform is it for Brighton, please?
    g I want to go to Cardiff. Where do I change?
    h Do you know if this train stops in Reading?
    i How much is a single to Hull, please?
    j ~~How can I get to Windsor?~~

    1 You Excuse me, how can I get to Windsor?
        Take the train at Platform 5 and change at Egham.
    2 You _____?
        No, this is a non-stop to Paddington.
    3 You _____?
        Number 7, sir.
    4 You _____?
        £22.
    5 You _____?
        Every half an hour – at ten to and twenty past the hour.
    6 You _____?
        No, this is the Liverpool train.
    7 You _____?
        It's not necessary – this bus goes all the way there.
    8 You _____?
        In ten minutes, at half past.
    9 You _____?
        Yes, take the next train from Platform 10.
    10 You _____?
        On a fast train? Just under an hour.

3 Ask for transport information.

08.10 Listen and ask the questions from Exercise 2 in the spaces. You will hear the correct questions after the spaces.

Writing and speaking

1 **About your country: public transport**

Write answers to these questions or prepare to tell a friend.

1 How do you go to work and/or the shops?

2 How do people travel long distances without a car?

3 What are the names of the big train and bus companies in your country?

4 Is public transport cheap or expensive?

5 Is there an underground railway in your town or capital?

6 On the buses does the fare depend on distance?

7 **a** When do you pay if you want to travel by bus?

   b Can you buy a return ticket?

   c If you need to take two buses, can you use one ticket?

2 **What would you say?**

1 You are a tourist in London. You are at a station. Someone asks you, *Excuse me, can you tell me how to get to Wimbledon, please?*

2 It's late at night. You want to get a train ticket from the machine – the ticket office is closed. You've only got a £20 note. On the machine it says, *Sorry, no change.*

Revision

WHAT IS IT IN YOUR LANGUAGE?

Here are some examples of the important points in this topic.

Translate the sentences below into your language.

Remember – translate the idea, not the words.

1 **a** Excuse me, can you tell me how to get to the centre of town, please?

   b Yes, you can go by bus, by train or by taxi.

2 Which part of the town are you going to?

3 **a** Where do I pay?

   b Over there, please, at the cash desk.

4 Where do I go to get a ticket?

5 Who are you talking to?

6 Which excursions would you like to go on?

7 You get a ticket before you get on the bus.

8 **a** Excuse me, have you got the time, please?

   b Yes, it's just after ten.

9 How often do the buses go to the station?

10 How long does it take to get to the centre?

11 Take the train at Platform 6 and change at the next stop.

University Hospitals of Derby and Burton NHS Foundation Trust Library and Knowledge Service

 Writing

Write to a friend about your round-the-world trip.

Look at the scheduled itinerary and your personal arrangements and plans.

From these notes write a full itinerary, together with your personal plans.

Remember to use:

- ▶ the present simple for the timetables/schedules
- ▶ the present progressive for the personal future arrangements
- ▶ *going to* for the future plans.

Start like this:

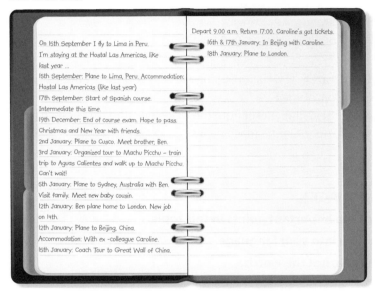

On 15th September I fly to Lima in Peru.
I'm staying at the Hostal Las Americas, like
last year ...

15th September: Plane to Lima, Peru. Accommodation:
Hostal Las Americas (like last year)

17th September: Start of Spanish course.
Intermediate this time.

19th December: End of course exam. Hope to pass.
Christmas and New Year with friends.

2nd January: Plane to Cusco. Meet brother, Ben.

3rd January: Organized tour to Machu Picchu – train
trip to Aguas Calientes and walk up to Machu Picchu.
Can't wait!

5th January: Plane to Sydney, Australia with Ben.
Visit family. Meet new baby cousin.

12th January: Ben plane home to London. New job
on 14th.

12th January: Plane to Beijing, China.
Accommodation: With ex-colleague Caroline.

15th January: Coach Tour to Great Wall of China.

Depart 9.00 a.m. Return 17:00. Caroline's got tickets.

16th & 17th January: In Beijing with Caroline.

18th January: Plane to London.

Speaking

08.11 **Now it's your turn to join the conversation.**

Listen again to the story 1 conversation.

Say Oliver's words in the spaces.

❓ Test yourself

Which one is right?

Choose a or b.

1 I go to work:
  a with car.
  b by car.

2 The bus:
  a leaves every hour.
  b is leaving.

3 a Do you know what is the time?
  b Do you know what the time is?

4 a How long does it take to get to the park?
  b How long takes it for go to the park?

5 A a How often go the trains to London?
    b How often do the trains go to London?
  B a Three times in an hour.
    b Three times an hour.

6 a How much is it for go and come back?
  b How much is a return ticket?

7 a What do I do now?
  b What I do now?

8 a Take that train and change at Broad Street.
  b You will take that train and then you are changing at Broad Street.

9 a West Road, 24.
  b 24, West Road.

10 My English friend has got a new baby.
  a What am I writing in this card?
  b What do I write in this card?

Write a dialogue.

Situation: You are at the ticket office at Waterloo Station.

You want two tickets to Hampton Court, a famous palace near London.

1 Travel clerk   **You**

> Next, please. Can I help you?

2 Respond.

3

> Single or return?

5

4 You want returns.

> That's £9.80, please.

7

6 Time of next train?

> In ten minutes, at twenty to eleven.

8 Return times – how often?

9

> From Hampton Court to Waterloo, there are two trains an hour, at ten past and twenty to the hour.

10

> Travelling time?

11

About half an hour

12

Thank you.

13 You are getting on to the train. You want to make sure it is the right one. You ask a station employee.

SELF-CHECK

I CAN . . .
. . . use prepositions at the end of questions
. . . ask for and give instructions
. . . ask for help
. . . ask for and understand travel information
. . . ask for and give the time
. . . use the present simple for timetables, schedules and itineraries.

Meeting friends

In this unit you will learn how to:
▶ *use impersonal* **it**
▶ *ask for opinions, using* **How was …?**
▶ *use adjectives +* **-ed** *or* **-ing**
▶ *say and respond to* **thank you**
▶ *express obligation and necessity, using* **have to**
▶ *use the imperative*
▶ *make and respond to offers, rejecting, insisting, accepting.*
▶ *introduce something negative in a polite way, using* **I'm afraid …**

VOCABULARY
▶ *large numbers; public signs*

PRONUNCIATION
▶ *intonation: expressing strong feelings*

CEFR: *Can describe plans, arrangements, habits and routines, past activities and personal experiences. Can make and respond to invitations, suggestions and apologies (A2). Can understand the main points of clear standard input on familiar matters regularly encountered in leisure. Can briefly give reasons and explanations for opinions and plans, and actions (B1). Can interact with a degree of fluency and spontaneity. Can take an active part in discussion in familiar contexts. Can explain a viewpoint giving the advantages and disadvantages of various options (B2).*

The story 1

 09.01* Tasha leaves customs. Who's there to meet her? What happens next?

Read the sentences. Only one is correct.

Listen to the conversation one, two or three times and choose the correct answer.

   a Tasha gets the bus with Oliver.

   b Tasha's friend, Helen, is at the airport to meet her.

   c Helen is at the airport with her husband and children.

   d Tasha goes to Helen's house by taxi.

Helen	Tasha, hi, how are you? It's lovely to see you again!
Tasha	Hello, Helen! It's great to see you, too. How are things?
Helen	I'm fine. We're all fine. How was your flight?
Tasha	It was all right – 13 hours is a bit long and tiring, but I'm here now. Thanks for picking me up, by the way.
Helen	That's OK. We're glad you could come. The car's in the car park, this way. David and the children are at home, waiting for you.

* For an American English version, listen to **11.15**.

Listening and reading 1

 1 **09.01 Listen and choose.**

Read the sentences.

Listen again and choose *True, False* or *We don't know*.

   1 Tasha's flight was terrible.   True/False/We don't know

   2 David is at home with the   True/False/We don't know
       children.

   3 Tasha knows David and the   True/False/We don't know
       children.

   4 Helen meets Oliver.   True/False/We don't know

   5 Tasha tells Helen about Oliver. True/False/We don't know

   6 Helen can't drive.   True/False/We don't know

 2 **09.01 Listen, read and complete.**

Read the sentences.

Listen again and complete the words.

Then read the text of the story 1 to check your answers.

   1 Helen says, *Hello* but Tasha says *H＿!*

   2 a Helen is happy to see Tasha.

        She says, *I＿'＿/I＿＿＿＿y/t＿/s＿＿you again.*

b Tasha is happy to see Helen.

She says, ___'_/g ____ t/__/____/you,/t __.

3 Helen asks, *How are you?* but Tasha asks *H__/a__/t____s?*

4 a Helen asks Tasha about her journey.

She says, *H__/w__/y__r/flight?*

b Tasha responds, *I_/w__/a__/____t.*

c Tasha talks about the flight.

She says *13 hours is a b__/l____/and t_____ but I'm here now.*

5 a Tasha is happy Helen is at the airport to meet her. During the conversation Tasha decides to thank her friend.

She says: *Thanks/f__/p_____g/m_/u_, b_/t__/w__.*

b When Tasha says, *Thanks*, Helen responds,

T___'_ OK. W_'__/g____/you/c____d/c__e.

Language discovery 1

 USING IMPERSONAL *IT*

Example from the story

Helen is happy to see Tasha again.

She says, *It's lovely to see you again*.

Tasha says, *It's great to see you, too.*

(Not: *Is lovely to see you again* OR *Is great to see you, too.*)

Q Why do we say *it* here?

A All verbs need a subject in English (except imperatives).

It is the impersonal subject.

Q What's the negative? Can I say, *It's nice to not work at the weekend*?

A No – not is before *to*. *It's nice not to work at the weekend.*

Summary – impersonal *it*			
Impersonal subject	Verb *be*	Adjective	Verb + *to/not to*
It	is	lovely	to see you again.
	's	frustrating	not to understand.

1 Complete the sentences.

Complete the sentences with one adjective from Box 1 and one verb from Box 2.

Use your dictionary, if necessary.

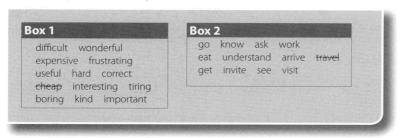

Box 1

difficult   wonderful
expensive   frustrating
useful   hard   correct
~~cheap~~   interesting   tiring
boring   kind   important

Box 2

go   know   ask   work
eat   understand   arrive   ~~travel~~
get   invite   see   visit

Example: It doesn't cost much – in fact, it's quite *cheap* to *travel* by coach.

1 It's too _____ by plane. Let's go by train.

2 A Is it _____ to _____ *Where are you live?* or *Where do you live?*

   B *Where do you live?*

3 At first it's _____ to _____ a foreign language because people speak fast.

4 For some people it's very _____ to _____ museums – they really enjoy it.

   For others it's the opposite. They find it really _____ .

5 I've got an invitation to stay with my friend abroad. It's very _____ of him to _____ me.

6 When you travel abroad, it's always _____ to _____ a few words of the language.

7 It's _____ not to _____ late for an exam.

8 It's _____ to _____ long hours.

9 It's _____ to see old friends after a long time.

10 Every time I try to telephone him there's no reply It's really _____ not to _____ an answer.

11 If you are on a diet, it's _____ not to _____ sweet things!

It's **+ adjective + verb with** *to/not to*

2 Write these words in the correct order.

   1 to/again/nice/talk/it's/you/to

   2 better/not/it's/go/to

   3 with/contact/easy/to/it's/people/email

   4 for/wait/it's/someone/time/for/long/boring/to/a

   5 country/to/exciting/it's/visit/a/foreign

   6 normal/language/understand/not/it's/in/foreign/to/everything/a

ASKING FOR OPINIONS – *HOW WAS ...?*

Example from the story

Helen asks Tasha about her journey.

She says: *How was your flight?*

Tasha answers: *It was all right.*

Meaning and form

3 **Answer these questions about** *How was ...?*

  1 The flight is:

    a in the present.

    b in the future.

    c in the past.

  2 In *How was your flight?* Helen is asking:

    a for a long description of the flight.

    b if the flight was OK or not.

  3 *Was* is the past of:

    a verb *be*.

    b verb *do*.

Summary – past of *be*		
Affirmative		
I, he/she/it } was	you, we, they } were	
Negative		
I, he/she/it } wasn't	you, we, they } weren't	
Question		
Was { I? he/she/it?	Were { you? we? they?	

4 **Complete these mini dialogues with** *was* **or** *were* **+** *not* **where necessary.**

  1 **A** How _____ your holiday?

    B The hotel _____ bad but the food _____ terrible.

  2 **A** _____ your parents all right last night?

    B My mother _____ fine but my father _____ very well at all, actually.

  3 **A** _____ that film boring!

    B Yes, it _____ very good at all, _____ it?

  4 **A** (*On Monday morning*) How _____ your weekend?

    B Really relaxing and quiet thanks. And yours?

    A It _____ nice, very nice.

  5 **A** Why _____ you at school yesterday, David?

    B I _____ ill, Miss.

6 A How many people _____ at the party?

  B About twenty, I suppose.

7 A Nobody _____ at home – the answer machine _____ on.

How do you pronounce it?

 WAS

▶ The vowel *a* in *was* has two pronunciations.

  ▷ *weak / ə/ when* was *is with an adjective or noun.*

  ▷ *strong / a / when* was *is the important word.*

For example: *Was your flight OK? – weak / ə/.*

Yes, it was, thanks. – strong / ɐ /.

▶ The pronunciation of the *a* in strong *was* / ɐ / and *wasn't* is the same.

 1 09.02 Listen and decide.

Look at the text of the audio, with the stress shown.

What is the pronunciation of *was* in each one?

Choose *strong* or *weak*.

1 How was your <u>day</u>?   strong/weak

2 Your <u>par</u>ty – how <u>was</u> it?   strong/weak

3 It was fan<u>tas</u>tic, thanks.   strong/weak

4 Was your hotel <u>com</u>fortable? strong/weak

5 Yes it <u>was</u>, thanks.   strong/weak

 2 09.02 Listen again and repeat the sentences.

INTONATION – BIG FALLS TO EXPRESS STRONG FEELINGS

In Unit 4 we practised intonation to sound positive. In this topic we practise intonation to express strong feelings.

Examples from the story

Helen is happy to see Tasha.

She says, *It's lovely to see you again.*

Tasha responds, *It's great to see you, too.*

▶ Remember, with flat intonation you express that actually you are not very happy to see the person.

▶ To express strong feelings, the voice moves a lot on the syllable with stress.

3 **09.03 Listen and choose.**

Read the sentences.

Listen to the audio: you will hear each sentence twice.

Which expresses stronger feelings, a or b?

1 It's <u>wonderful</u> to see you again.	a/b
2 It's <u>great</u> to hear from you.	a/b
3 I think it's a good <u>idea</u>.	a/b
4 It's so <u>kind</u> of you to invite me.	a/b
5 I don't know <u>what</u> to do.	a/b
6 But I <u>can't</u>!	a/b
7 I'm so <u>sorry</u>!	a/b
8 Happy <u>Birth</u>day!	a/b

 4 **09.03 Listen and repeat.**

Listen again and repeat the sentences. Pay special attention to the big falls in the sentences with strong feelings.

Language discovery 2

 FEELINGS – ADJECTIVES + -*ED* OR -*ING*

Example from the story

Tasha talks about the flight. She says, *It was a bit long and tiring …*

In other words, Tasha is tired because the flight was tiring.

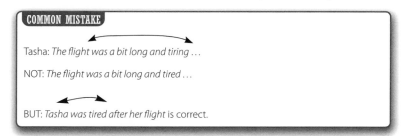

COMMON MISTAKE

Tasha: *The flight was a bit long and tiring …*

NOT: *The flight was a bit long and tired …*

BUT: *Tasha was tired after her flight* is correct.

Meanings and forms – adjectives + -*ed* and -*ing*

How is Tasha? She feels tired.

Why does Tasha feel tired?

What's the reason for her tiredness?

The flight. The flight was tiring.

Here's another example:

| How does John feel? | Interested. | The feeling + *-ed* |
| Why? | His book is interesting. | Reason or source of feeling + *-ing* |

Adjectives with *-ed/-ing*		
How? The feeling →	Tasha is tired.	adjective + *-ed*
Why? Reason or source of the feeling →	The flight was tiring.	adjective + *-ing*

1 Complete the dialogue.

Choose the correct form of the adjective in the brackets ( ) for each space.

Use your dictionary, if necessary.

A I feel a bit _____ (1) (tired/tiring) actually – it was a very long journey. And the plane was completely full!

B Oh! That's _____ (2) (surprised/surprising) at this time of year. When I travel, I go to sleep if I'm _____ (3) (bored/boring) on a plane. But sometimes it's _____ (4) (interested/ interesting) to talk to the person next to you.

A Oh, the man next to me on this flight was really _____ (5) (bored/boring). The conversation was all about his business trips – I wasn't very _____ (6) (interested/ interesting) at all, really.

A Yes, but it is _____ (7) (fascinating/fascinated) to travel and visit different countries, isn't it?

B Absolutely! I just find it _____ (8) (frustrated/frustrating) if I can't speak the language at all.

A Yes, I was a bit _____ (9) (disappointed/disappointing) with our last holiday because of that.

2 Correct the *-ed/-ing* adjectives in these sentences, if necessary.

1 The journey was very tired.

2 I'm very exciting about my trip.

3 I was really surprising about the new job.

4 The film was bored.

5 It's a fascinating story.

SAYING *THANK YOU*

Example from the story

Tasha is happy that Helen is at the airport to meet her.

She says, *Thanks for picking me up.*

Form

Summary – saying *thank you*		
	Preposition *for*	**Verb + *-ing* – gerund**
Neutral		
Thank you		
Thank you very much		
Formal	for	picking me up.
Thank you very much indeed		
Informal		
Thanks		
Many thanks		

Q Can I also say:

   a *Thank you to meet me?* ✗

   b *Thank you for meet me?* ✗ OR

   c *Thank you for to meet me?* ✗

A No, *Thank you for meeting me* is the only correct expression.

   Thank you + for + verb -ing.

3 Complete these sentences.

   1 Thanks _____ / _____ (help) me.

   2 Thanks _____ / _____ (come) to pick us up.

   3 Thank you very much _____ / _____ (wait) for me.

   4 Thank you _____ / _____ (meet) us.

   5 ❱ Thanks _____ / _____ (call).

4 Use the verbs in the box to say thank you in the situations.

let me know   go   tell   come   help   call   invite   wait   ask

Example: A friend tells you something very important.

You: *Thank you for telling me.*

   1 A friend in another country invites you for a holiday.
      You: _____

   2 You arrange to meet a friend at two o'clock. You arrive at 2.20.
      You: _____

   3 Your colleague shows you how to use the new computer in the office.
      You: _____

4 You've got an appointment for tomorrow – but something happens and you can't go. You telephone and tell them.

The other person says:

_____

5 Your colleague's partner was ill yesterday. Today you ask about her. Your friend says, _She's much better today._

You: _____

6 Your friend goes to the doctor's. You go with her. Later, at home,

she says: _____

7 You call a business friend. At the end of the conversation,

he/she says: _____

8 You invite some friends to your house. Later, when they leave,

You: _____

RESPONDING TO THANKS

5 Read and choose.

Read the formal, neutral and informal expressions in the box.

Choose an appropriate expression for the situations 1–6.

Formal – You're welcome	OR	Not at all
Neutral – That's OK	OR	That's all right
Informal – No problem	OR	Any time

1 Your friend says, _Thank you for helping me with my English._

You: _____

2 On the bus, you give your seat to an old lady. She says _Thank you so much. You're very kind!_

You: _____

3 A young person talks to you in the street. He says, _Excuse me, where's the station, please?_ You say, _Just there._ He says, _Thank you._

You: _____

4 The bus is at the bus stop. A woman is getting on the bus with three young children. You help her. She says, _Thank you ever so much._

You: _____

5 In a class you lend your dictionary to a friend. He/she says, _Thanks._

You: _____

6 You're in a shopping centre. You open the door for someone. The person says, _Thank you._

You: _____

Clothes

In your country, do you wear formal clothes to meet a friend or family member at the end of a journey? In Britain, it is usual to wear everyday clothes.

Saying *hello*

When we meet a family member or friend, it is common to **kiss them on the cheek (1)** and sometimes **hug them (2)**. Men often **shake hands (3)** or just say *Hello*. Good friends or family members sometimes shake hands and **hold the other person's arm (4)**, or **pat each other on the back (5)**. When we meet a business friend, it is common to shake hands. Adults often hug and/or kiss children. In Britain, some friends and families touch each other. Others don't. Touching isn't always the norm.

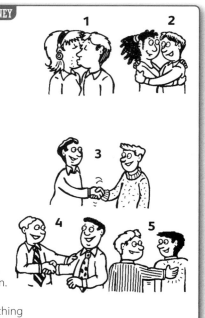

About your country: meeting people you know

Read the questions.

Write your answers or prepare to tell a friend.

What do you do when you meet someone after a journey?

- **a** a family member?
- **b** a friend?
- **c** business friend?
- **d** child?

Vocabulary builder 1

SAYING LARGE NUMBERS – *AND*

London Heathrow airport is one of the busiest international airports in the world with around 70 million passengers a year. This means an average of 191,200 people per day use the airport. Approximately 1,300 flights take off or land every day, with over 80 airlines flying to 184 destinations worldwide. There are 320 businesses in the airport (e.g. bars, restaurants and shops) and a total of 76,500 employees work there. Heathrow has five terminals; by far the biggest is Terminal 5, which is 353,020 m² (square metres).

1 How do we say these numbers?

Choose the correct expression from the box.

10　100　1,000　10,000　100,000　1,000,000　1,000,000,000

| a million　a hundred　ten thousand　ten　a billion |
| a hundred thousand　a thousand |

Look at the following numbers – where's the *and*?

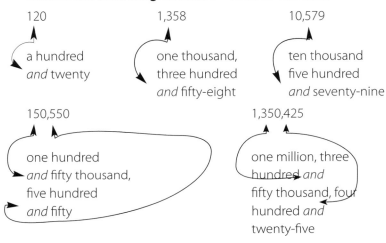

120
a hundred
and twenty

1,358
one thousand,
three hundred
and fifty-eight

10,579
ten thousand
five hundred
and seventy-nine

150,550
one hundred
and fifty thousand,
five hundred
and fifty

1,350,425
one million, three
hundred *and*
fifty thousand, four
hundred *and*
twenty-five

2 Read the sentence about *and*. Choose *True* or *False*.

With big numbers we say *and* before the *tens* (tens are *twenty, thirty, forty*, etc.).　　True/False

3 Write these numbers in words – don't forget the *and*.

1 594,000 _____

2 611,420 _____

3 4,601 _____

4 827 _____

5 32,158 _____

6 24,250,000 _____

7 6,368 _____

8 923,750 _____

4 Read aloud the numbers in the text about Heathrow Airport.

5 About your country: large numbers

Read the questions.

Either write your answers or prepare to tell a friend.

1 What is the population of your country/the capital/your town/village, etc.?

2 If you work, how much do you earn a year?

3 How much does a room/flat/house cost in your area – to rent a month/to buy?

4 How much does a new car cost in your country?

The story 2

 09.04* *Our story continues. Helen and Tasha go to the airport car park to get Helen's car.*

Read, listen and choose.

Read the sentences.

Listen and choose *True/False/We don't know*.

1	Tasha pays for the car park.	True/False/We don't know
2	They can't find the car.	True/False/We don't know
3	They ask a man for help with	True/False/We don't know the suitcase.

Helen	The car's on level 4. We can take the trolley in the lift. But first, I have to pay at the machine just here. Now, where's the ticket? Wait a minute … Oh, here it is, in my pocket. How much do I need? One hour – £6.00. Let me see if I've got the right money.
Tasha	I'm afraid I haven't got any change. I've only got notes.
Helen	No, don't worry. I'm getting this. Look, the machine gives change. Right, let's find the car. The lift is this way.
Helen	Here we are – it's the green Ford. Now, let's get your luggage in the boot. Can I help you with your suitcase?
Tasha	No, really, it's all right, thanks – I can manage. Could you just hold this bag for a minute while I get the suitcase in, then we can put the bag on top.
Helen	Come on! Let me help. Don't lift that suitcase on your own.
Tasha	OK – Thanks – it is quite heavy … Ready? One, two, three …
Helen	We can put our coats on the back seat.
Tasha	I think I'll keep mine on. I'm really cold.
Helen	I expect that's because you're tired after your long journey. Let's get home and you can have a rest.

* For an American English version, listen to **11.16**.

Listening and reading 2

 1 **09.04 *True* or *False*?**

Read the sentences. Five are true, five are false.

Listen and choose the five true sentences.

1 The car is on level 2.
2 First they pay, then they get the car.
3 The car park costs £3.60.
4 They take the lift.
5 They leave the trolley on the ground floor.
6 Helen's got a red Honda.
7 Tasha's suitcase is heavy.
8 They put the luggage on the back seat.
9 Helen helps Tasha with her luggage.
10 They put their coats in the boot.
11 They're going straight to Helen's house.

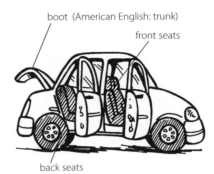

boot (American English: trunk)

front seats

back seats

2 **Now listen again and correct the wrong information in the false sentences.**

 3 **09.04 Listen, read and complete.**

Read the sentences.

Listen again and complete the words.

Then read the text of the story 2 to check your answers.

1 The car park isn't free. Helen says, *But first, I h _ _ _ / t _ / pay at the machine.*
2 Helen needs time to find the car park ticket. She says, *W _ _ _ _ / a / m _ _ _ _ _ _ .*
3 Helen needs time to see if she's got £6.00 in change. She says, *L _ _ / m _ / s _ _ _ / i _ / I've got the / r _ _ _ _ / m _ _ _ y.*
4 a Tasha is sorry she hasn't got change. She says,
    I' _ / a _ _ _ _ _ _ / I haven't got any change.
  b Helen tells her it isn't a problem.
    She says, *D _ _ ' t / w _ _ _ _ _ .*
5 Helen tells Tasha she's paying. She says,
    I' _ / g _ _ _ _ _ _ / t _ _ _ .
6 a Helen offers to help with Tasha's suitcase twice. The first time, she says, *C _ _ _ / I / h _ _ _ _ / y _ _ with your suitcase?*

b Tasha says no. She says, *No, / r _ _ _ _ _ _, / it's / a _ _ / _ _ _ _ _ t / thanks. / I / c _ _ / m _ _ _ _ _ e.*

c Helen insists. She offers Tasha help again. She says, *C _ _ _ _ / _ n! / L _ _ _ / m _ / help. D _ _ _ ' _ / l _ _ t / that big suitcase …*

d Tasha accepts. She says, *O _ _ . / T _ _ _ _ _ _ /. It / _ _ _ / q _ _ _ _ _ / h _ _ _ _ y.*

4 Read and complete.

Read the sentences.

Read the text of the story 2 and complete the words and phrases.

Think about your choice of prepositions.

1 Helen finds the car park ticket.
She says, *H _ _ _ _ / i _ / i _ /, _ _ / my p _ _ _ _ _ _.*

2 It's not necessary to pay the exact money because the machine gives c _ _ _ _ _ _ /.
You can pay with n _ _ _ _ _.

3 Tasha needs help with the bag. She says, *C _ _ _ _ _ / you / j _ _ _ _ / h _ _ _ _ / this bag for a minute?*

4 Helen holds the bag / w _ _ _ _ / Tasha puts the suitcase in.

5 They put the suitcase in the boot first.
Then they put the bag / _ _ _ / t _ _ _ / t _ _ .

6 Helen wants to help Tasha with the suitcase. She says, *Don't lift it / o _ _ / y _ _ _ _ / o _ _ .*

7 Is the suitcase very heavy? No, but it's q _ _ _ _ heavy.

8 Tasha decides not to take her coat off. She's cold.
She says, *I / think / I' _ _ _ / k _ _ _ _ / m _ _ _ _ / _ _ .*

9 Tasha's tired. When they get to the house she can go to her room and relax – she can
h _ _ _ _ / a / r _ _ _ t.

10 **Choose a, b or c.**

In the sentences i–iii below, the verb *get* means:

a go/arrive

b put – with difficulty

c pay

i Let's get your luggage in the car.

ii Don't worry! I'm getting this.

iii Let's get home.

5 Match 1–10 with a–j.

1 Why don't you take your jacket off?

2 Where's John?

3 Don't go on your own.

4 The boot is full.

5 I'll pay for the drinks.

a Yes, it's quite interesting, actually.

b I can give you two ten pound notes.

c with chocolate sauce on the top.

d Oliver is going to the centre by bus.

6 I love vanilla ice cream

7 Have you got change for £20?

8 Is that a good TV programme?

9 While Tasha is going to Helen's,

10 Do you need help with that?

e I'll go with you.

f I'll put the bag on the back seat then.

g No, thanks, it's all right. I can manage.

h He's upstairs, having a rest.

i I prefer to keep it on, thanks. I'm a bit cold.

j No, it's my turn. I'll get them.

LANGUAGE TIP

Q What's the difference between *car park* and *parking*?

A *Car park* is a noun. It's a public place to leave a car.

For example: *When I go to London, I leave the car in the car park at the station.*

NOT: *I leave the car in the parking.* **✗**

Park is a verb, for example *You can't park here.*

The phrase *No parking* means *You can't park here.* This is a verbal noun (a verb used as a noun).

Language discovery 3

 EXPRESSING OBLIGATION AND NECESSITY, USING *HAVE TO*

Example from the story

The car park isn't free. Helen says,

But first, **I have to** *pay at the machine just here.*

Meaning and form

Is it necessary to pay?   Yes, it is a regulation of the car park.

And if Helen doesn't pay? She'll have a problem – she is obliged to pay.

Summary – *have to* – obligation and necessity						
Positive			**Negative**		**Questions**	
I	have	to + *verb*	I don't	have to + *verb*	Do I	have to + *verb*?
He/she	has		He/she doesn't		Does he/she	

Look at these examples:

1 I **don't have to** go now. I can stay until 1.00.

   Meaning: It's not necessary for me to go now.

2 Do **I have to** enrol before the next course or can I just come on the first day?

   Meaning: Is it an obligation to enrol before the next course or is it possible to just go to the class on the first day?

LANGUAGE TIP

Q Learners of English often say, *Is it necessary for me to …?* Is this OK?

A This isn't wrong but it is very formal. *Do I have to …?* is more common.

Q What's the difference between:

   1 *Where do I have to go now?* and

   2 *Where do I go now?* (Unit 8).

A The difference is small:

   1 asks more about obligation – what are the rules or regulations?

   2 asks more about systems – what is the custom/norm?

In some situations both are appropriate.

Examples:

1 You are filling in a form:

Where do I sign? and *Where do I have to sign?* are both correct and appropriate.

2 You are using a new photocopier:

Which way do I put the paper? and *Which way do I have to put the paper?* are both correct and appropriate.

1 Complete these sentences with the correct form of *have to*.

1 My husband _____ travel a lot for his job. He's always away.

2 How many times a day _____ take this medicine, Doctor?

3 We _____ go if you don't want to. I really don't mind.

4 **Mother** Come on, Tommy – it's time for bed.

   Tommy Oh, Mum, _____? I'm not tired.

5 You _____ say *yes* or *no* now. You can tell me later.

6 I _____ come back again tomorrow, do I? Can't we finish all the work today?

7 **A** What time _____ be at the airport for your flight?

   B Half past ten.

8 I'm sorry but I really _____ go now, or I'll miss my train.

9 **A** Could you please tell me why I _____ fill this form in?

   B I'm sorry, sir. It's a company regulation.

10 Which number _____ phone to confirm my return flight?

THE IMPERATIVE

Examples from the story

Helen needs time to find the car park ticket.

She says, *Wait a minute.*

Tasha wants to help with the money. Helen says it isn't a problem.

She says, *Don't worry.*

Meaning and form

▶ *Wait*. Helen is telling Tasha to do something.

▶ *Don't worry*. Helen is telling Tasha not to do something.

▶ *Wait* is the imperative. *Don't worry* is the negative imperative.

Summary – the imperative		Examples
Positive imperative	Verb without *to*	Stop!
Negative imperative	*Don't* + verb without *to*	Don't forget!

2 Use the correct form of the verbs in the box below to complete the sentences.

> write   wait   forget   worry

1 _____ for me. I'll be home late tonight.

2 _____ it's Mum's birthday tomorrow.

3 _____ ! Everything will be all right.

4 _____ to me. It takes too long. Can't you email me instead?

LANGUAGE TIP

Be careful!

The imperative is a **danger zone** for communication in English.

In many languages, it is very common to use the imperative.

In English, we use the imperative only in specific situations.

In other situations it is impolite.

Q When is the imperative impolite?

A When we ask people to do things

For example:

a Give me some bread. ☹
  Can you give me some bread, please? ☺

b Put this on the table. ☹
  Could you put this on the table, please? ☺

(See Unit 7 for more practice with *Can you …?*, *Could you …?* for asking people to do things.)

Q When is it OK to use the imperative?

A Exercises 3, 4, 5, 6 show you specific examples.

---

3 Look at the examples 1–6 and match with a–f from the list.

Use your dictionary, if necessary.

1 A doctor: Just pull your sleeve up for me, please.

2 Come in!

3 Have a good weekend!

4 Be careful!

5 Stay in touch.

6 Go to the end of the road and turn right.

> **a invitations and offers**

> **b instructions – a person in authority asking someone to do something**

> **c giving street directions**

> **d asking for contact**

> **e hopes and wishes**

> **f warnings**

4 What are they saying? What are they communicating?

Match the situations (A–F) with the correct imperative phrase from Box 1 and the correct communication from Box 2.

Example: 'Have a good holiday!'
Hopes and wishes

Situation A

Situation B

Situation C

Situation D

Situation E

Situation F

Box 1	Box 2
1 Take the second on the left.	**a** Instructions
2 Go ahead. Help yourself!	**b** Street directions
3 Put the cup here and press that button.	**c** Offers and invitations
4 Write to me.	**d** Hopes and wishes
5 Enjoy yourselves!	**e** Warnings
6 Look out!	**f** Asking for contact

LANGUAGE TIP

For instructions and street directions, you can also use *you* + verb (the present simple, Unit 8). This form is also very common.

Instructions

1 You put your cup here, then you press that button.

2 First you fill this form in, then you pay over there.

Street directions

1 You take the second on the left.

2 You go as far as the station and then you turn right.

5 **Who uses the imperative? Match sentences 1–4 with situations a–d.**

1	Do your homework first.	**a**	with a close friend
2	Empty your pockets onto the table.	**b**	an adult to a child
3	Sit, Jack, sit.	**c**	a policeman
4	Don't go home yet! Stay a bit longer.	**d**	to an animal

▶ To make an imperative more polite, add *please*.

Example: *Please tell me* or *Tell me, please*.

6 **True or false?**

Read these sentences about the use of the imperative.

Choose *True* or False.

1 The negative imperative is appropriate in many situations, e.g. *Don't say that!*　　　　　　　　　　　　　　　True/False

2 The positive imperative can be impolite, e.g. *Sit here*.　　True/False

3 We use the positive imperative for wishes, e.g. *Have a good journey!*　　　　　　　　　　　　　　　　　　　True/False

4 We use the positive imperative for invitations and offers, e.g. *Come and join us*.　　　　　　　　　　　　　　True/False

5 We use the imperative with good friends and children.　True/False

Ⓥ Vocabulary builder 2

PUBLIC SIGNS – POSITIVE IMPERATIVE

The positive imperative is common in written instructions and warnings.

1 Look, read and match.

Look at the pictures and the imperative phrases in the box.

Write the correct imperative phrase for each picture.

Use your dictionary, if necessary.

Example

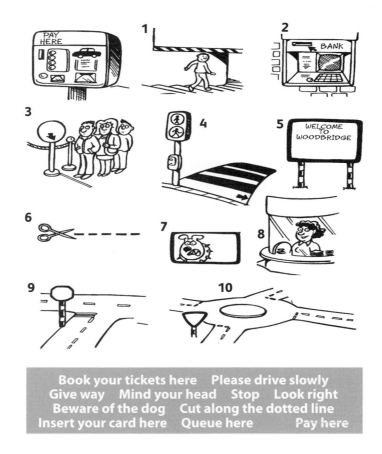

> **Book your tickets here   Please drive slowly**
> **Give way   Mind your head   Stop   Look right**
> **Beware of the dog   Cut along the dotted line**
> **Insert your card here   Queue here   Pay here**

USING THE VERB *MIND*

► In the previous exercise, *mind* means *be careful of* ... This verb is common for warning people.

You can use the verb *mind* with both:
  a the person or thing in danger:
  For example, *Mind your head.*
  b the dangerous thing:
  For example, *Mind the door.*

2 Write an expression with the verb *mind* for the following situations.

1 You are crossing the road. A bus is coming. Warn your friend.

2 There's a step. Warn your friend.

3 A child is sitting in a car, his legs outside the car. You want to shut the car door.

4 Your friend is in the car with the door open. Another car is coming.

PUBLIC SIGNS – NEGATIVE IMPERATIVE

▸ The negative imperative is not common in signs.

▸ *No* + verb + *-ing* or *No* + noun is more common.

3 Look and choose.

Label the signs with the correct expression from the box.

Use your dictionary, if necessary.

No entry	No parking	No photography	No left turn
	No bathing	No smoking	

Language discovery 4

OFFERS: REJECTING, INSISTING, ACCEPTING

Examples from the story

a Helen offers to help Tasha with her suitcase.

She says, *I'll help you with that suitcase.*

b Tasha says no – she **rejects** the offer.

She says, *No, really, it's all right thanks. I can manage.*

c Helen **insists**. She offers Tasha help again.

She says, *Come on! Let me help.*

d Tasha says yes – she **accepts** the offer.

She says, *OK Thanks. It is quite heavy.*

(For more practice with *I'll* for offers, see Unit 6.)

LANGUAGE TIP

The verb *manage*

In sentence **b**, Tasha uses the verb *manage* when she rejects Helen's offer of help. *I can manage* is a very common way to reject help.

Here, *manage* means that it's difficult for Tasha to lift the suitcase because it's heavy, but she can lift it with effort.

We use *manage* when the action is difficult but possible.

Manage is about effort and success.

 1 09.05 Rejecting offers of help with *manage*. Listen and repeat.

Listen to these mini dialogues and repeat B's responses in the spaces.

1 A Can I help you with that?

   B Thanks very much, but I think I can manage it on my own.

2 A Let me do that.

   B No, honestly, I can manage thanks.

3 A I'll take that if you like.

   B No, really, I'm fine thanks. I can manage.

4 A Shall I do that?

   B It's OK. I can manage, thanks.

5 A Would you like me to carry that for you?

   B Thanks for the offer but I think I can manage it.

2 Complete the mini dialogues with the correct sentence a–i from the box.

Example: **A** How often do you go home to see your parents?

          B I usually *manage to go about once a month.*

1 A The meeting is now at three o'clock and not four. Can you manage to get here one hour earlier?

   B _____

2 A That's a big box! Mind your back!

   B _____

3 A I'm sorry I can't help.

   B _____

4 A I've got no idea how to do this.

   B _____

5 A Tom worries so much about exams.

   B _____

6 A How much do you understand when you watch a film in English now?

   B _____

7 A Do you do any sport?

   B _____

8 A Do you see your children in the evenings?

   B _____

a I try to get to the gym twice a week but I don't always manage it.

b Don't worry! I'll manage on my own.

c It's all right. I think I can manage it. Where shall I put it?

d If we work together, we'll manage something.

e Yes, I usually manage to spend an hour or so with them before they go to bed

f I usually manage to go about once a month.

g I can try.

h Yes, but he always manages to get good marks.

i I manage to understand quite a lot, actually.

Example from the story: insisting

Helen insists. She offers Tasha help again.

She says, *Come on! Let me help.*

> **LANGUAGE TIP**
> **The verb *let***
> We can use *let* to offer help and also to offer again if the person says *no* the first time.
> **Form:** Verb *let* – imperative form   person   verb
> **Example:** *Let*   *me*   *carry that for you.*
> The expressions *Come on!* and *Go on!* make the phrase stronger.
> The meaning of *let* is *to give permission*.

3 Complete the dialogues.

Look at the situations 1–7. You are the person **.**

Complete the dialogues with sentences from the box.

Let me call an ambulance.

No, it's heavy. Let me take it!

Wait a second. Let me open the door for you.

Come on! It's my turn. Let me pay this time.

Come on! Let me have a look at it.

No, really. Let me do something to help.

Come on, it's late! Let me take you.

1 **A** Can I carry that for you?

B I'm all right, thanks.

A _____

B Thank you. It is very heavy, actually.

2 **A** I'll get this.

B _____

A OK, thanks.

3 **A** Can I take some of those for you?

B No, it's all right. I can manage

A _____

B Thanks.

4 **A** Can I just sit down for a minute?

B Of course. Would you like me to get you anything?

A No, I'm… oh, the baby…

B _____

5 **A** Do you know where the nearest bus stop is?

B It's OK, I've got the car. I can drive you home.

A No, I can get the bus. It's no problem.

B _____

A Thanks. It's really nice of you to offer but I can get the bus.

6 A Can I do anything?

B No, you go and sit down.

A _____

B Thanks, could you peel the vegetables?

7 A Oh! My eye!

B What's the matter?

A I think I've got something in it.

B _____

INTRODUCING SOMETHING NEGATIVE IN A POLITE WAY, USING *I'M AFRAID …*

Example from the story

Tasha is sorry she hasn't got change. She says, *I'm afraid I haven't got any change.*

▶ Use *I'm afraid* to introduce something negative in a polite way.

4 Match 1–8 with the correct response, a–h.

1 Excuse me, are you the manager?

2 Could you tell me the time, please?

3 Excuse me, where I can get a taxi?

4 Could I borrow your dictionary?

5 Come on! Have another glass of wine.

6 Would you like to come to dinner on Saturday?

7 Do have some more cake.

8 What's the matter?

a I'm afraid I can't. I'm driving.

b I'm afraid I don't know. I'm not from here.

c I'm afraid I've got some bad news.

d I'm afraid we can't. We're going to my mother's.

e No, actually I'm not. I'm afraid he's not here at the moment.

f I'm afraid I can't eat another thing!

g I'm afraid I haven't got a watch.

h I'm afraid I haven't got one.

> **LANGUAGE TIP**
>
> **Short answers – *I'm afraid so, I'm afraid not***
> ▶ To respond to questions with *Yes* or *No* alone can sound rude.
> ▶ To express that you are sorry about a situation, use *I'm afraid so* and *I'm afraid not.*

▶ *I'm afraid so* means *I'm sorry but yes.*

Examples:

He's drunk, isn't he?
He isn't ill, is he?
It's a big problem, isn't it?   }   Response: *I'm afraid so.*
It's too expensive, isn't it?

▶ *I'm afraid not* means *I'm sorry but no.*

Examples:

Is he here?
You haven't got a car, have you? }
Have you got any change?   Response: *I'm afraid not.*
Can you help me?

5 **Respond with *I'm afraid so* or *I'm afraid not.***

    1 **A** It's a bad accident, isn't it?

        B _____

    2 **A** This isn't right, is it?

        B _____

    3 **A** Do you know where he lives?

        B _____

    4 **A** You don't like this, do you?

        B _____

    5 **A** You can't swim, can you?

        B _____

    6 **A** Do we have to pay?

        B _____

Practice

USING *GET* FOR 'PAY' OR 'BUY'

Example from the story

Helen tells Tasha she's paying. She says,

I'm **getting** *this.*

▶ *Get* is an indirect verb for *pay.* (British English likes indirect language.)

> **LANGUAGE TIP**
>
> **Q** What's the difference between *I'll get this* and *I'm getting this*?
> **A** *I'll get this* is an offer. It is appropriate in both formal and informal situations. *I'm getting this* insists more. It is informal.

1 **Put the words in the right order to make sentences.**

    1 this/get/I'll

    2 No, I insist! getting/I'm/these

    3 It was your turn last week. me/ice creams/the/get/today/let

    4 card/get/I'll/on/credit/this/my

2 What would you say?

1 You come to England to stay with an English family. You don't know whether to use their first names or their surnames.

You ask: _____

2 Your friend hasn't got any change for the car park. You have.

You say: _____

Revision

WHAT IS IT IN YOUR LANGUAGE?

Here are some examples of the important points in this unit.

Translate the sentences into your language.

Remember – translate the idea, not the words.

1 It's lovely to see you again.

2 How was your journey?

3 I'm tired! My job is very tiring!

4 Thank you for inviting me.

5 Don't wait for me. I have to finish this.

6 a Shall I do that?

　　b Thanks but I think I can manage.

　　c Come on! Let me help you.

7 I'm afraid the manager's not here.

8 Have a good weekend!

Writing

Do you like watching films? Do you go to the cinema? Do you watch films on TV, on your laptop or tablet?

Write a) a summary of a film you know and b) a short review with your opinion of the film.

Write the story in the present simple and try to use the language points in the box.

> to let someone do something
>
> to thank someone for doing something
>
> to have to
>
> to manage to do something
>
> How was ...?
>
> it's + adjective + verb
>
> I'm afraid
>
> adjective ending in -ing   adjective ending in -ed
>
> the imperative

* Before you write, read the model answer in the **Answer key** to help you. The phrases from the box are in **bold**.

Speaking

09.06 Now it's your turn to join the conversation.

Listen again to the Story conversation.

Say Tasha's words in the spaces.

Test yourself

Read and choose.

Which one is right? Choose a or b.

1 **a** It's nice to have a holiday.
   b Is nice to have a holiday.

2 **a** How was your day?
   b How were your day?

3 **a** I'm very interesting in football.
   b I'm very interested in football.

4 **a** Thank you for to ask me to go with you.
   b Thank you for asking me to go with you.

5 **a** I'm have to leave now.
   b I have to leave now.

6 **a** I'll pay this.
   b I'll get this.

7 **a** Please come with us today.
   b Please to come with us today.

8 **a** Let me to do that.
   b Let me do that.

9 Can you come with us?
   a I afraid no.
   b I'm afraid not.

10 Can I help with that?
   a Thanks but I can manage.
   b Thanks but I manage.

Write a dialogue.

Meeting someone after a journey.

Situation: You travel to visit a friend. Your friend is at the station to meet you.

Your friend

1 She greets you. She is happy to see you.

3 She asks about your journey.

5 She replies and shows you the way to the taxis.

7 She responds and then says:

> Look, here's a taxi.
> Go on! You get in first.

9 You offer to pay.

You

2 Greet your friend. You are happy to see her.

4 Say something positive. Ask about her life in general.

6 Thank her for meeting you.

8 You arrive at your friend's house. Your friend asks the driver how much it is.

10 Your friend insists she's paying.

I CAN . . .

- . . . use impersonal *it*
- . . . ask for opinions, using *How was . . . ?*
- . . . use adjectives + *-ed* or *-ing*
- . . . say and respond to *thank you*
- . . . express obligation and necessity, using *have to*
- . . . use the imperative
- . . . make and respond to offers, rejecting, insisting, accepting
- . . . introduce something negative in a polite way, using *I'm afraid . . .*

10 Finding accommodation

In this unit you will learn how to:

▶ *talk about length of time, and prices*
▶ ask **Who …?** *and respond using short answers*
▶ *talk about the number of people, using* **how many …**
▶ *talk about the same thing, using* **one, ones**
▶ *ask for an alternative, using comparatives.*
▶ *make negative comparisons using* **not as … as**
▶ *make decisions – buying things, using* **I'll**
▶ *use the verb* **hope** *+ present simple*
▶ *talk about the past, using the past simple*
▶ *talk about life experiences and results using the present perfect.*

VOCABULARY
▶ *hotel language; ordinal numbers*

PRONUNCIATION
▶ **schwa / ə /**

CEFR: *Can find specific, predictable information in simple everyday material such as advertisements (A2). Can understand the main points of clear standard input on familiar matters regularly encountered in work and leisure. Can briefly give reasons and explanations for opinions and plans, and actions. Can deal with most situations likely to arise while travelling. Can connect phrases in a simple way to describe experiences, events and hopes (B1). Can interact with a degree of fluency and spontaneity. Can engage in extended conversation on most general topics in a clearly participatory fashion. Can explain a viewpoint giving the advantages and disadvantages of various options (B2).*

The story 1

 10.01* *Oliver is at the hotel reservations desk in the tourist information centre at Victoria Station in Central London. He needs a room.*

Read the sentences.

Listen and choose *Yes* or *No*.

1 Oliver books a hotel room.   Yes/No

2 They talk about:
      type of room   Yes/No
      hotel facilities   Yes/No
      prices   Yes/No
      one particular hotel   Yes/No

Assistant	Who's next, please?
Oliver	I think I am. I'd like to book a room, please.
Assistant	Yes, how many of you are there?
Oliver	It's just for me.
Assistant	And how long is it for?
Oliver	I need a room from tonight until the end of next week.
Assistant	OK. So that's a single room for 14 nights altogether.
Oliver	Yes, that's right.
Assistant	In any specific area?
Oliver	I don't mind, as long as it's central.
Assistant	What sort of price are you looking to pay?
Oliver	Between £80 and £100 a night.
Assistant	There's the Trafalgar Hotel. It's very near here.
Oliver	How much is that one?
Assistant	£95 a night.
Oliver	That would be fine.
Assistant	I'll just see if they have any vacancies. Would you like to take a seat for a moment?
Oliver	Thanks.

* For an American English version, listen to **11.17**.

Listening and reading 1

1 **10.01** **Finding a room.**

Look at the table.

Listen and complete the table.

Number of nights	Oliver's price range	Location (where?)	Name of hotel	Price
	£ ___–£ ___			

2 **10.01** **Listen, read and complete.**

Read the sentences.

Listen again and complete the words.

Then read the text of the story 1 to check your answers.

1 **A** The assistant starts the conversation.
She asks, *W __ __ 's / n __ __ __ ?*

B Oliver responds, *I think __ / __ m.*

2 **A** The assistant asks about the number of people.
She says, *H__ __ / m __ __ y / o __ / y __ __ / a __ e / t __ __ r __ ?*

B Oliver responds, *It's j __ __ __ / for m __.*

3 **A** The assistant suggests the Trafalgar and Oliver asks the price.
He says, *How much is t __ __ __ / o __ __ ?*

B The assistant responds, *£95 / __ / n __ __ __ t.*

3 Read and complete the words and phrases.

Read the sentences.

Read the text of the story 1 and complete the words and phrases.

1 Oliver is looking for a room.
He says, *I'd like to / b __ __ k / a room, please.*

2 **a** The assistant asks about the number of nights.
She says, *H __ __ / l __ __ g / s / i __ / f __ r?*

b Oliver responds, *F __ __ __ / tonight / u __ __ __ __ / the end of next week.*

3 Oliver needs a room for one person. He needs a s __ __ __ __ __ / room.

4 The location of the hotel isn't very important to Oliver, but he wants to be in the centre. He says, *I don't mind, / a ___ / l ___ ___ ___ / a ___ / it's central.*

5 a The assistant asks how much Oliver wants to pay. She says, *W ___ ___ ___ / s ___ ___ ___ / o ___ / price / are / you / l ___ ___ ___ ___ ___ g / t ___ / p ___ ?*

    b Oliver's minimum is £80 and his maximum £100. He says, *B ___ ___ ___ ___ ___ n / £80 and £100 / ___ / n ___ ___ ___ t.*

6 When you need a room, you can say, *Have you got any rooms free?* or *Have you got any v ___ ___ ___ ___ ___ ___ ___ ___ ?*

7 The assistant asks Oliver to sit down. She says, *Would you like to t ___ ___ ___ / a / s ___ ___ ___ / for a moment?*

Language discovery 1

ASKING QUESTIONS WITH '*FOR*' AT THE END

Example from the story

The assistant asks about the number of nights.

She says, *How long is it for?*

▶ *How long* asks about the number of days.
▶ It refers to the room.
▶ She can also say, *How long for?* but this is more direct. It can sound abrupt.

Form

How many	is	it/this/that	
How long		they/these/those	for?
When	are		
Who			

1 Complete these dialogues. Make questions from the words in the table.

1 **A** Good evening, sir. _____ ?

 B There are four of us.

 A If you would like to follow me, I'll show you to your table.

2 **A** Here are our tickets to New York.

 B _____ ?

 A Next Wednesday.

3 **A** Here's the bill.

 B Let's pay half each. _____ ?

 A £35.

4 **A** They're beautiful. _____ ?

 B Oh, that's my little secret.

5 **A** If you want to go out on the lake, you can hire a boat. It costs £50.

 B _____ ?

 A One hour.

AS LONG AS

The location of the hotel isn't very important to Oliver, but he wants to be in the centre.

The assistant asks, *In any specific area?*

Oliver says, *I don't mind, as long as it's central.*

▶ *As long as* talks about condition. It means *if*, but we use *as long as* when the condition is important to us.

2 Complete the mini dialogues.

 Use *as long as* + the correct phrase from the box.

 Change the verb if necessary.

as long as …	be too noisy
	get there by twenty past
	be back before eleven o'clock
	go to London
	find me a room
	rain
	take me home afterwards
	~~be careful~~

Example:

A Dad, can I borrow the car?

B Yes, as long as you're careful.

 1 A Can we go on a trip to England?

 B Why not? _____ we _____ .

 2 A Could you babysit for us on Saturday evening?

 B Of course, _____ you _____ .

3 A We're going to the open-air theatre this evening.

   B That can be really good, _____ it _____ .

4 A The train leaves at half past three.

   B So, _____ we _____ we'll be OK.

5 A Would you like a table by the window, sir?

   B I don't mind, _____ it _____ .

6 A Mum, can I go out?

   B Yes, _____ .

7 A I'm sorry, sir, but the hotel is full. I understand you've got a booking but …

   B I don't mind how long I have to wait, _____ you _____ .

PRICES: TALKING ABOUT HOW MUCH YOU WANT TO SPEND

Example from the story

The assistant asks Oliver how much he wants to pay.

She says, *What sort of price are you looking to pay?*

Q What's the difference between

  a *How much do you want to pay?*

    and

  b *What sort of price are you looking to pay?*

A The grammar is correct in both questions. The meaning is the same.

  a *How much do you want to pay?* is more direct.

  b *What sort of price are you looking to pay?* is indirect.

▶ Question b is common in shops and when you are buying a service.

  a Can I say, *What kind of price …?* instead of *sort*.

  b Yes, *What kind of …?* and *What sort of …?* are the same.

Responses – the price

Oliver's minimum is £80 and his maximum is £100.

He says, *Between £80 and £100.*

Other possible responses:

Anything up to £100 is all right.
Anything under £100 is OK.
As long as it's less than £100.
} These expressions mean £100 is your maximum.

About £100.
Around £100.
} It can be a little more or a little less than £100.

Prices: quantities and time

How much is a room at the Trafalgar? £95 a night.

▶ We use *a/an* for measurements of time, units of quantity, etc.
Example: *90p a packet.*

3 Complete the mini dialogues.

Example: **A** He's very good at his job. How much does he charge?

　　　　　B £65 an hour.

Use one picture and one word from the box.

Use your dictionary, if necessary.

1 **A** How much does it cost to have a car?

　　B About ＿＿＿＿＿＿＿ . Expensive, isn't it?

2 **A** Can you tell me how much those flowers cost, please?

　　B Yes, ＿＿＿＿＿＿＿

3 **A** How much are these bananas, please?

　　B ＿＿＿＿＿＿＿

4 **A** Those strawberries look nice. How much are they, please?

　　B ＿＿＿＿＿＿＿

5 **A** Can you tell me the price of these biscuits, please?

　　B ＿＿＿＿＿＿＿

6 **A** Let's get some more of that wine, shall we? How much is it?

　　B ＿＿＿＿＿＿＿

£ 2.10 £ 7.50 £ 6.99 £ 2.00 £ 1.35

Car expenses
Jan. £ 130
Feb. £ 130

BISCUITS

| month | kilo | bunch | packet | bottle | box | hour |

Q Can I also say *per*, for example *£20 per hour*?

A *A/an* is normal in spoken English.

　　Per is formal. It is more common in written English.

How do you pronounce it?

Schwa / ə /

▶ This is the most common sound in English.

▶ Why? The vowel in unstressed syllables is often pronounced *schwa*.

▶ In the following words and phrases, all the letters with the *schwa* symbol /ə/ on the top have the same sound *schwa*.

 10.02 Listen and repeat the words and phrases.

The stress is underlined in each phrase.

Pay special attention to the pronunciation of the *schwa* /ə/.

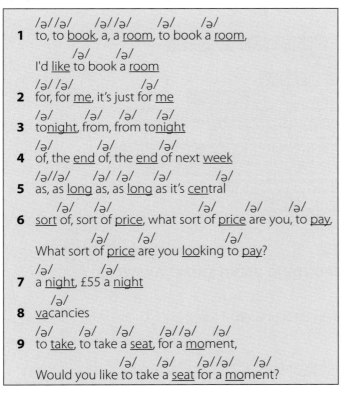

```
        /ə/ /ə/    /ə/ /ə/    /ə/     /ə/
    1   to, to book, a, a room, to book a room,
              /ə/    /ə/
        I'd like to book a room
        /ə/ /ə/              /ə/
    2   for, for me, it's just for me
        /ə/     /ə/   /ə/   /ə/
    3   tonight, from, from tonight
        /ə/      /ə/       /ə/
    4   of, the end of, the end of next week
        /ə//ə/    /ə/ /ə/   /ə/        /ə/
    5   as, as long as, as long as it's central
           /ə/   /ə/           /ə/    /ə/    /ə/
    6   sort of, sort of price, what sort of price are you, to pay,
               /ə/    /ə/          /ə/
        What sort of price are you looking to pay?
        /ə/        /ə/
    7   a night, £55 a night
            /ə/
    8   vacancies
        /ə/     /ə/     /ə/   /ə//ə/  /ə/
    9   to take, to take a seat, for a moment,
                    /ə/   /ə/   /ə//ə/   /ə/
        Would you like to take a seat for a moment?
```

Vocabulary builder 1

IN A HOTEL

Complete these mini dialogues with the correct response from the box.

Use your dictionary, if necessary.

1   **A**   There are two of us.
    B   _____

2   **A**   Does the room have a private bathroom?
    B   _____

3   **A**   Is it half board?
    B   _____

4   **A**   Do you do full board?
      B   _____

5   **A**   I see B & B signs everywhere. What does B & B mean?
      B   _____

6   **A**   What does 'No vacancies' mean?
      B   _____

7   **A**   I'm very sorry but the lift isn't working.
      B   _____

8   **A**   Don't I need a key to open the door of my room?
      B   _____

9   **A**   Where could I have a business meeting, please?
      B   _____

10   **A**   We're really thirsty and I'd like something to eat, too.
      B   _____

a   No, sir. Just put this card in the machine on the door.

b   Yes, the price includes dinner.

c   Do you prefer a double or twin room?

d   Yes, all our rooms have ensuite facilities, madam.

e   It means there are no rooms free. The hotel is fully booked.

f   The lounge is always open to visitors, madam.

g   Yes, that price includes a light lunch and a three-course dinner.

h   It stands for _bed and breakfast_. It's very common in Britain.

i   The bar is open all day for refreshments, sir.

j   Oh, dear! We'll have to go up the stairs.

Language discovery 2

ASKING _WHO ...?_ AND RESPONDING USING SHORT ANSWERS

Example from the story

The assistant asks, _Who's next?_ Oliver responds, _I think I am_.

▶ Short answers are very common in English.

Look at the examples.

Who works in this office?	→	I do.
Who likes coffee?	→	Peter does.
Who can drive?	→	David and Sally can.
Who hasn't got a sister?	→	Tom hasn't.
Who's hungry?	→	We are.
Who's going to Italy?	→	I am.

1 Complete the short answers in these mini dialogues. Choose from the box.

1　**A**　Who lives at No. 12?

　　　B　John and Sheila _____ . You don't remember them, do you?

2　**A**　Who's coming to the cinema with us tonight?

　　　B　I _____ . Have you got my ticket?

3　**A**　Who's not here yet?

　　　B　Sue _____ – she's always late.

4　**A**　Who's got a watch?

　　　B　I _____ . It's six o'clock.

5　**A**　Who can cook tonight?

　　　B　We _____ , if you like.

6　**A**　Do you all like pizza?

　　　　　I'm afraid Mike _____. He can't eat cheese.

7　**A**　Who has to go to work tomorrow?

　　　B　I _____ but my partner _____ . Isn't she lucky?

8　**A**　Who's using the computer?

　　　B　Robert _____, as usual.

9　**A**　Who thinks it's a good idea?

　　　B　I _____ – I think it's great!

10　**A**　Who understands her?

　　　B　No one _____ . She talks so fast.

11　**A**　Who's got a car?

　　　B　Kate _____ .

　　　A　Good! Perhaps she can take us there.

12　**A**　Who watches TV in your house?

　　　B　We all _____ .

am/am not	is/isn't	are/aren't
do/don't	does/doesn't	can/can't
have/haven't	has/hasn't	could/couldn't

TALKING ABOUT THE NUMBER OF PEOPLE, USING *HOW MANY?*

Example from the story

The assistant asks about the number of people.

She says, *How many of you are there?*

Oliver responds, *Just me.*

2 How many of you are there?

Answer the following questions about you.

1 How many of you are there in your family?
There are _____ of us.

2 How many of you are there in the room at this moment?
T_____ / are / _____ / o _____ / u _____ .
OR
J_____/ m_____ .

3 If you are a student – how many of you are there in your class?
_____

4 If you work – how many of you are there in the company?
_____

TALKING ABOUT THE SAME THING, USING *ONE/ONES*

Example from the story

The assistant suggests the Trafalgar Hotel and Oliver asks the price.

He says, *How much is that one?*

Meaning

▶ Don't repeat the noun. Use *one* or *ones* instead.

3 Read and complete.

Complete the speech bubbles 1–5 for the situations.

Choose from the sentences a–e in the box.

a I think I'll take this one.

b Have you got any smaller ones?

c I prefer the white one.

d A large one, please.

e Excuse me, can you tell me
   how much the small one is, please?

> **LANGUAGE TIP**
> Example from this exercise:
> *Is that a small or a large Coke?*
> Answer: ~~A large, please.~~ ✗
> *A large one, please.* ✓

Form

Look at these examples.

1   **A** Would you like a large Coke? **B** No, can I have a small one?

2   I like the green car but I prefer the white one.

3   This bag is too big. Can I see that one, please?

4   **A** Peter's out on his new bike. **B** A new bike? Who's got his old one?

5   **A** I like green apples. **B** Do you? I prefer red ones.

Let's look at Sentence 4, about the bike.

Q Can't I say, *The old is in the garage*?

A No, with *the* + adjective, say *one* or *ones*.

The old one is in the garage.

Example sentence	Summary: *one/ones*		
1	a		one
2	the		one/ones
3	this/that	adjective	one
4	my/your/his, etc.		one
5	no article		ones

4 Complete the mini dialogues. Use *a, the, my,* etc. + *one, ones*.

  1 A Would you like a hot or a cold drink?
   B Could I have _____ cold _____ , please?
  2 A Which umbrella is yours?
   B _____ black _____ .
  3 A Do you like your new computer?
   B Not really, I prefer _____ old _____ .
  4 A Do you like that blue hat?
   B It's too expensive. How about _____ red _____ ?
  5 A Are you going on a long trip?
   B No, it's just _____ short _____ this time.
  6 A Which shoes shall I wear?
   B Why don't you wear _____ new _____ ?

7 A Can I borrow a pen?

  B I've only got _____ red _____ .

8 A Where do I put the clean plates?

  B Here.

  A And _____ dirty _____ ?

  B They go over there.

9 A How many children have you got?

  B Two. They're both girls. The oldest one's called Marie and _____ other _____'s name's Danielle.

Q Where's the stress in the sentences?

A Stress is always on the important or new information.

So, in these sentences, the stress is on the adjectives, for example, *cold*, *black*, old, etc. A **cold** one, the **black** one, my **old** one, etc.

The story 2

 10.03* *Our story continues. The assistant telephones the Trafalgar Hotel, then talks to Oliver again.*

Read the sentences.

Listen and choose the correct answer for each question.

1 Does Oliver books a room at the Trafalgar Hotel?   Yes/No

2 How many hotels do they talk   two/three/four/five about?

Assistant	Sorry to keep you waiting, sir. I'm afraid the Trafalgar is fully booked. There are no vacancies until next week.
Oliver	Have you got anything else?
Assistant	How about these two? The Park Hotel is in the Holland Park area and the Royal is very central, near Oxford Street.
Oliver	Are they about the same price?
Assistant	Let me see. The Royal is £99 a night and the Park is a bit cheaper, £95. They're both three-star hotels so the facilities are about the same. Breakfast is included, of course, and all the rooms are ensuite, with free Wi-Fi, television, and tea and coffee facilities in the room.
Oliver	Which one is more central?
Assistant	The Royal, but the Park is smaller, it's in a quieter street and is perhaps a little more comfortable. It's more traditional, a family-run hotel. Breakfast at the Royal is Continental, buffet style, where you help yourself, but at the Park they also do a full, traditional English breakfast.
Oliver	I think I'll take the room at the Park. I prefer smaller, quieter hotels, and it's better for me because it's nearer the office where I'm working for the next two weeks.

* For an American English version, listen to **11.18**.

Listening and reading 2

 1 10.03 **Listen and complete the grid.**

Cover the text of audio 10:03.

Read the grid.

Listen again and choose the correct options.

Name of Hotel	The Park Hotel	The Royal Hotel
Price per night	£	£
Ensuite bathrooms	Yes/No	Yes/No
Free Wi-Fi	Yes/No	Yes/No
Tea and coffee facilities	Yes/No	Yes/No
Breakfast included	Yes/No	Yes/No
Type of breakfast	Continental/English	Continental/English
Oliver chooses	Yes/No	Yes/No

2 Read and complete.

Read the sentences.

10.03 **Listen again and choose the correct answers.**

Then read the story 2 and check your answers.

1 Oliver waits and the assistant comes back. She starts the conversation.
She says, *S___ ___ ___ y / t___ / k___ ___ p / y___ ___ / w___ ___ ___ ___ ___ g.*

2 When she says the Trafalgar is full, Oliver asks about other possibilities.
He says, *H___ ___ ___ / y___ ___ / g___ t / a___ ___ t h___ ___ g / e___ s___?*

3 The assistant compares the Royal and the Park. What does she say about the Park Hotel?
She says, *The Park is s___ ___ ___ ___ ___ r, it's in a q___ ___ ___ ___ ___ ___ /*
street and is perhaps a little m___ ___ ___ / c___ ___ ___ ___ ___ ___ ___ ___ ___ e.
It's m___ ___ ___ / t r___ ___ ___ ___ ___ ___ ___ ___ .

4 Oliver decides on the Park.
He says, *I'___ ___ / t___ ___ ___ / the room at the Park.*

Vocabulary builder 2

> ### ACCOMMODATION FOR VISITORS
>
> In Britain you can stay in a hotel, a guest-house or a 'bed and breakfast' (B&B).
> Hotels have one to five stars (* to *****). It depends on the facilities.
> A guest-house is a small hotel. It can be part of a private house. Visitors have breakfast and sometimes an evening meal in a guest house. Guest-houses are cheaper than big hotels.
> A bed and breakfast is also a private house. Sometimes it is just one or two rooms in a family home.
> *Tax (VAT – Value Added Tax):* it is common to include VAT in hotel prices.

HOTELS

1 Read about a London hotel and answer the questions.

Look at the map. Where is the Royal Scot Hotel? Read the text from a London Tourist brochure and choose A, B, C, D or E on the map.

Situated between the West End and the City of London, close to King's Cross Station, this modern hotel with 211 comfortable rooms, provides the ideal base for a shopping and sightseeing visit to the capital. London Zoo and Madame Tussaud's famous waxworks are within easy reach and local attractions include the British Museum and Sadler's Wells.

2 Read and decide.

Read the lists.

Read the text again and find all the right answers.

1 The Royal Scot is:

    small

    large

    traditional

    modern

    good for visiting London's shops

    good for tourists

    good for sports enthusiasts

    hot in the summer

    air conditioned

2 It has got:

    a swimming pool

    a big car park

    limited car parking

    three restaurants

    views of the park

    more than 200 rooms

3 Choose words from the box to complete these sentences.

Use your dictionary, if necessary.

1 My hotel is very _____ because it's _____ a park. There's not much traffic.

2 A How much is that hotel?

   B I don't know but it's in the centre of town. That means it's _____ .

   A I prefer to pay a bit more and be _____ so I can walk to the museums, shops and all the other places I want to visit. I also need a hotel that is _____ – being a tourist is tiring.

3 I really like my hotel. Everything looks so _____ and the staff are very _____ – they always talk to me.

| small | modern | traditional | big | comfortable |
| friendly | clean | central | expensive | quiet near |

Breakfast

4 Read the text and label the pictures.

Use your dictionary to help you, if necessary.

> Breakfast is usually included in the price of hotels in the UK.
>
> Continental breakfast can include cereals, yoghurt, rolls, croissants, toast, butter, cheese, jam, coffee, tea and hot chocolate.
>
> English breakfast includes fruit juice, cereals, eggs, bacon (sometimes tomatoes, sausages, mushrooms), toast, butter, marmalade, tea and coffee.
>
> Nowadays not many people in Britain eat a traditional full English breakfast at home. Sometimes it's a treat (something special) for weekends.

Continental breakfast

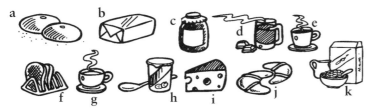

English breakfast

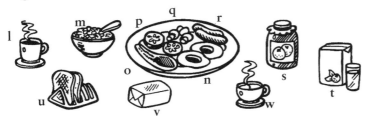

How do you pronounce it?

 10.04 Practise the pronunciation of *schwa* **in these words.**

Listen and repeat these words and phrases from the the story 2. You will hear each one twice.

Remember *schwa* **/ə/ is common in unstressed syllables.**

Pay special attention to the letters with the symbol /ə/ above them. The pronunciation is always *schwa* **/ ə/ – they are unstressed.**

Stressed syllables are <u>underlined</u>.

	/ə/
1	**Royal**
	/ə/
2	**Holland Park**
	/ə/
3	**Oxford Street**
	/ə/
4	**facilities**
	/ə/ /ə/ /ə/
5	**traditional**
	/ə/
6	**breakfast**
	/ə/
7	**continental**
	/ə/
8	**cheaper**
	/ə/
9	**smaller**
	/ə//ə/
10	**quieter**
	/ə/
11	**nearer**
	/ə/
12	**better**

 Language discovery 3

ASKING FOR AN ALTERNATIVE

Example from the story: a general alternative

The Trafalgar Hotel is full. Oliver asks about other possibilities.

He says, *Have you got anything else?*

▶ This question is very general.

▶ You can use it to ask about everything.

Example from the story: a more specific alternative

Look at this example.

Receptionist   I've got one room at £100 a night.

Client   Have you got anything cheaper?

▶ We can use the comparative with this question.

1 Ask questions in these situations. Use the comparative.

   1 In a shop

      You: _____?

   2 In a shop

      You: _____?

   3 Your travel agent suggests a flight at 22.00. It's too late.
      You: _____?

   4 You book a hotel room in London. Your friend tells you it's far from the centre.
      You phone your travel agent.
      You: _____?

MAKING NEGATIVE COMPARISONS

Example from the story

Oliver chooses the Park because it's **smaller**, **quieter**, **more comfortable**, it is **more traditional** and it's **nearer** the office than the Royal.

Why doesn't Oliver choose the Royal?

The Royal's **not as quiet** (as the Park) OR

The Royal **isn't as quiet** (as the Park).

▶ The pronunciation of *as* is also with *schwa* / ə/.

2 Complete the sentences. Use adjectives from the box.

| quiet | comfortable | big | traditional | good | near | expensive |

1 The Royal's not _____ / _____ . It's in a really busy street.
2 The Royal's _____ as _____ / _____ the Park.
   The beds are hard.
3 The Royal's _____ / _____ traditional. The style is more modern.
4 The Royal's _____ good _____ the Park for Oliver because
   it isn't / _____ / n_____ his office.

MAKING DECISIONS – BUYING THINGS

Example from the story

Oliver decides on the Park Hotel.

He says, *I'll take the Park*.

▶ Say, *I'll take* when you decide to buy.

3 Read and complete these decisions.

Situation: You are in a shop and you decide to buy.

1 You look at two boxes of chocolates, a big one and a small one.
   You decide to buy the small one.
   You: _____
2 You look at two pictures – one in black and white, one in colour.
   You decide to buy the one in black and white.
   You: _____
3 You look at two watches – a more expensive one and a cheaper one.
   You decide to buy the more expensive one.
   You: _____

The story 3

10.05* *Our story continues. Oliver arrives at the Park Hotel. He checks in.*

Read a–f.

Listen and choose *Yes* or *No*.

They talk about:

a	Oliver's passport	Yes/No
b	his room number	Yes/No
c	the restaurant	Yes/No
d	the breakfast room	Yes/No
e	the cost of the room	Yes/No
f	Oliver's luggage?	Yes/No

Receptionist	Good afternoon. Can I help you?
Oliver	Yes, I've got a room booked.
Receptionist	In what name, sir?
Oliver	Rees, R – double E – S, Oliver.
Receptionist	Yes, here it is, a single room for 14 nights.
Oliver	That's right.
Receptionist	Could you sign this registration card, please?
Oliver signs.	
Oliver	There you are.
Receptionist	Thank you. Here's your key. Room 508's on the fifth floor. Breakfast is served in the breakfast room downstairs from seven to ten o'clock and the lift is round the corner to your right. Do you need help with your luggage?
Oliver	No thanks, I'm fine.
Receptionist	I hope you enjoy your stay with us, Mr Rees.
Oliver	Thank you.

* For an American English version, listen to **11.19**.

Listening and reading 3

 1 **10.05 Listen and answer the questions.**

Cover the text again.

Read the questions.

Listen and answer.

1 What does Oliver sign?
2 What's his room number?
3 Where's the breakfast room?
4 What time's breakfast?
5 How much luggage has Oliver got?

 2 **10.05 Listen and complete the words.**

Read the sentences.

Listen again and complete the words.

Then read the text to help you, if necessary.

> **LANGUAGE TIP**
> Common mistake
> *On the first floor*
> NOT: *In the first floor*
> OR *At the first floor*
> To say where, *on*
> is the only correct
> preposition with *floor*.

1 Oliver says he has a reservation.
He says, *I've g __ __ / a / __ __ __ __ / b __ __ __ __ d.*

2 The receptionist asks his name.

She says, *I ___ / w ___ ___ ___ / n ___ ___ e, / sir?*

3 Where is room 508?

… / ___ n / the / f ___ ___ t ___ / floor.

4 Where can Oliver have breakfast?

She says, *Breakfast / i ___ / s ___ ___ ___ ___ d / in the breakfast room.*

5 Where's the breakfast room?

D ___ ___ ___ ___ ___ ___ ___ s.

6 Where's the lift?

R ___ ___ ___ ___ / the / c ___ ___ ___ ___ ___ / t ___ / y ___ ___ ___ / r ___ ___ ___ t.

7 The receptionist wants Oliver to enjoy his stay.

She says: *I / h ___ ___ ___ / you enjoy your stay with us, Mr Rees.*

Ⓥ Vocabulary builder 3

Ordinal numbers

Example from the story

Room 508 is on the fifth floor.

1 Look at this lift notice and complete the words on the right.

12th	twelfth
11th	eleventh
10th	___ ___ ___ th
9th	___ ___ ___ ___ h
8th	e ___ g ___ ___ ___
7th	___ ___ ___ ___ ___ ___ ___
6th	___ ___ ___ t ___
5th	___ ___ f ___ ___
4th	___ o ___ ___ ___ h
3rd	third
2nd – Restaurant	second
1st – Bar/Lounge	first
G – Reception	ground floor
LG – Breakfast room	lower ground

2 Look at the lift notice and complete these mini dialogues.

Example: ⟨617⟩ Where's your room? I'm *on the sixth floor.*

  1 A Excuse me, where's reception?
       B It's / __ __ / t __ __ / g __ __ __ __ __ / f __ __ __ __ .
  2 A Can you tell me where the restaurant is, please?
       B Yes, / i __ ' __ / o __ / t __ __ / s __ __ __ __ __ / floor.
  3 A Where do we go for breakfast?
       B Downstairs. The breakfast room's / __ n / t __ __ / l __ __ __ __ /
            g __ __ __ __ __ / floor.
  4 A Excuse me, where can I get a drink?
       B The bar's / on / t __ __ / f __ __ __ __ / f __ __ __ __ .

3 Complete the rule.

For ordinal numbers in English, add the letters __ __ to the number. The ordinals
f __ __ __ __ , s __ __ __ __ __ and __ __ __ __ d are irregular.

4 On which floor?

Answer these questions for you.

  1 If you live in a flat – where is your flat? On which floor?
       You: _____
  2 If you live in a house – where is your bedroom? On which floor?
       You: _____
  3 Where do you work or study – on which floor?
       You: _____
  4 Where are you now?
       You: _____

Language discovery 4

USING THE VERB *HOPE*

Example from the story

The receptionist wants Oliver to enjoy his stay.

She says, *I hope you enjoy your stay*.

Write sentences for these situations. Use the verb *hope*.

  1 It's the end of the week.
       What do you say to your colleagues when you leave work?
       I hope _____ .
  2 Your friend is going out for the evening.
       You: _____

> **LANGUAGE TIP**
> **Q** What's the difference between *I hope you have a good weekend* and *Have a good weekend* (Unit 9)?
> **A** They are very similar. Both are appropriate in most situations. *I hope …* can be more formal.

3 Your friend is going on holiday.

You: _____

4 Your friend is going on a journey.

You: _____

5 Your friend is taking an exam/having a baby/taking a driving test, etc.

You: _____

How do you pronounce it?

Practise the pronunciation of *schwa* in these phrases.

10.06 Listen and repeat the words and phrases from Oliver's conversation in the hotel.

Pay special attention to the letters with the symbol / ə/ above them. The pronunciation is always *schwa* / ə/. Stressed syllables are <u>underlined</u>.

    /ə/
1 Can I <u>help</u> you?

     /ə/
2 Oliver

     /ə/
3 <u>sin</u>gle

       /ə/
4 regis<u>tra</u>tion

  /ə/
5 of <u>course</u>

      /ə/ /ə/
6 <u>sig</u>nature

  /ə/
7 just <u>here</u>

  /ə/
8 to your <u>right</u>

      /ə/   /ə/
9 round the <u>cor</u>ner

    /ə/
10 Do you need <u>help?</u>

The story 4

10.07* *Our story continues. Oliver is in his hotel room in London. He phones his mother in Edinburgh.*

1 Listen and decide.

Cover the text.

Read the sentences.

Listen and choose *Yes* or *No*.

Oliver and his mother talk about:

a	the weather	**Yes/No**
b	Oliver's hotel	**Yes/No**
c	his trip	**Yes/No**
d	his work in London	**Yes/No**
e	Tasha	**Yes/No**
f	Oliver's father	**Yes/No**
g	a message	**Yes/No**

Oliver	Hi, Mum – it's Oliver. How are you?
Mother	Hello, dear. Where are you?
Oliver	I'm in a hotel in London, the Park. I haven't stayed here before. It's quite nice – small but comfortable and quiet. I've just got here from the airport.
Mother	How was your trip?
Oliver	It went quite well, actually. First, I visited our new representative in Chile, and then on Tuesday, Wednesday and Thursday I went to the Computer Fair in Buenos Aires. I talked to a lot of people there and had lots of meetings. And then on the flight on the way back I met a very interesting girl.
Mother	Oh, did you?
Oliver	Yes, she's an English teacher in South America. She's on holiday here, staying with friends, just outside London. I've got her number there so I can contact her again. I'm going to call her one day next week. We might have dinner together, or something. Anyway, how are you?
Mother	Did you get my message?
Oliver	What message?
Mother	I left a message at your hotel in Argentina two days ago.
Oliver	What was it about, Mum? Come on – what's happened?

* For an American English version, listen to **11.20**.

2 **10.07 Listen and choose.**

Read the sentences.

Listen again and choose the correct answer.

1   The name of Oliver's hotel is:
    a the Palmer.
    b the Park.
    c the Plaza.
    d the Spa.

2   **a** This is Oliver's first visit to this hotel.
    b This isn't Oliver's first visit to this hotel.
    c Oliver always stays at this hotel.

3   Oliver thinks the hotel is:
    a excellent.
    b good.
    c poor.

4   Oliver's business trip was:
    a good.
    b not very good.
    c terrible.

5   Oliver is thinking about inviting Tasha:
    a for lunch.
    b for a drink.
    c for dinner.
    d to the cinema.

6   Oliver doesn't know about:
    a a letter.
    b a problem.
    c a ticket.
    d an invitation.

 ## Listening and reading 4

1 **10.07 Listen and complete.**

Read the sentences.

Listen again and try to complete the words.

Read the text to help you, if necessary.

1   This is Oliver's first visit to the Park Hotel.
    He says, *I / h ___ ___ n ' ___ / s ___ ___ ___ ___ d / here before.*

2   Oliver talks about this trip.
    a He says, *First / I / v ___ ___ ___ ___ ___ d / our new representative …*
    b *… then on Tuesday, Wednesday and Thursday I / w ___ ___ ___ / to the Computer Fair …*

c He talks about his activities there.

He says, *I / t___ ___ ___ ___ d / t___ / a / l___ ___ / o___ / people there and h___ ___ / l___ ___ ___ / o___ / meetings.*

3 **a** Oliver tells his mother about Tasha.

He says, *On the flight on the way back / I / m___ ___ / a very interesting girl.*

b His mother is interested. She says, *Oh, d___ ___ / y___ ___ ?*

4 Oliver plans to phone Tasha next week.

He says, *I'___ / g___ ___ ___ ___ / t___ / call her one day next week.*

5 Oliver talks about the possibility of dinner with Tasha.

He says, *We / m___ ___ ___ ___ / h___ ___ ___ / dinner together.*

6 **a** Verb *get*: Oliver's mother asks him about her message.

She says, *Did you get my message?*

Here, *get* means find/buy/receive.

b Oliver says *no*. His mother gives more information about the message. She says, *I / I___ ___ ___ / a message at your hotel two days / a___ ___ .*

c Oliver asks about the message.

He says, *W___ ___ ___ / w___ ___ / ___ ___ / a___ ___ ___ ___ ?*

7 He wants to know what the situation is.

He says, *W___ ___ ___ ' ___ / h___ ___ p___ ___ e___ ?*

2 Listen, read and complete the phrases.

Read the sentences.

Read the text of the story 4 again and complete the words and phrases.

1 When Oliver's mother starts the conversation, she says, *Hello, d___ ___ ___* to her son.

2 **a** What's the hotel like? It's q___ ___ ___ ___ / n___ ___ ___ .

b Is there a lot of traffic noise? No it's a / q___ ___ ___ ___ / hotel.

▶ Older people often say *dear* to be friendly.

Q What's the difference in pronunciation between *quite* and *quiet*? (Sentences 2a and 2b.)

A *Quite* has one syllable / kwaɪt /.

Quiet has two (qui-et) / kwaɪət /.

Language discovery 5

Talking about the past, using the past simple

Example from the story

Oliver talks about his trip.

He says, *First I **visited** our new representative.*

*Then on Tuesday, Wednesday and Thursday I **went** to the Computer Fair. I **talked** to a lot of people there and I **had** a lot of meetings.*

*On the flight on the way back, I **met** a very interesting girl.*

All the verbs in **bold** are in the past simple tense.

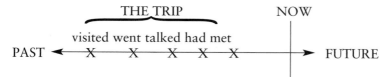

Meaning

Read these questions and answers about the past simple.

Q Is the trip:
   a in the past?
   b in the present?
   c in the future?

A In the past.

Q Oliver visited the new representative. Do we know when?

A Yes, during his trip. His trip is in the past.

Q Oliver went to the Computer Fair. Do we know when?

A Yes, on Tuesday, Wednesday and Thursday.

Q Oliver talked to lots of people and had lots of meetings. When?

A During the Computer Fair. The Computer Fair is in the past.

Q Oliver met Tasha. When?

A On the way back to England.

▶ All these activities were during Oliver's trip. His trip is in the past.

Are we saying anything about the present? No.

Form: past simple

Regular verbs – verb + -*ed*	Irregular verbs
visit – **visited**	go – **went**
talk – **talked**	have – **had**
	meet – **met**

Note: The verbs in **bold** are the past simple.

Grammar summary: past simple		
Positive		
I, you, he, she, it, we, they	talked (*verb + -ed or irregular verb*)	
Negative		
I, you, he, she, it, we, they	didn't	talk (*verb*)
Questions		
Did	I, you, he, she, it, we, they	talk? (*verb*)
Tag questions, echo questions and short answers		
I talked, didn't I? Yes, I did, etc.		

1   **Complete the dialogue, using the past simple.**

Situation: It's Monday morning. Two colleagues, Natalie and Dan are talking about the weekend.

Is the weekend in the past? Yes.

Is it finished? Yes.

So, the verbs are in the past simple.

Natalie   Hi, Dan, _____ (1) you _____ (2) (have/had) a good weekend?

Dan   Yes, I _____ (1) thanks. It _____ (2) (be/was) really nice, actually. On Saturday, I _____ (3) (wash) the car. Then in the afternoon I _____ (4) (take/took) the children to the park. Yesterday I _____ (5) (play) tennis in the morning and for lunch we _____ (6) (have/had) a barbecue in the garden.

Natalie   Great!

Dan	How about you? What _____ (1) you _____ (2)? (do/did)
Natalie	I _____ (1) (be/was) so tired after last week. I

I _____ (1) (be/was) so tired after last week. I
really _____ / _____ (2) (do/did) much
at all. I _____ (3) (see/saw) a good film on the
TV on Saturday night and yesterday I just
_____ (4) (relax) at home. My husband's sister _____
(5) (come/came) to see us. We _____ / _____ (6) (want)
to cook so we _____ (7) (get/got/got) an Indian takeaway. Later,
in the evening we _____ (8) (go/went) out for a drink and then
we _____ (9) (drive/drove) her home.

USING THE PRESENT PERFECT FOR (A) LIFE EXPERIENCES (B) PAST ACTIONS WITH PRESENT RESULTS

Examples from the story

a This is Oliver's first visit to the Park Hotel.
He says, *I haven't stayed here before.*

b Oliver asks what was in the message.

He says, *What's (has) happened?*

Now look at this example:

I've stayed in this hotel three times.

Meaning and form

Read these questions and answers about *I have stayed.*

Q Is the action of staying in the hotel in the past?

A Yes.

Q Do we know when in the past?

A No.

Q Why use the present perfect then?

A To show there is a connection between the past action (experience of staying) and the effect of the experience on the now.

Q So, what is the connection here?

A I have stayed in the hotel in the past so I know the hotel now. For example, I know where it is, what it looks like inside and outside. In other words, I am familiar with the hotel. It's also possible I will stay here again in the future.

Q So, why is the name of this tense 'present perfect'?

A Half the verb is present (*have*) and half is the past participle (*stayed*). It's this combination of present tense of *have* and past participle of the main verb that we use to show the connection.

Read these questions and answers about *What's happened?*

Q Is the action of 'happening' in the past?

A Yes.

Q Do we know when in the past?

A No.

Q Why the present perfect then?

A To show the connection between the past action (happened) and a result of this action/experience in the present.

Q So, what is the present result here?

A Perhaps there's a problem or perhaps there's very good news. We don't know. We only know that there is a new situation in the present.

Grammar summary – present perfect		
I/you/we/they	have ('ve)	+ past participle *(regular verb + -ed OR irregular)*
He/she/it	has ('s)	
Negative		
I/you/we/they	haven't	+ *past participle*
He/she/it	hasn't	
Question		
Have	I/you/we/they	+ *past participle*
Has	he/she/it	
Tag questions, echo questions and short answers		
Have(n't)	I/you/we/they?	
Has(n't)	He/she/it?	

▶ Asking questions with the present perfect

The present perfect is the same as all other two-word verbs in English. To make questions you change the word order.

For example: (1) *He* → (2) *has* → (3) *visited* ...

For questions, say (2) *Has* → (1) *he* → (3) *visited* ...?

(2) auxiliary, *Has* (1) the subject, *he* (3) the past participle, *visited* ...?

> **LANGUAGE TIP**
>
> **The past participle**
> The past participle of **regular verbs** is verb + -ed (you need to add -d only for verbs already ending in e.
> For example: I have worked, he has danced.
> For **irregular verbs**, you need to learn the past participle, as the third form to memorize:
> For example:
>
> | Infinitive | Past simple | Past Participle |
> |------------|-------------|-----------------|
> | see | saw | seen |
> | write | wrote | written |
> | speak | spoke | spoken |

2 Put the <u>underlined</u> words in the right order to make sentences about Oliver.

   1 <u>arrived/Oliver/has/</u> at his hotel.

   2 <u>spoken/has/he</u> to his mother.

   3 <u>called/he/has</u> Tasha? No, not yet. He's going to call her next week.

   4 <u>contacted/hasn't/he</u> the office. He's going there later.

   5 How many times <u>he/been/has</u> to South America? About six times.

3 Use the verbs in brackets in the present perfect to complete these mini dialogues.

   1 A _____ you _____ (see/saw/seen) the film *Titanic*?
      B Yes, I _____ .

   2 A How many times _____ you _____ (go/went/been) to France?
      B I' _____ / _____ lots of times.

   3 A How many countries _____ you _____ (visit)?
      B Me? I' _____ to the States but I _____ / _____ anywhere else.

   4 A How many jobs _____ your brother _____ (have/had/had)?
      B He _____ n't / _____ many, actually.

   5 A How many English books _____ you _____ (read/read/read)?
      B I' _____ / _____ hundreds!

   6 A _____ they _____ (finish)?
      B No, not yet.

   7 A You _____ / _____ (forget/forgot/forgotten), have you?
      B No, of course not.

   8 A My sister' _____ / _____ (buy/bought/bought) a new house.
      B Oh! _____ she? Whereabouts?

 Practice

LEAVING THE HOTEL

1 Put this conversation between a hotel receptionist and a guest in the right order. Use the letters.

A Certainly. What room number is it, please?

B Good morning. Can I help you?

C Room 201.

D Of course. If you wait at the front door, one will be here in a few moments. Goodbye. I hope you have a good flight.

E Let me see ... Here's your bill. How would you like to pay?

F Thanks. Goodbye.

G Morning. Yes, I'd like to check out, please.

H Could you possibly call me a taxi to go to the airport?

I No problem. Is there anything else I can do for you?

J By card, if that's OK.

 10.08 Listen and check your answers.

Receptionist	B	Good morning. Can I help you?
Guest	G	Morning. Yes, I'd like to check out, please.
Receptionist	A	Certainly. What room number is it, please?
Guest	C	Room 201.
Receptionist	E	Let me see … Here's your bill. How would you like to pay?
Guest	J	By card, if that's OK.
Receptionist	I	No problem. Is there anything else I can do for you?
Guest	H	Could you possibly call me a taxi to go to the airport?
Receptionist	D	Of course. If you wait at the front door, one will be here in a few moments. Goodbye. I hope you have a good flight.
Guest	F	Thanks. Goodbye.

 Writing

2 About your country: hotels.

Write answers to these questions or prepare to tell a friend.

1 When was the last time you stayed in a hotel?

2 Talk or write about:

   a the place.

   b how long you stayed.

   c who you went with.

   d why you went there.

3 What was the hotel like? Describe it and talk or write about the facilities.

4 How much did you enjoy your stay there?

Speaking

3 What would you say?

  1 You are in a hotel. You would like to watch TV. You turn the TV on and nothing happens. You call reception.

  2 You can't find the key card for your hotel room. You look everywhere but you can't find it. You're at reception.

Revision

WHAT IS IT IN YOUR LANGUAGE?

Here are some examples of the important points in this unit.

Translate the sentences into your language.

Remember – translate the idea, not the words.

  1 **A** Who's next?

     B I think I am.

  2 **A** How many of you are there?

     B There are four of us.

  3 How much is this one?

  4 £3 a packet.

  5 I don't mind where we go as long as you come, too.

  6 Have you got anything cheaper?

  7 On the sixth floor.

  8 I haven't been to Singapore.

  9 He telephoned last week.

 10 I got the letter yesterday.

Writing

Write the story of your life. Complete the gaps in the first paragraph and then write a paragraph for each topic. Follow the instructions for each topic.

My life story

My name is _____ . I was born in _____ (place) on _____ (date). I _____ (be) the _____ (first, second, third, etc.) of two, three, four, five, etc. children, so I've got _____ brother(s) and _____ sister(s).

OR: I am an only child.

I went/didn't go to a nursery and/but I _____ (go) to _____ primary school when I _____ (be) _____ years old. I really _____ (like) _____ when I _____ (be) there. My secondary school _____ (be) called _____ and I _____ (study) there from _____ to _____ years old. I _____ (take) exams in _____ , _____ , _____ .

Life experiences

Now write about your life experiences: use the present perfect to introduce the topic and the past simple to give details.

1 University

I have/haven't been to university. (If the answer is *yes,* give details of where, when and what you studied. Write these verbs in the past simple because we know *when.*

_____

_____

_____

2 Work

(Write about your experience of work, e.g. *I've worked as an office* administrator. Give details using the past simple.)

_____

_____

_____

I've also been a _____ . That was when _____ .

3 Personal life

(Write about your family situation and children.)

I _____ (be) single/ OR I _____ / _____ (be) married/separated/divorced for _____ years _____ .

4 Travel

(Write about places you've visited (present perfect) and details, e.g. when you went/what you did there (past simple).)

_____

_____

_____

5 Foreign languages

(Write about the language(s) you've learned and where/when/why you learned them.)

_____

_____

_____

Speaking

10.09 **Now it's your turn to join the conversation.**

Listen again to the Story 1 conversation.

Say Oliver's words in the spaces.

Test yourself

Which one is right?

Choose a or b.

1 I've seen that film on DVD.
   a Did you? What's it like?
   b Have you? What's it like?

2 a My room is in the first floor.
   b My room is on the first floor.

3 a This ice cream costs £3 a box.
   b This ice cream costs £3 the box.

4 a Could I see the red one, please?
   b Could I see the red, please?

5 a I hope you to enjoy your trip.
   b I hope you enjoy your trip.

6 a Yesterday I went to the cinema.
   b Yesterday I was to the cinema.

7 a Where you met my brother?
   b Where did you meet my brother?

8 a How would you like to pay?
   b How would you like to paying?

9 a With card, please.
   b By card, please.

10 a The bar is in the downstairs.
    b The bar is downstairs.

11 a What did you at the weekend?
    b What did you do at the weekend?

12 a When have you arrived?
    b When did you arrive?

13 a I'll take this one, please.
    b I buy this one, please.

14 a In which floor is the restaurant, please?
    b What floor is the restaurant on, please?

Write two dialogues.

Dialogue A: In a travel agency

1 The travel agent　　　　**You**

The travel agent asks about the type of hotel you want.

2 The only thing you don't like is noise.

3 She asks about the number of people.

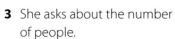

4 You and your partner.

5 She asks you about the price you want to pay.

6 Your maximum is £90.

7 She suggests the Plaza Hotel – £85.

8 Say *yes*.

9 She asks about method of payment.

10 You want to pay by card.

Dialogue B: In a shop

You pay and then you go to the shop next door to buy a suitcase. You are looking at a small suitcase:

The shop assistant | **You**

1 The shop assistant offers to help you.

2 You want the same suitcase but bigger.

3 The shop assistant says *yes* and shows it to you.

4 You decide to buy it.

SELF-CHECK

I CAN . . .

. . . talk about length of time, and prices
. . . ask *who?* and respond using short answers
. . . talk about the number of people, using *how many*
. . . talk about the same thing, using *one*, *ones*
. . . ask for an alternative, using comparatives
. . . make negative comparisons, using *not as . . . as*
. . . make decisions – buying things, using *I'll*
. . . use the verb *hope* + present simple
. . . talk about the past, using the past simple
. . . talk about life experiences and results, using the present perfect.

To the learner

We hope you have enjoyed learning with *Complete Teach Yourself English as a Foreign Language* and that you are happy with the progress you have made. We enjoyed finding a method to help you learn English in English, without a teacher, and writing this course for you.

We wonder what will happen to Oliver and Tasha in the future? Will Tasha enjoy her holiday? Will Oliver and Tasha meet again? What do you think?

We'll see!

With best wishes,

Sandra Stevens.

ANSWER KEY

KEY POINTS ABOUT ENGLISH PRONUNCIATION

1 1 b, 2 d, 3 f, 4 a, 5 c, 6 e

4 1 <u>sy</u>llables, 2 ex<u>am</u>ples, 3 conver<u>sa</u>tion, 4 ab<u>ove</u>, 5 im<u>por</u>tant, 6 infor<u>ma</u>tion

5 1 Some <u>Coke</u>. 2 To <u>Lon</u>don. 3 From <u>David</u>. 4 Are they <u>here</u>? 5 Does it <u>change</u>?

6 <u>Ask</u> them.

6 s<u>o</u>me, t<u>o</u>, fr<u>o</u>m, <u>a</u>re, d<u>oe</u>s, th<u>e</u>m

11 b The voice goes down.

13 1 One page (1), Two pages (2); 2 One box (1), Two boxes (2); 3 One bus (1), Two buses (2);

4 One house (1), Two houses (2); 5 One bridge (1), Two bridges (2); 6 One sandwich (2),

Two sandwiches (3); 7 One slice (1), Two slices (2); 8 One piece (1), Two pieces (2); 9 One

dish (1), Two dishes (2); 10 One glass (1), Two glasses (2); 11 One orange juice

(3), Two orange juices (4); 12 One kiss (1), Two kisses (2)

UNIT 1

The story
1 c, **2** b, **3** a

Listening and reading

1 a It's hot, isn't it?   b Yes, it is – very hot.

2 a Would you like a drink?   b Yes, please.

3 a What would you like?   b Some Coke, please.

Vocabulary builder

1

o	w	r	m	c	s	z
s	i	j	b	o	g	w
v	n	e	n	f	o	a
y	e	m	w	f	a	t
j	u	i	c	e	t	e
l	a	l	b	e	e	r
c	o	k	e	r	a	p

2

 rice
 crisps
 sandwich
 bread

 biscuits
 grapes
 soup
 hamburger

Language discovery 1

1 I'm not wrong, <u>am</u> I? He/She/It is English, <u>isn't</u> he/she/it? He/She/It <u>isn't</u> English, is he/she/it? We/You/They are happy, <u>aren't</u> we/you/they? We/You/They aren't happy, <u>are</u> we/you/they?

2 **1** It's really cold today, <u>isn't it</u>?

　　2 Nice and warm this morning, <u>isn't it</u>?

　　3 The weather's not bad today, <u>is it</u>?

　　4 Lovely day, <u>isn't it</u>?

How do you pronounce it?

2 **1** d This programme's not very interesting, <u>is it</u>?

　　2 g It's not very warm in here, <u>is it</u>?

　　3 a It's a very good film, <u>isn't it</u>?

　　4 b You're David, <u>aren't you</u>? My name's Sam.

　　5 h They're lovely, <u>aren't they</u>?

　　6 i He's a good singer, <u>isn't he</u>?

7 e   She's beautiful, <u>isn't she</u>?

8 c   The food's very nice, <u>isn't it</u>?

9 f   This isn't right, <u>is it</u>?

Language discovery 2

1   1 he isn't. 2 she is. 3 it isn't. 4 we are. 5 I am. 6 they aren't.

2   1 f Yes, it is. 2 h I am. 3 b Yes, it is. 4 c No, it isn't. 5 e Yes, she is. 6 g No, it isn't. or No, it's not.

7 i No, it isn't. or No, it's not. 8 a Yes, they are. 9 d Yes he is.

4   1 Some, some, some; 2 A, a, a

5

6   1   Would you like a hamburger?

  2   Would you like some bread?

  3   Would you like some soup?

  4   Would you like a sandwich?

  5   Would you like some grapes?

  6   Would you like a biscuit?

  7   Would you like some crisps?

  8   Would you like some rice?

8 1 <u>Another</u> drink? 2 Would you like <u>some more</u> crisps? 3 <u>More</u> wine? 4 Would you like <u>another</u> biscuit? 5 <u>Some more</u> milk?

9 1 ☺ **2** ☺☺ **3** ☺☺☺ **4** ☺☺☺

Speaking

Possible answers
1 Sorry, I'm not Chris. **2** Thanks, but the coffee's for my friend and the tea's for me.

Test yourself

Which one is right?

1	Starting a conversation	b Nice day, isn't it?
2	Offering	a Would you like a drink?
	Saying yes	b Yes, please.
3	Starting a conversation	b This food's not very hot, is it?
4	Starting a conversation	b This soup's delicious.
	Responding	a Yes, it is, isn't it?
5	Offering more	b Some more bread?
	Saying no	a No, thanks. I'm fine.

Dialogue: model answers

1	You	Cold, isn't it?
2	Your friend	Yes, it is – very cold.
3	You	Would you like a hot drink?
4	Your friend	Yes, please.
		Yes, please, that would be nice!
		Yes, please, I'd love one.

UNIT 2

The story 1

1 Yes, **2** No (he wants orange juice), **3** Yes, **4** Yes, **5** No, **6** No

Listening and reading 1

1 Excuse me. **2** Could I have a Coke and some orange juice, please? **3** Here you are. One Coke with ice and lemon and one orange juice.

Vocabulary builder

a beef, **b** pork, **c** chicken, **d** fish, **e** lamb, **f** vegetarian

The story 2

1 a chicken, **2** a beef, **3** a fish, **4** a lamb, **5** b beef, **6** b beef, **7** a or b we don't know,

8 c a sandwich

Listening, reading and speaking

1   1 Chicken, please. 2 Beef for me, please. 3 I'd like fish, please. 4 Could I have the lamb, please? 5 I'll have beef, please.

Language discovery 1

1   Passenger 6: The same for me too, please.

2   c

3   Nothing for me, thanks ... Could I have a sandwich instead?

4   1 I'll have fruit juice, please. 2 I'll have a slice of the chocolate one, please. 3 I think I'll have some bread and cheese. 4 I think I'll go to bed. 5 I'll go tomorrow.

5   1 Yes, could I have some coffee, please? 2 Yes, can I have a sandwich, please? 3 Can we have something cold, please? 4 Yes, could I have a small slice, please? 5 Excuse me, could I have a glass of water, please? 6 Could I have some grapes, please?

6

 02.04

> **Customer 1**   Three coffees and one tea, please.
> **Customer 2**   Could I have four Cokes, two orange juices and one hot
>   chocolate?
> **Customer 3**   We'd like two lemon teas, please.

Customer 1   3 coffees, 1 tea

Customer 2   4 Cokes, 2 orange juices, 1 hot chocolate

Customer 3   2 lemon teas.

How do you pronounce it?

1 A 1 P, 2 R

   B 1 R, 2 P

   C 1 R, 2 P

   D 1 P, 2 R

   E 1 R, 2 P

   F 1 P, 2 R

3 1 2Could I have some <u>wa</u>ter, please? (uncountable)

   2 Could I have some <u>bread</u>, please? (uncountable)

   3 Could I have an ice <u>cream</u>, please? (countable)

   4 Could I have another <u>sand</u>wich, please? (countable)

   5 Could I have some more <u>co</u>ffee, please? (uncountable) or Could I have another cup of

      <u>co</u>ffee, please? (countable)

The story 3

1 Passenger 1 – Apple juice. Passenger 2 – Beer. Passenger 3 – White wine.

2 Passenger 1 – Yes. Passenger 2 – Yes. Passenger 3 – No.

Language discovery 2

1 1 I've got some apple juice. 2 Have you got any cold beer? 3 I haven't got any more white wine.

2 Negative: I/you/we/they haven't got a drink. He/she/it hasn't got a drink.

Question: Have I/you/we/they got a drink? Has he/she/it got a drink?

Question tags: I/You/We/They've got a drink, haven't I/you/we/they? He/She/It's got a drink, hasn't he/she/it? I/You/We/They haven't got a drink, have I/you/we/they? He/She/It hasn't got a drink, has he/she/it?

Short answers: Yes, I/you/we/they have. Yes, he/she/it has. No, I/you/we/they haven't. No, he/she/it hasn't.

3 1 I've got water, juice, beer or wine.

2 We haven't got any more chicken.

3 A If you're hungry, I've got a pizza.

   B Have you? Could I have some now, please?

4 A Has he got any milk for the coffee?

   B Yes, he has. Here it is.

5 A We haven't got any bread.

   B Haven't we? OK, I'll go and buy some.

6 I haven't got chicken but I've got lamb.

7 They've got Coke, haven't they?

8 Why hasn't he got any rice?

4 1 Beer – yes. 2 Bread – yes. 3 Cheese – no. 4 Biscuits – we don't know. 5 Crisps – no. 6 Grapes – yes.

Practice

1 1 I've got some wine but there isn't any beer. 2 A Is there any more pizza? B No, but

there's some bread. 3 A Are there any hamburgers?

B No, but there are some sandwiches. 4 A Have you got any biscuits? B No, and there isn't

any chocolate either. 5 A Is there any soup? B Sorry, I haven't got any more.

2 1 C What would you like to eat? There's chicken or I've got some beef too.

2 F I'd like some chicken, please.

3 H With peas or carrots?

4 B I really don't mind. I like all vegetables.

5 E And would you like something to drink? I've got some wine if you'd like some.

6 A Actually, I don't drink alcohol, so could I have some Coke, fruit juice or something like

that instead, please?

7 D We've got some apple juice in the fridge. Could you get it for me?

8 G Of course. Here you are.

The story 4

1 False, **2** True, **3** False, **4** False, **5** True

Listening and reading 2

1 This fish isn't very nice at all.

2 What's the chicken like?

3 Nicer than the beef?

4 I think so.

5 Beef is more popular than chicken. In fact, beef is the most popular dish on the plane.

6 a Could I change this fish then, please?

b Is it all right if I have a different dinner?

c Can I try the chicken, please, if that's OK?

Language discovery 3

1 1 It's bigger than New York. 2 Which is the tallest building in the world? 3 Which is more difficult, understanding English or speaking it? 4 He's the most interesting person I know.

2 1 Can I / Could I / Is it all right if I use the phone?

2 Can I / Could I / Is it all right if I use the toilet?

3 Can I / Could I / Is it all right if I smoke?

4 Can I / Could I / Is it all right if I have some more bread?

5 Can I / Could I / Is it all right if I watch TV?

3 1 Yes, of course. 2 I'm sorry. 3 Yes, go ahead. 4 I'm sorry, I don't think that's possible.

Speaking

Possible answers

Situation 1: I'm sorry, I'm a customer here, too. (Advanced alternative: I'm sorry but I don't work here.)

Situation 2: Excuse me, could I have beef and not chicken, please? (Advanced alternative: Excuse me, would it be possible for me to have beef instead of chicken, please?)

Revision

Writing: model answers

1 Dear Chris, I'm planning a party with friends at home next Saturday.

2 I've got some bread, cheese and beer but I haven't got any wine. I'll buy some tomorrow.

3 I've got a small problem – I haven't got any glasses. Can I/Could I borrow some, please?

4 If lots of friends decide to come, is it all right if I have the party at your house? Your house is bigger than my flat.

5 I'll call you tomorrow and we can talk about it.

6 Until tomorrow, Pat.

Test yourself

Which one is right?

1 b, **2** a, **3** a, **4** a, **5** b, **6** a, **7** b, **8** a, **9** b, **10** b

Dialogue: model answers

1	You	Would you like tea or coffee?
2	Friend	Coffee for me, please.
3	You	Excuse me, (can/could I have) two coffees, please?
		Have you got any ice cream?
4	Waiter	No, I'm sorry, we haven't.
5	Waiter	Two coffees.
6	You	Would you like some more coffee?
7	Friend	No thanks, I'm fine.
8	You	Excuse me, can/could I have the bill, please?
9	You	Is it all right if I pay by card?
10	Waiter	Yes, of course.

UNIT 3

The story

a countries, **c** nationalities, **e** languages

Listening and reading

1 1 Yes, 2 Yes, 3 Yes, 4 We don't know. 5 No – she lives in South America. 6 We don't know.

7 Yes, 8 Yes, 9 No, 10 Yes

2 a   Where are you from? b I'm English. c I'm from England too.

3 a   Oh, really? b Actually, I live in South America, in Uruguay. Do you?

c   Do you speak any foreign languages? I can speak a bit of French. Can you?

4 1   a And you? b How about you?

2   Actually, I live in South America.

3   I'm not very good at it.

Practice

1 1, 2, 3 And you? or How about you?

2 1 d, 2 c, 3 b, 4 e, 5 a

Language discovery 1

1 1 She speaks Spanish. 2 She lives in South America. 3 She likes it there.

4 He uses French in his job sometimes.

2

1	Does she live in South America?	Yes, she does.
2	Does she like it there?	Yes, she does.
3	Does the man speak Spanish?	No, he doesn't.
4	Does he speak French?	Yes, he does.
5	Does he live in South America?	No, he doesn't.
6	Do they work together?	No, they don't.
7 and 8	Yes, I do, or No, I don't.	

3 1 The man can speak French but he can't speak Spanish.

   2 Can the woman speak Spanish? Yes, she can.

   3 Can they both speak English? Yes, they're English.

   4 I can speak some English.

Language discovery 2

1 1 Yes.

   2 Yes.

   3 No. If the verb in the first sentence is positive, the short question is positive. If the verb in the first sentence is negative, the short question is negative.

   4 Yes.

How do you pronounce it? (1)

1 b I

2 a I, b NI

3 a I, b NI

4 a NI, b I

5 a I, b NI

6 a NI, b I

Speaking

1

1	A	I can play the guitar.
	B	Oh, can you? What sort of music do you play?
2	A	My brother's new job's very interesting.
	B	Is it? What does he do?
3	A	My father lives in the States.
	B	Does he? Whereabouts?
4	A	My children don't like ice cream.
	B	Don't they? It's very popular in my house.
5	A	I'm thirsty.
	B	Are you? Would you like something to drink?

6	A	Sue's not here today.
	B	Isn't she? Look, isn't that her over there?
7	A	I like this cold weather.
	B	Do you? I prefer the summer myself.
8	A	Jessica can't drive.
	B	Can't she? So, how does she get to work?
9	A	I don't drink tea.
	B	Don't you? I have about five cups a day.
10	A	I'm not very well.
	B	Aren't you? What's the matter?

Vocabulary builder

a 2 B, **b** 11 G, **c** 7 A, **d** 9 J, **e** 4 F, **f** 10 H, **g** 12 E, **h** 5 A, **i** 3 B, **j** 8 A, **k** 1 C, **l** 6 F, **m** 14 D, **n** 13 I

How do you pronounce it? (2)

1

a •o	b o•	c •o o
Egypt	Brazil	Mexico
China	Japan	Italy
		Portugal
Poland		Germany
d o•o o	e o o o o•	
Australia	The United States	

2

English	Japan<u>ese</u>	<u>I</u>talian	<u>A</u>rabic
<u>S</u>panish	Chin<u>ese</u>		
<u>P</u>olish	Portug<u>ue</u>se		
<u>G</u>erman			

Speaking and writing

2 1 Can you speak Arabic?   No, not at all.

2 And do you speak Italian?   Yes, not too badly.

3 How about Japanese?   Yes, but not very well.

4 And what's your native language?   (Yours)

4

Possible answers

1 I'm sorry but I don't understand. 2 Excuse me, that's my dictionary. Advanced alternative:

Excuse me, I think that dictionary's mine.

Revision

Writing, model answer

Name: Daniela Castro

Contact details: Mob: 07964 001330

Email: DanJones84@fastmail.com

I can use Microsoft Word, Excel and PowerPoint.

My native language is Spanish and I speak English and Portuguese fluently. I can also speak a

little Japanese but I can't write it.

I can play the guitar and I like dancing. I'm interested in foreign travel.

Test yourself

Which one is right?

1 a, **2** b, **3** b, **4** b, **5** a

Dialogue: model answers

1	You	Where are you from?
2	Claudia	I'm from Italy. And you?
3	You	I'm [your nationality].
4	Claudia	Are you? That's interesting.
5	You	Which languages do you speak?
6	Claudia	Italian, of course, some English and a little Chinese.
7	You	Chinese? Really? Isn't it difficult? Can you write it too?

UNIT 4

The story

1 He works in marketing computers. **2** She teaches English.

Listening and reading

1 1 b, c; 2 b, d

2 a aWhat do you do? I work in computers.

   b What's your job? I'm a teacher.

   c What sort of work do you do in computers?' I'm in marketing.

   d I work for a big company.

3 a Do you like your job? Yes, I really enjoy teaching.

   b Do you enjoy working in marketing? It's OK.

   c I'm not very keen on all the travelling.

4 a You're not an English teacher, by any chance, are you?

   b Whereabouts?

   c What about you?

   d In fact, I'm on my way home now from a fair in Argentina.

Practice

1 1 b, 2 e, 3 a, 4 f, 5 c, 6 d

2 1 No, I'm on my way back. 2 They're on their way to school. 3 She's on her way home.

   4 He's on his way to work. 5 We're on our way to the airport. 6 I'm on my way there right now.

How do you pronounce it?

4 1 I'm fine, thanks. How are <u>you</u>?

   2 I'm Carol. And <u>you</u>? What's <u>your</u> name?

   3 I live in London. Where do <u>you</u> live?

   4 My birthday's in April. When's <u>yours</u>?

5 I don't smoke. Do <u>you</u>?

6 I'd like some coffee. Would <u>you</u> like a drink?

7 I live with my parents. Do you live with <u>yours</u>?

6

1	a P	5	a P
	b NP		b NP
2	a P	6	a NP
	b NP		b P
3	a NP	7	a NP
	b P		b P
4	a NP		
	b P		

Vocabulary builder 1

1 taxi driver **2** waiter **3** doctor **4** receptionist **5** mechanic **6** dentist **7** actor **8** shop assistant

9 tour guide **10** hairdresser **11** travel agent **12** cashier **13** student

Language discovery 1

1 1 What does Dan do? He's a waiter.

2 What's Pat's job? He's a hotel receptionist.

3 What does Carl do? He's a mechanic.

4 What's Kate's job? She's a shop assistant.

5 What does Jo do? OR What's Jo's job? She's a tour guide.

6 What's Jim's job? OR What does Jim do? He's a travel agent.

3 1 in politics. 2 in banking. 3 in education. 4 in publishing.

4 1 Sue works for Amazon.

2 Which company does your brother work for?

3 Do you know who she works for?

6 1 Yes, I quite like it.

2 No, I'm not very keen on it, actually.

3   I really enjoy it.

4   I don't mind it.

5   Actually, I don't like it at all.

6   Yes, I quite like it.

7 Interviewer: Like doing … don't like doing …

Sophie: enjoy going out … like inviting … don't mind doing … not very keen on helping

8

1	A	doing.
	B	watching TV, reading
2	B	hoovering, ironing
3	A	cooking
	B	making cakes
4	B	not very keen on going
5	B	don't mind waiting

Vocabulary builder 2

1 e, **2** i, **3** b, **4** g, **5** f, **6** d, **7** a, **8** j, **9** k, **10** c, **11** h, **12** l

Speaking

Possible answers

1 'I'm sorry but John doesn't work here any more.'

2 'No, I'm not in again until Wednesday.'

Revision

Writing: model answer

1 I really enjoy the computer work. It's very interesting

2 I quite like the secretary and the receptionist. They're very friendly

3 I don't mind working extra hours. We're very busy sometimes.

4 I'm not very keen on travelling to work by bus but there isn't a car park here.

5 And I really don't like the food in the canteen. It's very expensive and not very

international.

Test yourself

Which one is right?

1 b, **2** b, **3** a, **4** b, **5** a, **6** b, **7** a

Dialogue: model answers:

1 I'm a … What do you do? OR What's your job?

2 What sort of work do you do in television?

3 I think I know you. You're David West, aren't you?

4 Do you like working in television?

5 I … [details about you]

6 I really enjoy it OR I quite like it OR I don't mind it OR I'm not very keen on it actually OR

Actually I don't like it at all.

7 Would you like some more wine? OR Would you like another glass of wine?

UNIT 5

The story

a yes, **b** yes, **c** no, **d** yes, **e** yes, **f** yes

Listening and reading

1 1 Oliver, 2 Tasha, 3 Russia, 4 mother, 5 Edinburgh, 6 2 weeks … London,

7 some friends, 8 near, 9 America… 6 months, 10 goes, 11 her family

2 1 And yours? 2 a I'm staying in London ... b Because of my job.

3 Yes, I'm going to England to see some friends of mine. 4 My father's working in the

States at the moment. 5 My mother organizes her work so that she can travel with him.

6 Because I need to see …

3 1   Tasha is short for Natasha.

2   So, whereabouts … .

3   I live in Scotland, actually.

4   I'm staying in London for a couple of weeks.

5   She's on holiday.

6   Oh, right.

7   He works abroad.

8   Not all the time but quite a lot of the time.

9   She goes to England even if her parents aren't there.

10 Every year.

4 1   Uni is short for university.

2   The baby spends a lot of the time asleep.

3   She phones home from Uni every weekend.

4   My brother is staying with us for a couple of months

5   They're going on holiday to Italy

Language discovery 1

1

Girls	Boys
1 Abi/Abigail	Ollie/Oliver
2 Beth/Bethany	Chris/Christopher
3 Ellie /Eleanor	Nick/Nicholas
4 Sam/Samantha	Dom/Dominic
5 Kathy/Katherine	Sam/Samuel
6 Ros/Rosalyn	Josh/Joshua
7 Chris/Christine	Mike/Michael
8 Mel/Melanie	Finn/Finley
9 Jess/Jessica	Tom/Thomas
10 Becky/Rebecca	Matt/Matthew

2 Two: Chris and Sam

3 What's your name short for?

5

Jo	My name's Jo, and yours?
Sam	Sam.
Jo	**So,** where do you come from Sam?
Sam	I'm from New York. I work in a bookshop there.
Jo	Do you like it?
Sam	Yes, I really enjoy it, actually. I love books. **So,** do you know this town well?
Jo	Quite well. I come for a holiday from time to time. How about you? Where do you go on holiday?
Sam	I like going to Europe for my holidays – I love London and I know Paris and Rome and a few other places. **So,** how do you know John and Jean?
Jo	John's my brother.
Sam	Oh, right.

6 1 (Actually), I work for Panasonic, (actually).

2 (Actually), it's not mine, (actually).

3 (Actually), I don't drink alcohol, (actually).

4 (Actually), I can't drive, (actually).

5 (Actually), I'm from Italy, (actually).

6 (Actually), I don't know him, (actually).

7 (Actually) I'm her mother, (actually).

8 (Actually) I'm not very keen on it, (actually).

9 (Actually) I'm not married, (actually).

8 1 No, she's abroad. 2 No, she lives abroad. 3 Oliver travels abroad a lot for his job.

4 Tasha's father works abroad quite a lot. 5 I enjoy travelling abroad.

How do you pronounce it?

1 b: 'organizes' has four syllables – or-gan-iz-es.

3 I close (1) … the supermarket closes (2)

I finish (2) … she finishes (3)

I wash (1)… she washes (2)

I fix (1) … she fixes (2)

I relax (2) … she relaxes (3)

I watch (1) … Kate watches (2)

I dance (1) … my wife dances (2)

I use (1) … my wife uses (2)

I change (1) … Kate changes (2)

I sneeze (1) … she sneezes (2)

I organize (3) … she organizes (4)

I kiss (1) my wife and my wife kisses (2) me.

5 1 Who washes the dishes? (NOT: Who does wash the dishes?)

2 Who finishes work at 9.00 (NOT: Who does finish …)

3 Who watches sport on TV? (NOT: Who does watch ...)

4 Who fixes things? (NOT: Who does fix ...)

6 Touch, cross, mix, pass, manage, pronounce, wish. All these words have an extra syllable in 3rd person singular.

Vocabulary builder

1 1 husband, 2 son, 3 brother, 4 partner, 5 related to (preposition! NOT: *related with*), 6 daughter, 7 wife, 8 brother, 9 twin brother, 10 girlfriend, 11 Daddy, 12 relative/relation, 13 Mum, 14 sister, 15 a children, b kids, 16 Dad, 17 Mummy, 18 brother and sister, 19 married to (preposition! NOT: *married with*), 20 going out with/boyfriend

2 1 Mike's son. 2 Karen's husband. 3 Daniel's mother's name's Karen. 4 Josh's father's name's Mike. 5 Mike's daughter's name's Naomi. 6 What's Karen's daughter's name? 7 Who's Daniel? A friend of Jack's.

Language discovery 2

1

Subject	Possessive adjective	Possessive pronoun
I	my	mine
he	his	his
she	her	hers
you	your	yours
we	our	ours
they	their	theirs

2 1 yours, 2 ours, 3 his, 4 theirs, 5 yours, 6 a mine, b his, c hers, d theirs, e ours

Language discovery 3

1 1 b (the present), 2 b (temporary)

3

Positive		Negative	
I am		I am not	
(I'm)		(I'm) not	
He is		He is not	
She is		She is not OR She isn't	
It('s)	working.	It('s) not OR It isn't	working.
You are		You are not	
We are		We('re) not	
They('re)		They're not OR They aren't	

Questions		Question tags – to make conversation Echo questions – to express interest	
		Positive	Negative
Am I		Am I?	Aren't I?
Is he		Is he?	Isn't he?
Is she		Is she?	Isn't she?
Is it	working?	Is it?	Isn't it?
Are you		Are you?	Aren't you?
Are we		Are we?	Aren't we?
Are they		Are they?	Aren't they?

4 1 Yes, 2 No, 3 Yes, 4 Yes, 5 Yes, 6 Yes (aren't I?)

5 Mark   Where's Dad?

   Dave   He's washing the car. This water's for him.

   Mark   And Mum?

   Dave   She's in the kitchen – making a cake for your birthday.

   Mark   What's Jamie doing?

   Dave   Watching TV in his room.

   Mark   Is he?

        Is Sharon doing her homework?

   Dave   Of course she isn't. She's upstairs with some friends. They're listening to music.

Mark	They aren't listening to my new CD, are they?
	Sharon, what are you listening to?
Sharon	Your new CD. It's great! I'm really enjoying it!
Mark	Are you? Now come on. Give it back to me.
Sharon	Sorry! Here you are.

6 1 I'm teaching. 2 I'm staying. 3 Is living. 4 You're being … You are. 5 I work … I'm not.

6 Does your daughter live?

7 1 c (future), 2 a (in the past), 3 a (personal), 4 a yes, b yes

8 A What are you doing this evening?

B I'm going to the cinema with Don. Would you like to come with us?

A No, thanks. Jim's arriving/coming in a minute. We're going out for a drink.

B Which pub are you going to?

A The one by the river.

Practice

1 1 Present, 2 Future, 3 Future, 4 Present, 5 Future, 6 Present, 7 Future, 8 Future, 9 Future,

10 Future

2 A So, **what are you doing** next weekend?

B Well, on Saturday morning **I'm visiting** a friend. Then, in the evening **we're having**

dinner in the new pizza restaurant. On Sunday **my parents are coming** for the day.

3 A Are you coming to class tomorrow?

B No, I'm not.

A Why can't you come?

B Because tomorrow my mother is coming from Germany. I'm going to the airport to

meet her.

Language discovery 4

1 a So that she can buy new books for her job.

b Because of her friends and relatives.

c Because it's her country.

d So that she can have a holiday.

How do you pronounce it?

1 1 I'm phoning to tell you about the party.

2 I go to the coffee bar to talk to my friends and have a snack.

3 I need some change to make a phone call.

4 I'm going to the kitchen to have some tea.

5 You call 999 to get an ambulance.

6 I swim to relax and keep fit.

7 She's in Italy to learn Italian.

8 I'd like to go to London to visit the museums.

Speaking

Possible answers

1 I think it's my turn, actually OR Excuse me, I think I'm next.

2 (I'm) coming.

Revision

Writing: model answer

1 are/'re having, **2** are/'re staying, **3** am/'m writing, **4** go, **5** relax, **6** sunbathe, **7** are/'re taking,

8 is living, **9** are/'re meeting, **10** is/'s taking, **11** to visit, **12** are/'re going

Test yourself

Which one is right?

1 b, **2** b, **3** b, **4** b, **5** a, **6** b, **7** a, **8** b, **9** b ,**10** b ,**11** b, **12** a

Dialogue: model answers

1 You   Hello, My name's … What's yours?

2 Gloria   I'm Gloria.

3 You   Why are you studying English?

4 Gloria   Because of my job. How about you?

5 You   I'm studying English because I want to work in tourism in my country. What are you doing after the class?

6 Gloria   I'm going to the library to do my homework. And you?

7 You   I'm having lunch in the cafeteria with some friends.

UNIT 6

The story
1 Yes, **2** Yes, **3** Yes, **4** Yes, **5** No, **6** Yes, **7** Yes

Listening and reading

1 1 b. 2 a Rees, b --, c 0769 1894304, d 020 7402 3277, e orees@starmail.com, 3 a Harrison,

b --, c --, d 020 8549 6682, e --, 4 a visit relatives, b do other things, c spend time with her

friends, 5 a d e f.

2

1 a We could meet for a drink …

b Yes, that would be nice.

2 a Shall I give you ...?

b I'll give you ... you can phone me and we can arrange something.

3 Or you could email me.

4 a I'll send you a text.

b I can give you ...

5 a I'll phone you ...

b I'll look forward to it.

6 When would you like me to call?

7 I'm going to visit relatives and do other things but I'm going to spend time at home with

my friends, too.

3 **1** We could meet one evening. **2** a if you like, b if that's OK. **3** we can arrange something.

4 extension, **5** too, **6** Just a minute. **7** by the way, **8** a I don't mind. b any time, **9** Right then.

10 Some time next week. **11** a This is a 'fasten your seatbelts' sign. Is it on? b land,

12 a take, b contact

Vocabulary builder 1

1 0 – zero; 1 – one; 2 – two; 3 – three; 4 – four; 5 – five; 6 – six; 7 – seven; 8 – eight; 9 – nine; 10 – ten

2 The odd numbers are 1, 3, 5,7, 9. The even numbers are 2, 4, 6, 8, 10. Even numbers are numbers you can divide by two.

3 1 b, 2 b, 3 a

Practice

1 1 Some time tomorrow. 2 Any time you like. 3 Any time between 10 a.m. and 9 p.m. 4 Some time next Wednesday.

2 In each question, by the way can go at the beginning or the end of the question. 1 What's your boyfriend's name, by the way? 2 By the way, how's your baby? 3 By the way, I've got a new computer. 4 Is it OK if my new girlfriend comes to the party, by the way? 5 Are you going to England, by the way? 6 By the way, have you got X's phone number? 7 By the way, do you like fish? 8 Hello. My name's X, by the way.

How do you pronounce it? (1)

2 1 **3**210. 2 55 31 **3**1. 3 41**7**8. 4 01**5**32.

4 1 **sis**ter, 2 **Wed**nesday, 3 fant**ast**ic, 4 **lots,** 5 **un**der, **floor,** 6 **my, I'll, you**

Language discovery 1

1 1 f, 2 h, 3 i, 4 c, 5 a, 6 e, 7 b, 8 g, 9 d

2 1 b; 2a Take the children to school, b Make a cup of tea, c Phone a doctor, d Cook dinner; 3a yes, b yes, c yes, d no

3 1 I can take the children to school for you if you like. She says, 'That's very kind of you.' 2 I'll make you a cup of tea. 3 Shall I call the doctor? She says, 'Could you?' 4 Where can I find the number? 5 Would you like me to cook (for you all)? 6 The children could eat at my house. She says 'Thanks for the offer, but it's alright.'

5 1 We can / We could / Shall we; 2 We can / We could / Shall we; 3 I can / I could /I'll / Shall I / Would you like me to; 4 Could you / Would; 5 I can / I could /I'll / Shall I / Would you like me to; 6 I can / I could /I'll / Shall I / Would you like me to

6 1 Yes, 2 Yes, 3 Yes, 4 No

Vocabulary builder 2

1 1 Hello, my name's Williams. (family name)

2 A What's your name? B Daniel. (first name)

3 Hi! I'm Peter. (first name)

4 A And your name is …? B Richards. (family name)

5 A Could I have your name, please sir? B Yes, it's Stevens. (family name)

6 Is that Hugh? (first name)

7 Her father's name's Matthews. (family name)

8 No, Edward's his other name. (first name)

2 The international code for Britain is 0044.

Emergency (fire, police and ambulance): 999.

Directory enquiries (national) 118 500.

Directory enquiries (international) 118 505.

Language discovery 2

1 1 c, 2 e, 3 a, 4 d, 5 b

3 1 Tom   Hi, this is Tom. Is that Andrea?

Vicky   Hello, Tom. No, this is Vicky … Andrea, it's Tom on the phone ....

2 Speaking OR This is David (speaking).

How do you pronounce it? (2)

1

06.11

Teacher	So, could you tell me your surnames, please? Lesley, What's your surname?
Lesley	Crowley.
Teacher	How do you spell that, Lesley?
Lesley	C – R – O – W – L – E –Y.
Teacher	And yours, Denise?
Denise	My family name's Farnish.
Teacher	Is that with an 'F' or a 'V'?
Denise	With an 'F'. F – A – R – N – I – S – H.
Teacher	And how about you, Matt? What's your other name?
Matt	Hannant. That's H – A double N – A – N – T.
Teacher	Anne, your surname is …?
Anne	Johnson, spelt J – O – H – N – S – O – N.
Teacher	Simon, yours next, please.
Simon	Lawrence.
Teacher	How do you spell it?
Simon	L – A – W – R – E – N – C – E.
Teacher	And John? I've got Pierson here. Is that right?
John	Yes. P – E – A – R – S – O – N.
Teacher	Oh, I've got P – I – E.
John	No, it's P – E – A at the beginning.
Teacher	And Joan – How about you? What's your other name?
Joan	Rawlings. R – A – W – L – I – N – G – S.
Teacher	And the last one is Liz, please.
Liz	My surname's Thompson-Smith.
Teacher	Is that Thompson with a 'P' or without?
Liz	With a 'P' and 'Smith' at the end.
Teacher	Thanks very much everybody. Now let's start the lesson.

1 Lesley Crowley, 2 Denise Farnish, 3 Matt Hannant, 4 Anne Johnson, 5 Simon Lawrence,

6 John Pearson, 7 Joan Rawlings, 8 Liz Thompson-Smith.

2 How do you spell it? (NOT: How do you write it?)

Speaking and listening

2 'S' for Sierra

'A' for Alpha

'K' for Kilo

'O' for Oscar

286

'T' for Tango

'A' for Alpha

3

06.13

1 A My name's Hallis.

    B Double R is that?

    A No, double L, H – A – double L – I – S.

2 A The name's Frazer.

    B Do you spell that with an S or a Z?

    A With a Z.

3 A My name's Stevens.

    B Is that with PH or a V?

    A With a V.

4 A My name's Simms.

    B Is that one M or two?

    A S – I – double M – S.

5 A Her name's Helen Stubbs.

    B Is that P for Papa or B for Bravo?

    A Double B for Bravo.

6 A What's your initial?

    B S.

    A Is that F for Foxtrot or S for Sierra?

    B S for Sierra.

1 a, 2 b, 3 b, 4 a, 5 b, 6 b

4

1 Piper, that's P–I–P–E–R.

2 My name's Snaithe, spelt S–N–A–I–T–H–E.

3 Yes, it's Smeaton, S–M–E–A–T–O–N.

4 And my surname is Taylor, T–A–Y–L–O–R.

5 The family name's Sheridon, S–H–E–R–I–D–O–N.

6 And the second name is Reeder, that's spelt R–E–E–D–E–R.

7 Samuels, S–A–M–U–E–L–S.

Possible answers

1 I'm very sorry. I've got the wrong number.

Advanced alternative: Sorry to disturb you. I think I've got the wrong number.

2 I'm sorry, the signal is bad. I can't hear you.

Advanced alternative: I'm sorry, this signal's terrible. Could you speak up a bit, please?

Revision

Writing: model answer

Hi guys,

Great news! Jo and I have just got a new flat.

We're going to paint it next weekend. Jo's brother's going to help us and we're going to paint

all the rooms white. We're going to buy a new sofa and we also need a small table for the

kitchen

We're going to move in at the end of the month. My Dad has got a van so he's going to help

us. The flat's near the centre of town and it's not far from my office so I'm going to sell my car

and buy a bike.

When the flat's ready we're going to have a house-warming party so …

So watch this space for an invitation!

Test yourself

Read and choose

1 b, **2** a, **3** b, **4** a, **5** b, **6** b, **7** i, b, ii a, **8** b, **9** a, **10** b, **11** b, **12** b, **13** b, **14** b, **15** b, **16** b, **17** a, b, c

Dialogue: model answers

1	You	We could have a Chinese meal and watch a DVD at your house.
2	Your friend	Yeah, why not?
3	You	Shall I get the food and the DVD on the way?
4	Your friend	That would be good. Could you get me a Chinese chicken with rice, please?
5	You	No problem. I could get some beer, too.
6	Your friend	No, don't worry about that. I've got some.
7	You	What sort of film would you like to see?
8	Your friend	I don't mind.

UNIT 7

The story

a c d e f

Listening and reading

1 1 b, 2 b, 3 a

2 1 ladies and gentlemen, 2 This is, 3 Captain, 4 If you would like to adjust your watches,

5 estimated time of arrival, 6 forecast.

Vocabulary builder 1

1

11 eleven
12 twelve
14 fourteen
15 fifteen
16 sixteen
17 seventeen
18 eighteen
19 nineteen
20 twenty
30 thirty
40 forty
50 fifty
60 sixty
80 eighty
90 ninety

2 Ninety-nine – 99; Twelve – 12; Forty-three – 43; Thirty-one – 31; Eleven – 11;

Seventy-six – 76; Eighty-five – 85; Twenty-two – 22; Sixty-four – 64; Fifty-seven – 57;

Seventeen – 17; A hundred – 100

3

18 eighteen
93 ninety-three
86 eighty-six
19 nineteen
14 fourteen
59 fifty-nine
15 fifteen
16 sixteen
37 thirty-seven
68 sixty-eight
13 thirteen
21 twenty-one
45 forty-five
12 twelve
100 a hundred

4 1 Nine and six is fifteen, and twenty-three is thirty-eight and eighteen is fifty-six.

2 Four and twelve is sixteen, and two is eighteen and fourteen is thirty-two.

5 a Two, four, six, eight, ten, twelve, fourteen, sixteen, eighteen, twenty

b One, three, five, seven, nine, eleven, thirteen, fifteen, seventeen, nineteen

c Five, ten, fifteen, twenty, twenty-five, thirty, thirty-five, forty, forty-five, fifty

d Three, six, nine, twelve, fifteen, eighteen, twenty-one, twenty-four, twenty-seven, thirty,

thirty-three, thirty-six

e One eight is eight.   Two eights are sixteen.

Three eights are twenty-four.   Four eights are thirty-two.

Five eights are forty.   Six eights are forty-eight.

Seven eights are fifty-six.   Eight eights are sixty-four.

Nine eights are seventy-two.   Ten eights are eighty.

6 a $20 + 10 = 30$. b $12 - 1 = 11$. c $4 \times 6 = 24$. d $27 \div 3 = 9$.

Language discovery 1

1 1 shop, 2 dinner party, 3 school, 4 office, 5 shop, 6 dentist's, 7 office, 8 dentist's,

9 dinner party, 10 school

2 1 d, 2 b, 3 c, 4 e, 5 a

The story 2

1 1 d, 2 e, 3 f, 4 b, 5 c, 6 a

2 1 Passport control, 2 Trolleys, 3 Information desk, 4 Baggage reclaim, 5 Customs,

6 Arrivals.

3 1 D, 2 E, 3 F, 4 C, 5 A, 6 B

4 1 b, 2 a, 3 b

5 1 Now let's find ... 2 a Would you mind waiting for just a minute?

b Of course not. c Could you look after my trolley and can you take my coat, please? d

Sure. Go ahead. 3 a Can I help you? b Could you tell me where the ladies' is please?

6 1 Tasha's got quite a lot of luggage. 2 No, not yet. 3 The suitcases aren't there yet,

anyway. 4 'Is that it?''Is that everything?' 5 It's this way. 6 a You haven't got anything to

declare, have you? b No nothing. 7 It's been really nice talking to you, Tasha. 8 Tasha

thanks Oliver for his help... 9 I'll be in touch next week. 10 b.

Vocabulary builder 2

1 1 baggage, 2 hand luggage, 3 pieces of luggage, 4 (suit)cases (Luggage is wrong here

because the verb is plural – *are*.)

2 1 for (Thank someone for something), 2 to (Talk to someone) (American English uses 'talk

with someone'), 3 in (be/stay in touch with someone)

3 1 by, 2 at, 3 in, 4 on, 5 to, 6 in, 7 on, 8 to, 9 in

Language discovery 2

1 Suggestions: 1 Let's have a drink. 2 Let's go and visit Hilary this afternoon, shall we? 3 Let's

not watch the football. Why don't we watch the film on Channel 5 instead? 4 Let's go to

Mexico. Let's invite Sam, too.

5 Let's not go to the party. Let's stay here instead.

Responses

☺: any of the following positive responses: Yes, let's!/OK/All right/Yes, why not?/that's a

good idea./Yes, why don't we?

☺ any of the following negative responses: No, let's not./Do you really want to?/I'm not too

sure./Perhaps not./Actually, I'm not too keen.

Practice 1

1 1 Can you say that again, please? *This is more common than 'Can you repeat that, please?' 2 Could you pass the water, please? Yes. Here you are. 3 Mum/Dad, can you help me with my homework? Of course. What is it? 4 Would you mind taking a photo of us, please? Not at all. What do I do? 5 Can you call me back in 10 minutes, please? I'm sorry but I'm going out right now and it's urgent. 6 Would you mind not smoking in the kitchen? Oh, sorry! 7 Could you spell that for me, please? Yes, it's T – H – A …etc.

2
07.04

1 Passengers are requested to remain in their seats with their seat belts fastened – we are entering an area of turbulence.

2 Passenger Smith going to Rome is requested to go immediately to Gate 12 where the flight is now closing.

3 All transfer passengers are requested to report to the transfer desk.

4 All passengers are requested to return to their seats. We are beginning our descent.

5 Passengers are requested to put all hand luggage in the storage space above your heads.

6 All passengers are required to complete a landing card for the immigration authorities.

7 Passengers are requested to remain in their seats until the plane comes to a complete halt.

a 4, b 7, c 5, d 2, e 1, f 6, g 3

Language discovery 3

1 Excuse me, can you tell me where the coffee bar is, please?

2 Excuse me, could you tell me where the toilets are, please?

3 Excuse me, could you tell me how much this is, please?

4 Excuse me, would you mind telling me how much these are, please?

5 Excuse me, can you tell me how much this magazine is, please?

6 Excuse me, could you tell me how much these crisps are, please?

The story 3

1 1 2, 2 No

2 1 b, 2 b, 3 c, 4 c, 5 d, 6 a

Vocabulary builder 3

1 a <u>pa</u>cket of <u>crisps</u>; 2 a <u>can</u> of <u>Coke</u>; 3 a <u>bar</u> of <u>choc</u>olate, 4 a <u>pa</u>cket of <u>chew</u>ing gum; 5 a

<u>pa</u>cket of <u>bis</u>cuits; 6 a <u>bott</u>le of <u>wa</u>ter; 7 a <u>car</u>ton of <u>fruit</u> juice; 8 a <u>pa</u>cket of <u>sweets</u>

How do you pronounce it?

1 b, 2 a, 3 b, 4 a, 5 b, 6 a, 7 b, 8 a

Practice 2

1 1 Excuse me, how much is this, please? (Direct), 2 How much does this cost, please?

(Direct), 3 Do you know how much this is, please? (Indirect), 4 Excuse me, could you tell

me how much this costs, please? (Indirect)

3 1 b, 2 a, 3 b, 4 a, 5 b, 6 b, 7 b, 8 a, 9 b, 10 b, 11 a, 12 b

Speaking

Possible answers

1 How much is it again? or I'm sorry but I don't think this change is right. Advanced

alternative: I'm sorry but I think there's a mistake here.

2 Excuse me, I don't know where my suitcase is. Could you help me, please?

Revision

Writing

1 1 In the morning we could go on a tour of London.

2 Let's go by car.

3 Who are you talking to?

4 Is it going to be on TV?

5 Stand next to your brother.

6 How many passengers are there on this plane?

7 Don't they have dinner together at the end of the flight?

8 Bye! I'll see you in five minutes.

9 Would you mind signing on page 2, please?

10 You can change your mind at any time.

2 Talking to a friend: Can you ...?

Asking an office colleague for help: Could you ...?

Asking a hotel receptionist for help: Would you mind ...?

A friend: 1 Can you turn the TV off (please)? 3 Can you pass me the bread (please)?

8 Can you lend me £20?

An office colleague: 2 Could you show me how to use the new photocopier (please)?

6 Could you take a message for me? 9 Could you lend me your stapler?

A hotel receptionist: 4. Would you mind signing here please, sir? 5. Would you mind not

using your mobile in here, please, madam? 7. Would you mind taking a seat for a moment?

10 Would you mind calling a taxi for me, please?

Speaking

Tasha	That would be a good idea – I've got quite a lot of luggage.
Tasha	Would you mind waiting for just a minute, Oliver?
Tasha	Could you look after my trolley, oh, and can you take my coat, please?
Tasha	Yes, could you tell me where the ladies' is, please?
Tasha	The suitcase, the small bag and my handbag – yes that's everything.
Tasha	Yes and thanks for the help with the luggage.

Test yourself

1b, **2**b, **3**b, **4**a, **5**b, **6**b, **7**b, **8**b, **9**a, **10**b, **11**b, **12**b

Dialogue: model answers

1 Barbara   Could you take the children to school, please? I'm working this morning.

2 Eva   Of course. Would you like me to go to the supermarket on the way back?

3 Barbara   Could you? Can you get some bread, some milk and some cartons of fruit juice?

4 Eva   Fine. Do you need anything else?

5 Barbara   No, thanks. Could you take the children to the park after school and would you mind working on Saturday evening?

6 Eva   I can take the children to the park but I'm sorry, I can't work on Saturday evening – I'm going to a party.

7 Child   Let's all have an ice cream!

UNIT 8

The story 1

1 By bus

2 c and d

Listening and reading 1

1 1 c, 2 b, 3 b, 4 d, 5 a

2 1 a Could you tell me how to get to the centre of town, please? (preposition!) b You can go by bus, by train or by underground. 2 a Which part of London are you going to? b I need to get to Victoria Station. 3 You can take the A1 Airbus. 4 a Where do I get the bus from? b You follow the sign that says 'Airbus'. 5 No, the A1 bus goes all the way to Victoria Station. 6 How long does it take to get there?

How do you pronounce it?

1 Vic<u>to</u>ria

2 <u>Pad</u>dington

3 <u>Mar</u>ylebone

4 King's <u>Cross</u>

5 St <u>Pan</u>cras

6 <u>Eus</u>ton

7 <u>Liv</u>erpool Street

8 Water<u>loo</u>

Listening and reading 2

1 Corrections to false sentences are given in brackets. 1 True. 2 False (270 lines). 3 False (each line has a name). 4 False (the fare depends on the number of zones). 5 True 6 True. 7 False (it's quite expensive).

2 1 Marble <u>Arch</u>, 2 <u>Ox</u>ford Street, 3 Piccadilly <u>Circ</u>us, 4 Green <u>Park</u>, 5 Buckingham <u>Pa</u>lace, 6

Trafalgar <u>Square</u>, 7 <u>Down</u>ing Street, 8 The Houses of <u>Par</u>liament, 9 The London <u>Eye</u>, 10 St

Paul's <u>Cath</u>edral, 11 Tower <u>Bridge</u>, 12 The Tower of <u>Lon</u>don

How do you pronounce it?

1

08.09

Park <u>Road</u>	<u>High</u> Street	Eton <u>Avenue</u>
Buckingham <u>Gardens</u>	Tudor <u>Drive</u>	Moor <u>Close</u>
West <u>Hill</u>	Elm <u>Cres</u>cent	Rose <u>Walk</u>
River <u>Lane</u>	Church <u>Grove</u>	Esher <u>Place</u>
Orchard <u>Way</u>	Maple <u>Court</u>	Nova <u>Mews</u>

2 1 c Road/Rd, 2 f Gardens/Gdns, 3 i Lane/La. 4 e Street/St, 5 b Drive/Dr. 6 l Crescent/Cres.

7 j Grove/Gr. 8 h Court/Ct, 9 a Avenue/Ave. 10 d Close/Cl. 11 k Walk/Wk 12 g Place/Pl.

Language discovery 1

1 d, **2** g, **3** c, **4** k, **5** j, **6** a, **7** i, **8** b, **9** f, **10** l, **11** h, **12** e

Vocabulary builder

1 1 Train/station/platform, 2 underground (train)/station/platform, 3 bus/bus stop, 4 coach/

coach station, 5 taxi/taxi-rank

2 1 map, 2 timetable, 3 ticket, single, return, 4 ticket office, ticket machine, 5 platform, 6 fare,

7 zone, 8 line, 9 journey, 10 fast, 11 direct, 12 announcements, 13 excursion, 14 tip

3 1 fare, 2 timetable, 3 map, 4 ticket machine, 5 ticket office

4 1 journey, 2 travel, 3 travel, 4 journey

5 1 First you find out about times and prices. 2 Then you book a ticket. 3 You can either

change your ticket or cancel the trip. 4 a You get on the coach b You get off the coach.

Language discovery 2

1 1 c, 2 a

2 All the questions are correct.

3 1 how do I get to, 2 where can I book, 3 how could I find out about,

4 how to buy, 5 how I get to, 6 how I can open, 7 how I could change

4 1 you follow, 2 you go down, 3 you collect, 4 you go through, 5 you wait, 6 you go up, 7

you get on, 8 you put, 9 you look for, 10 you go to

5 1 Where do I sign? 2 Can you tell me what to write/what I write in this card? 3 Where do

I pay, please? 4 correct 5 correct 6 How do I open this door? 7 correct 8 Do I give a tip or

not?

6 1 b, 2 e, 3 c, 4 a, 5 f, 6 g, 7 h, 8 d

7 1 i, 2 d, 3 h, 4 c, 5 e, 6 b, 7 a, 8 f, 9 g, 10 l, 11 k, 12 j

8 1 c, 2 a

The story 2

1 b

2 1 Excuse me, can you tell me the time, please? 2 Yes, it's five to eight.

3 Many thanks.

Language discovery 3

1 Watch hands should show the following times: 1 11:00, 2 3:30, 3 4:15, 4 5:45, 5 8:50,

6 10:25

2 The first train in the morning leaves at 6.22, then there's another at 7.49, one at 8.13, and another at 9.56. To come back you can leave at 13.05, or 14.50, or there are later trains at 15.32 and 16.09.

To go   To come back

1 6.22 (six twenty-two)   1 13.05 (thirteen 'o' five)

2 7.49 (seven forty-nine)   2 14.50 (fourteen-fifty)

3 8.13 (eight thirteen)   3 15.32 (fifteen thirty-two)

4 9.56 (nine fifty-six)   4 16.09 (sixteen 'o' nine)

3 a 3 A Every hour, on the hour. b 2 C Twice an hour, at a quarter past and quarter to each hour. c 1 B Four times an hour, at five past, twenty past, twenty-five to and ten to the hour.

4 1 b, 2 d, 3 a, 4 c

5 1 c, 2 a, 3 d, 4 b

7 1 How long does it take you to have breakfast? 2 How long does it take you to get to work? 3 How long does it take you to get to the nearest supermarket? 4 How long does it take the children to walk to school?

8

08.08

1	A	Dad, what's the time?
	B	It's a few minutes to one.
2	A	Excuse me, could you tell me the time, please?
	B	Of course. Er, actually, it's exactly one o'clock.
3	A	John, have you got the time?
	B	Yeah, it's just before one.
4	A	Could you tell me what the time is, please?
	B	Yes, it's just after one.
5	A	Excuse me, can you tell me what time it is, please?
	B	Sorry, I haven't got a watch but I think it's around one.
6	A	Do you know what the time is, Sharon?
	B	Let me see, it's almost one.

a 1, 3, 5, 6; b 2, 5; c 4, 5

9 1 Dad, what's the time? 2 Excuse me, could you tell me the time, please? 3 John, have you got the time? 4 Could you tell me what the time is, please? 5 Excuse me, can you tell me what time it is, please? 6 Do you know what the time is, Sharon?

10

London King's Cross d	08:24	08:45	09:00	09:24	09:54	10:00	10:25
Cambridge a	09:28	09:42	10:12	10:16	10:46	11:09	11:16

11 1 c, 2 a

12 1 a in the past. 2 a in the past. For example, you've got your ticket.

Practice

1 1 fly, 2 leaves, 3 picks you up, 4 drive, 5 takes, 6 get, 7 happens, 8 do we get?, 9 meets, 10 takes, 11 show, 12 leaves, 13 are, 14 come, 15 do we get?

2 1 j, 2 h, 3 f, 4 i, 5 b, 6 e, 7 g, 8 c, 9 a, 10 d

3

08.10

1	You	Excuse me, how can I get to Windsor? Take the train at Platform 5 and change at Egham.
2	You	Do you know if this train stops at Reading? No, this is a non-stop to Paddington.
3	You	Which platform is it for Brighton, please? Number 7, sir.
4	You	How much is a single to Hull, please? £22.
5	You	How often do the trains run to Waterloo? Every half an hour – at ten to and twenty past the hour.
6	You	Is this the right train for Birmingham? No, this is the Liverpool train.
7	You	I want to go to Cardiff. Where do I change? It's not necessary, this bus goes all the way there.
8	You	When's the next coach to Glasgow, please? In ten minutes, at half past.
9	You	Could you tell me how to get to London from here, please? Yes, take the next train from Platform 10.
10	You	How long does it take to get Cambridge from London? On a fast train? Just under an hour.

Writing and speaking

2 Possible answers

1 I'm sorry but I'm not from here. 2 Excuse me, have you got change for a £20 note, please? I need to buy a ticket from the machine.

Revision

Writing: model answer

On 15th September I fly to Lima in Peru. I'm staying at the Hostal Las Americas, like last year. Then, two days later, on the 17th, my Spanish course starts. I'm doing intermediate this time. On 19th December I take my end of course exam. I hope I pass. I'm spending Christmas and New Year with friends and then on 2nd January I fly to Cusco where I'm meeting my brother Ben. The next day we take a train to Aguas Calientes and walk up to Machu Picchu. I'm really looking forward to it! On 5th January Ben and I fly to Sydney in Australia. We're going to visit our family there and meet our new baby cousin. A week later, on the 12th, Ben flies home to London because he's got a new job and he starts on the 14th. On the same day I go to Beijing in China where I'm staying with Caroline, an ex-colleague. Caroline's got tickets for us to go on a coach tour of the Great Wall of China on the 15th. We leave in the morning and come back around five. Then I'm spending two days visiting Beijing with Caroline. Finally, on 18th January I fly home to London. I think I'm going to need a holiday after all that travelling!

Test yourself

Which one is right?

1 b, **2** a, **3** b, **4** a, **5** A b, B b, **6** b, **7** a, **8** a, **9** b, **10** b

Dialogue: model answers

2	You	Two tickets to Hampton Court, please.
3	Clerk	Single or return?
4	You	Return, please.
5	Clerk	That's nineteen pounds eighty please.
6	You	When's the next train? OR At what time does the next train leave?
7	Clerk	In 10 minutes, at twenty to eleven.
8	You	And to come back, how often do the trains run?
9	Clerk	There are two trains an hour, at ten past and twenty to the hour.
10	You	How long does the journey take?
11	Clerk	About half an hour.
12	You	Thank you.
13	You	Excuse me. Is this the right train for Hampton Court, please?
		OR
		Excuse me. Does this train go to Hampton Court, please?

UNIT 9

The story 1

b

Listening and reading 1

1 1 False, 2 True, 3 We don't know, 4 False, 5 False, 6 False

2 1 Hi, 2 a It's lovely to see you again. b It's great to see you too. 3 How are things, 4 a How was your flight? b It was all right. c 13 hours is a bit long and tiring but I'm here now. 5 a Thanks for picking me up, by the way, b That's OK. We're glad you could come.

Language discovery 1

1 1 expensive to go. 2 correct to ask. 3 difficult/hard to understand. 4 interesting to visit; boring. 5 kind of him to invite. 6 useful to know. 7 important not to arrive. 8 tiring to work. 9 wonderful to see. 10 frustrating not to get. 11 difficult/hard not to eat

2 1 It's nice to talk to you again. 2 It's better not to go. 3 It's easy to contact people with email. 4 It's boring to wait for someone for a long time 5 It's exciting to visit a foreign country. 6 It's normal not to understand everything in a foreign language.

3 1 c, 2 b, 3 a

4 1 A was B wasn't, was, 2 A were B was, wasn't, 3 A wasn't B wasn't, was it?, 4 A was A was, 5 A weren't B was (Children call their teachers Miss or Sir). 6 A were, 7 was, was

How do you pronounce it?

1 1 weak, 2 strong, 3 weak, 4 weak, 5 strong

3 1 a, 2 a, 3 b, 4 a, 5 b, 6 b, 7 a, 8 b

Language discovery 2

1 1 tired, 2 surprising, 3 bored, 4 interesting, 5 boring, 6 interested, 7 fascinating, 8 frustrating, 9 disappointed

2 1 tiring – reason/source, 2 excited – feeling, 3 surprised – feeling, 4 boring – reason/

source, 5 Correct

3 1 Thanks for helping me. 2 Thanks for coming to pick us up. 3 Thank you very much for

waiting for me. 4 Thank you for meeting us. 5 Thanks for calling.

4 1 Thanks for inviting me. 2 Thanks for waiting for me. 3 Thank you for helping me. 4 Thanks

for letting me know. 5 Thank you for asking. 6 Thanks for going with me. 7 Thanks for

calling. 8 Thanks for coming.

5 1 Informal: EITHER No problem OR Any time 2 Formal: EITHER You're welcome OR Not at

all 3 Neutral: That's OK OR That's all right 4 Neutral: That's OK OR That's all right 5 Informal:

No problem OR Any time 6 Formal: You're welcome OR Not at all

Vocabulary builder 1

1

10 – ten

100 – a hundred

1,000 – a thousand

10,000 – ten thousand

100,000 – a hundred thousand

1,000,000 – a million

1,000,000,000 – a billion

2 True

3 1 Five hundred and ninety-four thousand. 2 Six hundred and eleven thousand, four

hundred and twenty. 3 Four thousand, six hundred and one. 4 Eight hundred and

twenty-seven. 5 Thirty-two thousand, one hundred and fifty-eight. 6 Twenty-four million,

two hundred and fifty thousand. 7 Six thousand, three hundred and sixty-eight. 8 Nine

hundred and twenty-three thousand, seven hundred and fifty.

4 Seventy million (passengers a year), a hundred and ninety-one thousand, two hundred (people a day), one thousand, three hundred (flights), eighty (airlines), a hundred and eighty-four (destinations), three hundred and twenty (businesses), seventy six thousand, five hundred (employees), three hundred and fifty-three thousand and twenty (square meters).

The story 2

a False, **b** False, **c** False

Listening and reading 2

1 The True sentences are: 2, 4, 7, 9 and 11.

2 1 The car is on level 4. 3 The car park costs £6.00. 5 They take the trolley in the lift. 6 Helen's got a green Ford. 8 They put the suitcase in the boot. 10 Helen puts her coat in the back but Tasha keeps her coat on.

3 1 But first, I have to pay ... 2 Wait a minute. 3 Let me see if I've got the right money. 4 a I'm afraid I haven't got ... b Don't worry. 5 I'm getting this. 6 a Can I help you with your suitcase? b No, really, it's all right, thanks. I can manage. c Come on! Let me help. Don't lift that big suitcase. d OK. Thanks. It is quite heavy.

4 1 Here it is, in my pocket. 2 change; notes 3 Could you just hold this bag ... 4 while 5 on the top 6 on your own 7 quite 8 I think I'll keep mine on. 9 have a rest 10 i b ii c iii a.

5 1 i, 2 h, 3 e, 4 f, 5 j, 6 c, 7 b, 8 a, 9 d, 10 g

Language discovery 3

1 1 has to. 2 do I have to. 3 We don't have to. 4 Do I have to? 5 you don't have to. 6 I don't have to. 7 do you have to. 8 have to. 9 have to. 10 do I have to.

2 1 Don't wait. 2 Don't forget. 3 Don't worry! 4 Don't write.

3 1 b, 2 a, 3 e, 4 f, 5 d, 6 c

4 A: 2 c, B: 6 e, C: 4 f, D: 5 d, E: 3 a, F: 1 b

5 1 b, 2 c, 3 d, 4 a

6 1–5 are all True.

Vocabulary builder 2

1 1 Mind your head, 2 Insert your card here, 3 Queue here, 4 Look right, 5 Please drive

slowly, 6 Cut along the dotted line, 7 Beware of the dog, 8 Book your tickets here, 9 Stop,

10 Give way

2 1 Mind the bus! 2 Mind the step! 3 Mind your legs! 4 Mind your door! OR Mind the car!

3 1 No smoking, 2 No parking, 3 No bathing, 4 No entry, 5 No left turn, 6 No photography

Language discovery 4

2 1 g, 2 c, 3 b, 4 d, 5 h, 6 i, 7 a, 8 e

3 1 No, it's heavy. Let me take it! 2 Come on! It's my turn. Let me pay this time. 3 Wait a

second. Let me open the door for you. 4 Let me call an ambulance. 5 Come on, it's late! Let

me take you. 6 No really. Let me do something to help. 7 Come on! Let me have a look at it.

4 1 e, 2 g, 3 b, 4 h, 5 a, 6 d, 7 f, 8 c

5 1 I'm afraid so. 2 I'm afraid not. 3 I'm afraid not. 4 I'm afraid not. 5 I'm afraid not.

6 I'm afraid so.

Practice

1 1 I'll get this. 2 I'm getting these. 3 Let me get the ice creams today. 4 I'll get this on my

credit card.

2 Possible answers

1 What shall I call you? Advanced alternative: What would you like me to call you? 2 I've got

some change. Here you are.

Revision

Writing: model answer

The phrases from the box are in bold.

TITANIC

The film *Titanic* is about a real passenger ship. The producer creates a love story to show what happens when the huge ship hits an iceberg and sinks in the North Atlantic. This was on 15th April 1912, during the ship's first voyage, from England to New York, with 2,224 people on board.

The film begins with 101-year-old Rose Calvert on a boat around the wreck of the *Titanic*. She tells the story of when she was a 17-year-old first-class passenger, travelling with her rich fiancé Cal and her mother, Ruth. Young Rose is unhappy with her life and tries to jump off the ship but Jack Dawson (a third-class passenger) **doesn't let her**. Later Cal gives Rose a present, a necklace with an enormous and extremely expensive, heart-shaped blue diamond, called 'The Heart of the Ocean'.

Rose goes to find Jack **to thank him for saving** her. They become close and spend time having fun, drinking and dancing in third class.

The next day Rose's mother, Ruth, tells her daughter that **she has to marry Cal** because they have no money. Rose knows this but she loves Jack. That evening Jack draws a picture of Rose wearing her 'Heart of the Ocean' necklace.

Suddenly, the ship hits an iceberg. It rips a big hole in the ship and water begins to rush in. Rose finds Jack but there aren't enough lifeboats and the ship is going to sink. They go to the back and jump off as the ship goes down. Jack dies in the water but Rose **manages to survive** and she finds the 'Heart of the Ocean' diamond in her coat pocket. She changes her name to Rose Dawson and never has contact with Cal again.

At the end of the film, Rose is 101 years old. She goes to the edge of the salvage boat and throws the 'Heart of the Ocean' diamond into the water - her love for Jack is still alive. She goes to her cabin and goes to sleep: she is with Jack again.

Review: How was the film for me?

It's very easy to see why *Titanic* is such a famous film. The main actors, Kate Winslet (Rose) and Leonardo di Caprio (Jack) are **amazing** but **I'm afraid it's difficult** to follow the story in places because it jumps from the past to the present and back to the past etc. I was very **impressed** by the music. It's not a new film but if you don't know it, **let me recommend** it. **Don't miss** it!

Test yourself

Which one is right?

1 a, **2** a, **3** b, **4** b, **5** b, **6** b, **7** a, **8** b, **9** b, **10** a

Dialogue: model answers

1	Your friend	Hello, X. It's great to see you again.
2	You	Hi, X. It's lovely to see you too.
3	Your friend	How was your journey?
4	You	It was good thanks. How are things with you?
5	Your friend	I'm fine. The taxis are this way.
6	You	Thank you for picking me up, by the way.
7	Your friend	That's OK. Look, here's a taxi. Go on!
		You get in first.
8	Your friend	How much is it, please?
9	You	Let me pay.
10	Your friend	No, I'm getting this.

UNIT 10

The story 1

1 No; **2** a Yes, b No, c Yes, d Yes

Listening and reading 1

1 Number of nights: 14; Price range: £80 – £100 a night; Location: central; Name of hotel:

Trafalgar; Price: £95

2 1 a Who's next? b I think I am. 2 a How many of you are there? b It's just for me.

3 a How much is that one? b £95 a night.

3 1 I'd like to book a room, please. 2 a How long is it for? b From tonight until the end of

next week. 3 He needs a single room. 4 I don't mind, as long as it's central. 5 a What sort

of price are you looking to pay? b Between £80 and £100 a night. 6 Have you got any

vacancies? 7 Would you like to take a seat ...

Language discovery 1

1 1 How many is it for? ('it' refers to 'table') 2 When are they for? 3 How much is it for?

4 Who are they for? 5 How long is that for?

2 1 as long as we go to London.

2 as long as you take me home afterwards.

3 as long as it doesn't rain.

4 as long as we get there by twenty past.

5 as long as it isn't too noisy.

6 as long as you are back by eleven o'clock.

7 as long as you find me a room.

3 1 £130 a month, 2 £7.50 a bunch, 3 £1.20 a kilo,, 4 £2.00 a box, 5 £1.35 a packet, 6 £6.99 a

bottle

Vocabulary builder 1

1 c, **2** d, **3** b, **4** g, **5** h, **6** e, **7** j, **8** a, **9** f, **10** i

Language discovery 2

1 1 John and Sheila do. 2 I am. 3 Sue isn't. 4 I have. 5 We can. 6 I'm afraid Mike doesn't.

7 I do but my partner doesn't. 8 Robert is. 9 I do. 10 No one does. 11 Kate has. 12 We all do.

2 All answers: There are XXX of us. If you're alone, the answer to Question 2 is: Just me.

3 1 e, 2 d, 3 c, 4 a, 5 b

4 1 a cold one. 2 the black one. 3 the/my old one. 4 the/this/that red one. 5 a short one. 6

the/your new ones. 7 a red one. 8 the dirty ones. 9 the/my other one's.

The story 2

1 1 No 2 3

Listening and reading 2

1

Name of Hotel	The Park Hotel	The Royal Hotel
Price per night	£95	£99
Ensuite bathrooms	Yes	Yes
Free wifi	Yes	Yes
Tea and coffee facilities	Yes	Yes
Breakfast included	Yes	Yes
Type of breakfast	Continental/English	Continental
Oliver chooses	Yes	

2 1 Sorry to keep you waiting. 2 Have you got anything else? 3 The Park is smaller, it's in a

quieter street and is perhaps a little more comfortable. It's more traditional. 4 I'll take the

room at the Park.

Vocabulary builder 2

1 C – Close to (near) King's Cross Station.

2 The Royal Scot is: large, modern, good for visiting London's shops, good for tourists

(sightseeing). It has got: more than 200 rooms.

3 1 quiet … near, 2 expensive … central … comfortable, 3 clean … friendly

4 a rolls, b butter, c jam, d hot chocolate, e coffee, f toast, g tea, h yoghurt, i cheese, j croissants, k cereal, l coffee, m cereal, n eggs, o bacon, p tomatoes, q mushrooms, r sausages, s marmalade, t fruit juice, u toast, v butter, w tea

Language discovery 3

1 1 Have you got anything smaller? 2 Have you got anything longer? 3 Have you got anything earlier? 4 Have you got anything nearer the centre? / more central?

2 1 not as quiet. 2 not as comfortable as. 3 not as traditional. 4 not as good as, as near.

3 1 I'll take the small one, please. 2 I'll take the black and white one please. 3 I'll take the more expensive one, please.

The story 3

a passport – no, **b** room number – yes, **c** restaurant – no, **d** breakfast room – yes, **e** cost – no, **f** luggage – yes

Listening and reading 3

1 1 the registration card. 2 508. 3 downstairs. 4 7.00 – 10.00. 5 Not much.

2 1 I've got a room booked. 2 In what name? 3 … on the fifth floor. 4 Breakfast is served in the breakfast room. 5 Downstairs. 6 Round the corner to your right. 7 I hope you enjoy your stay.

Vocabulary builder 3

1 10th – tenth; 9th – ninth; 8th – eighth; 7th – seventh; 6th – sixth; 5th – fifth; 4th – fourth

2 1 It's on the ground floor. 2 Yes, it's on the second floor. 3 Downstairs, the breakfast room's on the lower ground floor. 4 The bar's on the first floor.

3 For ordinal numbers, add the letters 'th' to the number. The ordinals first, second, and third are irregular.

Language discovery 4

1 I hope you have a good weekend. **2** I hope you have a nice evening. **3** I hope you enjoy your holiday. **4** I hope you have a good journey. **5** I hope everything goes well.

The story 4

1 a No, b Yes, c Yes, d No, e Yes, f No, g Yes

2 1 b, 2 a, 3 b, 4 a, 5 c, 6 b

Listening and reading 4

1 1 I haven't stayed here before. 2 a First I visited our new representative … b then on Tuesday, Wednesday and Thursday I went to the Computer fair. c I talked to a lot of people there and had lots of meetings 3 a On the flight on the way back I met a very interesting girl. b Oh, did you? 4 I'm going to call her one day next week. 5 We might have dinner together. 6 a Here, *get* means *receive* b I left a message at your hotel two days ago. c What was it about? (preposition!) 7 What's happened?

2 1   Hello dear.

2   a Quite nice, b No, it's a quiet hotel.

Language discovery 5

1 Natalie   Hi, Dan, did you have a good weekend?

Dan   Yes, I did thanks. It was really nice, actually. On Saturday, I washed the car. Then in the afternoon I took the children to the park. Yesterday I played tennis in the morning and for lunch we had a barbecue in the garden.

Natalie   Great!

Dan   How about you? What did you do?

Natalie   I was so tired after last week. I really didn't do much at all. I saw a good film on the TV on Saturday night and yesterday I just relaxed at home. My husband's sister came to see us. We didn't want to cook so we got an Indian takeaway.

Later, in the evening we went out for a drink and then we drove her home.

2 1 Oliver has arrived. 2 He has spoken. 3 Has he called. 4 He hasn't contacted. 5 has he been.

3 1 A Have you seen the film *Titanic*?

   B Yes, I have.

2 A How many times have you been to France?

   B I've been lots of times.

3 A How many countries have you visited?

   B Me? I've been to the States but I haven't been anywhere else.

4 A How many jobs has your brother had?

   B He hasn't had many actually.

5 A How many English books have you read?

   B I've read hundreds.

6 A Have you finished?

   B No, not yet.

7 A You haven't forgotten, have you?

   B No, of course not.

8 A My sister's (has) bought a new house.

   B Oh! Has she? Whereabouts?

Practice

1 B, G, A, C, E, J, I H, D

3 Possible answers

1 The television in my room doesn't work. 2 I'm very sorry but I can't find my key card.

   Advanced alternative: I'm terribly sorry but I think I've lost my key card.

314

Revision

Writing: model answer

MY LIFE STORY

My name is Nicolette Smith. I was born in Edinburgh on 5th April 1982. I am the first of two children, so I've got one sister.

I didn't go to a nursery but I went to Fernhill primary school when I was four years old. I really liked reading and art when I was there. My secondary school was called Teddington High School and I studied there from 11 years to 18 years old. I took exams in Maths, Chemistry and English.

I haven't been to university OR I've been to university. I studied English in York and got my degree in 2003. I lived in student accommodation for the first year and after that I shared a house with three friends. I've never lived on my own. Every year, during the summer holidays, I worked as a tourist guide.

I've also worked as a hotel receptionist. That was in the evenings during my university course. After my degree my first job was as a trainee manager in a pharmaceutical company. I worked there for three years, from 2003 to 2006. After that I moved to my present job as a research assistant in the same company.

My husband and I have been married for three years and we have one child, a girl.

I've travelled quite a lot. As my mother is French, I've spent a lot of time with my grandparents in France. I've also been to Kenya, Korea and some Latin American countries. In Brazil I went on a trip down the Amazon. It was amazing.

My mother has always spoken to me in French so I speak it fluently. I've also learnt some Mandarin. I did an evening course for beginners a few years ago. I love foreign languages and cultures.

Test yourself

Which one is right?

1 b, **2** b, **3** a, **4** a, **5** b, **6** a, **7** b, **8** a, **9** b, **10** b, **11** b, **12** b, **13** a, **14** b

Dialogues: model answers

A

1	Travel agent	What sort of hotel are you looking for?
2	You	I don't mind, as long as it's quiet.
3	Travel agent	How many of you are there?
4	You	There are two of us.
5	Travel agent	What sort of price are you looking to pay?
6	You	Anything up to £90.
7	Travel agent	How about the Plaza Hotel? That one's £85 a night.
8	You	OK.
9	Travel agent	How would you like to pay?
10	You	By card, please.

B

1	Shop assistant	Can I help you?
2	You	Yes, have you got a bigger one like this?
3	Shop assistant	Yes, I have – this one.
4	You	I'll take that one, please.

Glossary

Auxiliary (verb) A verb used with another verb. The auxiliary (verb) shows tense etc. For example:

She **is** reading	Present progressive
He **can** drive	Modal auxiliary/ability
I **have** finished	Present perfect

Reading, *drive* and *finished* are the main verbs – they give the meaning. *Is*, *can't*, *have* are the auxiliaries.

▶ The auxiliary for the present simple is *do/does*.
▶ The auxiliary for the past simple is *did*.
▶ Auxiliaries are always part of the verb in all other tenses.

We use auxiliaries to make questions. We change the word order: the auxiliary goes *before* the person. For example:

She is reading.

Is she reading?

She likes Coke.

Does she like Coke?

To make the verb negative, we add *n't* (*not*) to the auxiliary. For example:

*He **can't** drive.*

*She **doesn't** like Coke.*

Some auxiliaries have a short form or contraction (see **Contraction**), for example *he**'s**, they**'re**, we**'ve**.* Contractions are common in spoken English and informal written English.

Auxiliaries are very important in English because we use them a lot to make conversation: **Question tags** and **short answers** both use **auxiliaries**.

Some examples of **auxiliaries in question tags** are:

*He's working, **isn't** he?*

*They're married, **aren't** they?*

*She's got a cat, **hasn't** she?*

And here are some examples of **auxiliaries** in short **echo questions**:

A He's here.		**B** Oh, is he?	
A They can't come.		**B** Can't they? Why not?	
A She's had the baby.		**B** Has she? Is it a boy or a girl?	

Comparative Comparing two things. For example:

*Peter is older **than** his brother.* Short adjective *old* + *er* (*than*)

*A house is **more** expensive than a flat.* Longer adjective, *more* + adjective (+ *than*)

Contraction A short form of verbs *be* and *have*, some auxiliary verbs and *us* in *let's*. We write an apostrophe (') in the place of the missing letters. For example:

I am = **I'm**

It is and *it has* = **it's**

He would not = *He* **wouldn't**

Contractions are very common in spoken and informal written English.

Direct language can be impolite in English. For example: *Give me a glass of water* is often impolite. It is more polite to use indirect language, for example: *Could you give me a glass of water, please?*

Echo questions help conversation. They show you are interested and want to continue the conversation. Echo questions have two words: the auxiliary + subject. For example:

A *I live in Paris.*   **B** *Do you?*

A *He hasn't got a car.*   **B** *Hasn't he?*

Formal language is appropriate with people you don't know, people in authority and official situations and documents (see **Informal language** and **Neutral language**). For example: *Thanks* is informal language. *Thank you very much indeed* is formal.

Gerund The verb + *-ing*, used like a noun. For example:

I enjoy travelling.

Imperative The verb without *to*, for example, *Wait a minute*.

Remember the imperative is a danger zone for learners of English. We often use other forms of the verb to ask/tell someone to do something.

The imperative is common for:

Wishes:	*Have a nice day!*
Instructions:	*Take this train.*
Directions:	*Turn left at the end of the road.*
Warnings:	*Be careful!*

Informal language Appropriate with family, friends and children. For example, *Bye/See you later* is informal and *Goodbye* is neutral/formal.

Intonation is the music or movement of the voice on the syllable with stress. English expresses different meanings through intonation. For example:

Yes ➤

Flat intonation. The person isn't interested.

Yes ↘

A big movement in the pitch of the voice. The person is interested.

Less direct language English uses indirect language a lot. It helps conversation and communication. Direct language with flat intonation can sound rude. For example:

Dialogue 1 – direct	**Dialogue 2 – less direct**
A *Where's John?*	*Do you know where John is?*
B *I've got no idea.*	*I'm afraid I've got no idea.*

The words in Dialogue 1, with flat intonation, can sound rude. The words in Dialogue 2 are less direct.

Neutral language Appropriate in most situations. For example, *Thank you* is appropriate with people you know, people you don't know, people in authority and children; *Thanks* is informal and *Thank you very much* indeed is formal (see **Formal language** and **Informal language**).

Past participle The verb + *ed*. The third part of an irregular verb, for example *see/saw/**seen – seen***, is the past participle. We use the verb *have* + past participle to form the perfect tenses. For example, *I have eaten* – present perfect.

Plural More than one. For example: *sandwiches*, *grapes*.

Preposition Little words that connect nouns, etc., with other words. For example, ***to*** *the station* (direction), ***at*** *the restaurant* (place), ***before*** *two o'clock* (time).

The preposition is sometimes part of a phrase. For example: *interested **in**, I'm interested **in** sport* or *to be married **to**, She's married to a Frenchman.*

There are lots of prepositions in English. They are a problem zone for learners because it's often difficult to know which preposition to use. To help you:

▶ Try to learn the meanings of the prepositions (for example direction = *to*)

▶ When you learn a phrase with a preposition, remember to learn the preposition, too!

Question tag A short question form at the end of a sentence. This question form with falling intonation isn't really a question. It is a way of starting or making conversation.
For example:

    A *Terrible weather, **isn't it?***   **B** *Yes. It's not very good, **is it?***

The speakers know that the weather is terrible. They are not really asking questions. They are using question tags to start/continue the conversation.

Schwa The vowel sound / ə/, as in *a* book. It is the only sound in English with a name!

Short answers *Yes* and *No* alone can often sound rude in English. Short answers are: *Yes/No* + person + auxiliary. For example:

    A *Is Sue here?*   **B** ***Yes, she is.***

    A *Can you drive?*   **B** ***No, I can't.***

Singular One only, for example, *a bus, a biscuit.*

Stress Emphasis or force on a syllable or word. In all words with two syllables or more in English, one syllable has stress. Example, ***Eng*** - *lish*, *fan* – ***tas*** – *tic.*

In sentences, the stress is on the important words, the words with a lot of meaning. For example, *I've bought some **bread**, some **cheese** and some **fruit**.*

In English we also use stress to give a particular meaning or emphasis: *Could I have a **cold** drink?* (meaning not a *hot* one).

We also use it to correct people. For example, *The books **on** the desk, not **under** it.*

Syllable Part of a word with a vowel sound. For example, the word *question* has two syllables, *ques – tion*. And the word *popular* has three, *pop – u – lar.*

Uncountable Nouns that you can't count – mass nouns. For example, *rice* and *money* are uncountable nouns. You can't say *one, two, three* + noun.

Weak form In some short, common words (for example *but, for, from, to, was, does*), the vowel has two pronunciations: one strong (when the word has stress), for example, *who is it **for**?*; and one weak (when the word doesn't have stress), for example, *it's for you*. Read the following phrases: *it's for **you**, but not **now**, from **Tom**, to **Paris**, **Was** it **good**? **Does** she **know**?* In all the words that are not stressed - those not in bold - the pronunciation of the vowel is *schwa* – it is very short and weak. *Schwa* is the most common weak form vowel sound.

Quick reference: communicative functions

The figure in brackets ( ) is the unit number.

Ability (3)

Questions:	*Can you + verb?*
	Do you + verb?
Responses:	*No, not at all*
	Yes, but not very well
	Yes, not too badly

Asking about the same topic (3)

And you?

How about you?

Asking for an alternative – general (10)

Have you got anything else?

Asking for an alternative – specific

Can I / Could I have X instead, please? (2)

Have you got anything + short adjective + *-er?*

Example: *Have you got anything cheaper?* (10)

Have you got anything + *more* + long adjective

Example: *Have you got anything more suitable?*

Asking for help – indirect questions (7)

Can you tell me where X is, please?

Do you know how much X costs, please?

Could you tell me if ...

Asking for help, systems – present simple (8)

What/Where/When/How do I ... + verb?

Example: *Where do I sign?*

Asking for information (6)

Could you tell me ...? I'd like (to know)... What's the ...?

Example:

Could you tell me
I'd like (to know)   }   *the time of the next train,*
What's   *please?*

Asking for opinions (9)

How is/was …?

Example: *How was your meal?*

Asking for things (2)

Could I have …?

Example: *Could I have a glass of water, please?*

Asking someone to do something

Can you …, Could you …, Would you mind + verb + -ing (7)

Examples: *Can you/Could you wait a moment, please?*

                   Would you mind waiting a moment?

                   If you would like to … (very indirect) (7)

Example: *If you would like to call again tomorrow …*

Attracting attention (1)

Excuse me …

Example: *Excuse me, could I have the bill, please?*

Buying things, decisions (10)

I'll take …

Example: *I'll take this one*

Choosing – responding to offers (2)

X, please

X for me, please

I'd like X, please

Could I have X, please?

I'll have X, please

Decisions (2)

I'll …

Negative decisions – *I don't think I will* (2)

Decisions, buying (10)

I'll take …

Negative decision – *I think I'll leave it*

Insisting, offering help (9)

Come on! Let me … + verb

Example: *Come on. Let me do that!*

Response: Yes: *Thank you / Thanks*

               No: *No thank you / thanks. I can manage*

Invitations and offers

Question:		*Would you like a …? (1)*
Example:		*Would you like an ice cream?*
Responses:	Yes:	*Yes, please. That would be nice*
		Yes, please. I'd love one/some
	No:	*No, thank you*
		No, thanks. I'm fine
Question:		*Would you like to …? (7)*
Response:	Yes:	*Yes, that would be nice*
	No:	*I'm sorry, I'm …* (reason)
Question:		*If you would like to …* (a very indirect way of asking someone to do something)
Responses:	Yes:	*Thank you*
		Yes, of course
		Yes, that's fine
		Yes, I'll …
	No:	*I'm sorry but I can't*

Likes and dislikes – like, enjoy, mind, be keen on (4)

Question:		*Do you like/enjoy X/verb + -ing?*
		Do you like your job?
		Do you enjoy being a mother/father?
Responses:		
	Very positive:	*Yes, I really enjoy it*
	Yes:	*Yes, I quite like it*
	Neutral:	*I don't mind it*
	No:	*I'm not very keen on it, actually*
	Very negative:	*Actually, I don't like it at all*

Making conversation

actually (3)	*Actually, I + verb OR I + verb, actually*
Example:	*I live in London, actually*
echo questions (3)	
auxiliary + person	

Do you? / Have you? / Can she? / Aren't they? etc.

Number of people, talking about the (10)

Question:	*How many of you are there?*
Response:	*There are X of us*

Offers (*see* **Invitations and offers**)

Offering help (6)

Offers:		I can…
		I could…
		I'll …
		Shall I …?
		Would you like me to …?

Example: I can
　　　　　 I could } do that for you (, if you like).
　　　　　 I'll

Example: Shall I
　　　　　 Would you like me to } do that for you?

Responses:	Yes:	Thanks
		Thank you
		That's very kind of you
		Can you? Could you? Would you?
	No:	Thanks for the offer but it's all right
		Thanks but I can manage

Offering more

(some) more, another (1)

Question:	Would you like some more coffee?
	Would you like another sandwich?
Responses:	(see **Invitations**)

Permission, asking for (2)

Questions:	Is it all right if I …?
	Could I …?
	Can I …?

Example: Is it all right if I
　　　　　 Could I } use your phone?
　　　　　 Can I

Responses:	Yes:	Of course. Go ahead.
	No:	I'm sorry but …+ reason

Possibilities and suggestions (6)

We could …

Example: *We could go to the cinema*

You can …

Example: *You can tell me tomorrow*

Possibilities, suggestions and offers (*see* Offering help)

Price, talking about the (10)

Question: *What sort of price are you looking to pay?*

Response: Maximum: *Anything up to XXX*

Anything under XXX

As long as it's less than XXX

Approximately: *About XXX*

Around XXX

Rejecting an offer of help (9)

No, really. It's all right thanks

No, really. I can manage

Requests (*see* Asking for things/Asking people to do things)

Same, asking for the (2)

The same for me, please

I'll have X, too, please

Starting a conversation – question tags (1)

Adjective,+ *isn't it?*

Example: *Nice, isn't it?*

Not very + adjective, + *is it?*

Example: *Not very interesting, is it?*

Sentence + question tag

Examples: *He isn't playing very well, is he?*

It was a good film, wasn't it?

Suggesting doing something together (7)

Let's ... + verb

Example:		*Let's go to the cinema*
Responses:	Yes:	*OK*
		All right
		Yes, why not?
		That's a good idea
		Yes, why don't we?
	No:	*Do you really want to?*
		I'm not too sure
		Perhaps not
		Actually, I'm not too keen
Negative suggestion:		*Let's not ...*
Example:		*Let's not go to the party. I'm too tired*

Suggestions, possibilities and offers (*see* Offering help)

Thanking (9)

Neutral:	*Thank you*	*for* + verb + *-ing*
	Thank you very much	e.g. *for inviting me*
Formal:	*Thank you very much indeed*	
Informal:	*Thanks*	
	Many thanks	
	Thanks a lot	
Responses:		
Neutral:	*That's OK*	
	That's all right	
Formal:	*You're welcome*	
	Not at all	
Informal:	*No problem*	
	Any time	

Why, saying (5)

Question:		*Why are you …?*
Responses:		*to … + verb*
		because I want to …
		because I need to …
		because I like to …
		so (that) (I can)
		because …
		because of … + noun
Example:	A	*Why are you going to Italy?*
	B	*To*

Because I want to
Because I need to
Because I like to } *visit my Italian friends*
So (that) (I can)

Because of my friends – they're Italian
Because I'm going to visit my Italian friends

Quick reference: English grammar

Grammar is about the job of each word or phrase in a sentence. Let's look at eight of the main parts of speech.

1 Nouns

Nouns – e.g. *table*, *John*, *happiness* – are people, things, animals, places and abstract concepts.

1.1 Nouns can be common or proper, e.g. *bus* is a common noun and *July* is a proper noun, i.e. it starts with a capital letter

1.2 Nouns can be singular or plural, e.g. *a dictionary* (singular = one), *three clocks* (plural = more than one). We usually add *s* or *es* to make a noun plural but there are some exceptions, e.g. *one child*, *two children*.

Some nouns are singular in English and plural in some other languages, e.g. *news*, *information*, *advice*, *furniture*.

1.3 Nouns can be countable (= you can count the things) or uncountable (= you can't count it), e.g. *one brother*, *two brothers* but *water*, *rice*, *happiness*.

> **LANGUAGE TIP**
> ▶ Some nouns can be both. *Coffee* is uncountable but we often say *three coffees* as a short way of saying *three cups of coffee*.
> ▶ We often use unit words with uncountables, e.g. *a loaf of bread*.

1.4 Genitive or possessive 's is about possession, e.g. *the manager's office* means *the office belonging to the manager*. Apostrophe *s* is also used with some expressions of time e.g. *yesterday's newspaper*, *in two years' time* and for buildings, e.g. *St Paul's (cathedral)*, *the optician's (shop)*.

> **LANGUAGE TIP**
> **'s or s'?**
> *My brother's teacher* = one brother but, *My brothers' teacher* = two + brothers.
> Similarly *in a year's time* (singular) – but *in a few years' time* (plural).

1.5 Compound nouns are two nouns together that make one, e.g. *car key*, *wine glass*, *river bed*.

> **PRONUNCIATION TIP**
> The stress falls on the first part, e.g. **finger** nail, **rain** hat.

1.6 Gerunds (verb + *-ing*) are verbs used as nouns, e.g. *Eating fruit and vegetables is good for you* (subject) or *I like swimming* (object).

2 Pronouns

Pronouns (*pro-noun* = instead of a noun) are words used in the place of a noun.

2.1 Personal pronouns can be the subject or object of a verb, e.g. *She* (subject) *sings*. *I like her* (object). Object pronouns can be direct or indirect, e.g. *Eat it!* (direct), *Give me* (indirect) *a call*.

LANGUAGE TIP
Verbs need a subject in English. If there isn't one, use *it* or *there* – e.g. It's raining again. *It's difficult to say. There's a meeting at 3.30.*

2.2 Possessive pronouns (e.g. *mine, yours, his*, etc.), are 'owners', e.g. A: *Whose glasses are these?* B: *They're mine*. Possessive pronouns replace the noun.

2.3 Reflexive pronouns are used when the subject and the object of the verb are the same person or thing, e.g. *Oh no! I've cut **myself***. *The washing machine turns **itself** off automatically.*

2.4 Pronouns *one/ones* are used to avoid repeating a countable noun, e.g. A: *Which cake?* B: *The big* ***one**, please* … or *I'd like some trousers like the **ones** in the window.*

2.5 Relative pronouns. These 'relate' or link two parts of a sentence, e.g. *A lady called. She's here.* To join these two sentences together we say, *The lady **who/that** called is here* … *Lady* is subject – must use *who/that*.

3 Quantifiers

Quantifiers tell us about the quantity or number.

3.1 Articles – look at the three types of article in the table.

Zero article	Indefinite article *a/an*	Definite article *the*
e.g. *I like peas and cheese* (in general)	e.g. *I've bought a car.* (We don't know which car.)	e.g. *The car's here.* (We know which car – the car you've bought.)
With plural and uncountable nouns Meaning: unspecific/general	With singular nouns Meaning: unspecific – new information/first mention	With singulars, plurals and uncountable nouns Meaning: particular, common knowledge/old information

LANGUAGE TIP
Some languages don't have articles so this can be a completely new area for some learners of English. Remember that a singular noun always needs something in front of it, e.g. the word *hat* can be *a hat* (general), *the hat* (particular), *this hat* (demonstrative) or *her hat* (possessive), but there must be something in front of the noun.

3.2 Other expressions of quantity, e.g. *some/any/a little/anyone/nobody*.

***Some** people were late for the meeting because of the transport strike* (quantifier + noun). ***Others** walked and got there on time* (quantifier as pronoun + verb).

LANGUAGE TIP
Remember to use a singular verb with *anyone/anybody*, *everyone/everybody* and *no one/nobody*.

4 Adjectives

Adjectives give information about a noun.

4.1 Ordinary adjectives go in front of the noun, e.g. *a **young** girl*.

They don't change in English, i.e. we don't add *s* to the adjective with a plural noun, e.g. *Two **expensive** rings*.

4.2 The order of adjectives

Look at the categories in the three example sentences below:

	Personal evaluation	Size	Shape/	Quality/ colour	Origin	Material	
A	beautiful	large	oval		French	beech	dining table
Some	amazing	small		brown	forest		mushrooms
The		king- size		white	Egyptian	cotton	sheets

4.3 Comparative and superlative adjectives

Comparative adjectives

She's younger than Paul (short adjective = adjective + *-er* + *than*).

This restaurant is more expensive than the other one (long adjective = *more* + adjective + *than*).

Superlative adjectives

*La Paz is **the highest** capital in the world* (short adjectives = *the* + adjective with *-est*).

*This is **the most frightening** film I've ever seen* (long adjectives = *the* + *most* + adjective).

> Form – two-syllable adjectives. Some use *-er/est* for the comparative and superlative, e.g. *lovely*, *lovelier*, *the loveliest*. Others use *more/most* + adjective, e.g. *famous*, *more famous*, *the most famous*.

> **LANGUAGE TIP**
> If in doubt, use the long form.

Some comparatives and superlatives are irregular: e.g. *good*, *better*, *best* and *bad*, *worse*, *worst*.

> **LANGUAGE TIP**
> To compare three or more things, use the superlative.
> The pronunciation of the *a* in *than* is the same as the second *a* in the word *Africa*.

5 Verbs

Verbs tell us about action or situation and time.

5.1 Verb tenses

There are 12 tenses in English, four present tenses, four past tenses and four future tenses. Each of these groups has a simple tense:

▶ Present simple: *I **swim** a lot*.
▶ Past simple: *I **went** to Africa last year*.
▶ Future simple: *I'**ll see** you tomorrow*.

To these three base tenses we can add one or two extra pieces of information about the action or situation.

5.1.1 Continuous/progressive tenses

One piece of extra information we can show in the verb is that the action or situation continues over time. To do this we use a continuous/progressive tense:

Present continuous, e.g. *Daniel's (= is) using the computer*. This action is happening 'now' or 'around now'.

Past continuous, e.g. *At 10.00 last night Barbara was watching television*. This action continued over time in the past.

Future continuous, e.g. *At this time tomorrow I'll be taking my driving test*. This action will continue over time in the future

> Form of the six progressive tenses: verb *be* in the appropriate tense + verb + *-ing*.

5.1.2 Perfect tenses

The other piece of information we can show in the verb is that, with a perfect tense, we make a connection between two points in time, e.g. *I've cut the grass*, i.e. the speaker is looking for a reaction in the present about his/her past action of cutting the grass.

Present perfect – e.g. *I've (have) made some cakes* (past action/present result). The next sentence may be about the cakes, e.g. *Would you like one?*

Past perfect – e.g. *When we got to the cinema the film had started*. This is like a double past – an action before another action in the past, used for looking back from the second action to the first. We're looking back from 'getting to the cinema' to the film starting, which happened before we arrived.

Future perfect – e.g. *By the time I get home, everyone will have gone to bed*. This tense looks back from a point in the future (getting home) to a connected action before it (everyone going to bed).

> Form of the six perfect tenses: verb *have* in the appropriate tense + past participle.

5.1.3 Perfect continuous progressive tenses

Lastly we can combine both the 'continuous' form for 'happening over time' and the perfect form for showing a connection between two points in time. These are the three **perfect continuous tenses**:

Present perfect progressive, e.g. *I've (= have) been working in the garden for three hours* – an action that started in the past and has continued up to now.

Past perfect progressive, e.g. *I was tired because I'd been studying* – looking back from a situation in the past (*I was tired*) to the action before that caused it (*I'd been studying*).

Future perfect progressive, e.g. *When we arrive in Australia next Wednesday, we'll have been travelling for 24 hours* – looking back from the time of arriving in Australia, which is in the future, to the action of *travelling* which will continue up to that time.

> **LANGUAGE TIP**
>
> As languages vary greatly in the number of tenses and their meanings, learning to use English tenses correctly can take time. To help you decide which tense to use, ask yourself these questions about the action or situation:
> **a** When? – use a past, present, or future.
> **b** Over time? No = use a simple tense. Yes = use a continuous tense.
> **c** Showing a connection between two points in time? Yes = use a perfect tense.
> **d** Both over time and Yes – use a perfect continuous tense.

5.2 Modal auxiliary verbs

Modal auxiliary (helping) verbs go between the subject and main verb. They tell us about:

▶ ability – *My son **can** play the guitar*.
▶ probability – *We **might** go on holiday next month*.
▶ requests – ***Could** you open the door for me please?*
▶ obligation – *You **have to** turn left here*.
▶ prohibition – *You **mustn't** say that!*
▶ advice – *You **should** give her a call*.

▶ condition – *If we won the lottery,* **we'd (would)** *go round the world.*

> **LANGUAGE TIP**
> Don't put *to* after a modal, e.g. *I should go* NOT *I should to go.*
> We also use modals to deduce from evidence or knowledge:
> *The two people in the photo* **might be** *brother and sister. They look alike.*
> *They* **must be** *going on holiday tomorrow – their car is fully loaded.*
> *I* **must have** *left my glasses at home. They're not in my pocket.*
> Past = modal + *have* + past participle.

5.3 The passive

We use the passive when the 'receiver' of the action has more importance than the person doing the action:

Shopping **is delivered** *free of charge.*

Food and medical supplies **are being sent** *to the disaster area.*

> Form: *Be* in the appropriate tense + past participle of the main verb.

The passive is common in formal written English such as formal letters, reports, books and technical documents.

A reduced passive is used in headlines e.g. *Election* **won** *by the Democrats.*

To include the 'doer', use the preposition *by*, e.g. *The President was attacked by a tall man in his thirties.*

5.4 Multi-word verbs (also known as **phrasal verbs**)

Multi-word verbs are a verb + particle that changes the meaning of the verb.

There's a large number of phrasal verbs in English. They are informal and therefore common in spoken English.

There are four types:

1 *My car's* **broken down**. – intransitive, i.e. no object.

2 *Can you* **turn** *the TV* **on**, *please?*
OR
Can you **turn on** *the TV, please?* This is a little more formal.

With pronoun = *Can you* **turn it on**? NOT *Can you* **turn on it**?

3 *I'll* **look after** *the children* – no change of order with pronoun = *I'll* **look after** *them* NOT *I'll look them after.*

4 *I can't* **put up** *with her shouting any more* – two particles. With pronoun, no change of word order – *I can't* **put up** *with it any more.*

> **LANGUAGE TIP**
> The particle can sometimes give an indication of the meaning, e.g *In* = a movement in – *Join in when you're ready.*
> Pronunciation: The stress is usually on the particle, e.g. *Turn it off.*
> With two particles, stress the first one – e.g. *I can't put up with this any more!*

6 Adverbs

Adverbs describe or add to the meaning of a verb or adjective. They tell us the manner, place or time of the action or how often it happens.

6.1 Adverbs can be one word e.g. *She sings **beautifully*** (i.e. adjective + *ly*) or a phrase, e.g. *They come to the club **every week***.

6.2 Adverbs with adjectives

Adverbs give extra meaning to adjectives:

*This book is **really** interesting.*

*Paul's **unbelievably** fluent in French.*

7 Prepositions

Prepositions – e.g. ***at** the bank*, ***before** 1.00*, ***to** the supermarket*, *it's **for** you* – are words that tell us about place, time, directions and purpose, etc.

7.1 Many verbs are followed by a particular preposition, e.g. *to believe **in** something*, *to suffer **from** an illness*, *to congratulate someone **on** something*.

7.2 Prepositions are also used in many fixed expressions, e.g. ***at** home*, ***in** hospital*, ***for** example.*

7.3 When a verb follows a preposition, add *-ing* to the verb e.g. *Please lock the door **before** lea**ving**.*

> **LANGUAGE TIP**
> Prepositions are known for giving learners problems. If a verb takes a preposition, try to learn both together.

8 Conjunctions

These words and phrases link two parts of a sentence, one sentence to another or one paragraph to another. (Conjunction = con + junction.)

8.1 Conjunctions signal addition, contrast, result, an opposing view, etc:

Addition: *He opened the door **and** saw that the window was open.*

Contrast: *My sisters went to the party **but/whereas** I stayed at home.*

Result: *She had a free day **so** she went to the beach.*

> **LANGUAGE TIP**
> Learning to use conjunctions is an important part of writing well in English.

The story – American English audio transcripts

 11.01

Our story begins on a plane.

Man	It's hot, isn't it?
Woman	Yes, it is – very hot.
Man	Would you like a drink?
Woman	M'm, yes, please.
Man	What would you like?
Woman	Some Coke, please.

 11.02

The two passengers would like a drink.

Man	Excuse me.
Flight attendant	Yes, sir?
Man	Could I have a Coke and some orange juice, please?
Flight attendant	Of course. Would you like the Coke with ice?
Woman	Yes, please.
Flight attendant	Ice for you, sir?
Man	No, thanks.
Flight attendant	Here you are. One Coke with ice and one orange juice.
Man and woman	Thank you/Thanks.

 11.03

Our story continues. The flight attendant serves dinner to eight passengers.

1	**Attendant**	Chicken or beef, sir?
	Passenger	Chicken, please.
2	**Attendant**	Beef or vegetarian, madam?
	Passenger	Beef for me, please.
3	**Attendant**	Would you like fish or pork, sir?
	Passenger	I'd like fish, please.
4	**Attendant**	What would you like to eat, madam, fish or lamb?
	Passenger	Could I have lamb, please?
5	**Attendant**	Is it fish or beef for you, madam?
	Passenger	I'll have beef, please.
6	**Attendant**	And for you, sir?
	Passenger	The same for me too, please.

7 Attendant	Would you like vegetarian or chicken, sir?
Passenger	I don't mind. I like both.
8 Attendant	Would you like fish or chicken, madam?
Passenger	Nothing for me, thanks. I'm not very hungry. Could I have a sandwich instead?
Attendant	Of course.

 11.04

Our story continues. The flight attendant serves drinks.

Passenger 1

Attendant	Would you like a drink with your meal? I've got some apple juice.
Passenger	Yes, please.

Passenger 2

Attendant	What would you like to drink with your meal, sir?
Passenger	Have you got any cold beer?
Attendant	Of course … Here you are.

Passenger 3

Passenger	Could I have some white wine, please?
Attendant	I'm sorry, madam. I haven't got any more white wine. Would you like red instead?

 11.05

The story continues. The passengers have a meal. The flight attendant talks to a passenger.

Passenger	This fish isn't very good at all. What's the chicken like?
Attendant	I think it's very good.
Passenger	Better than the beef?
Attendant	I think so, but the beef is more popular. In fact, beef is always the most popular dish on the plane.
Passenger	Could I exchange this fish then, please? Is it all right if I have a different meal?
Attendant	Of course. What would you like instead?
Passenger	Can I try the chicken, please, if that's OK?

 11.06

The conversation on the plane continues.

Tasha	Where are you from?
Oliver	The United States. And you?
Tasha	I'm from the US, too.
Oliver	Oh, really? But your book isn't in English.
Tasha	Well, actually, I live in South America, in Uruguay and so I speak Spanish.

Oliver	Do you? That's interesting!
Tasha	Yes, I like it there. How about you? Do you speak any foreign languages?
Oliver	I can speak a bit of French.
Tasha	Can you?
Oliver	Yes, I use it in my job sometimes – but I'm not really very good at it.
Tasha	Oh, aren't you? I really like languages.

 11.07

The two passengers continue their conversation. They talk about their work.

Tasha	What do you do?
Oliver	I work in computers. And you? – what's your job?
Tasha	I'm a teacher.
Oliver	You're not an English teacher by any chance, are you?
Tasha	Yes, I am, actually. I teach in a school in Uruguay.
Oliver	Really? Whereabouts?
Tasha	In a town about 75 miles from the capital. I teach in an International School.
Oliver	Do you? Do you like your job?
Tasha	Yes, I really enjoy teaching and the students are lovely. What about you? What sort of work do you do in computers?
Oliver	Well, I'm in marketing. I work for a big company, so I travel a lot as part of my job. In fact, I'm on my way home now from a computer fair in Argentina.
Tasha	And do you enjoy working in marketing?
Oliver	It's OK, but I'm not very enthusiastic about all the travelling.

 11.08

The conversation on the plane continues. They exchange names, talk about their families and the reasons for their trips.

Tasha	What's your name?
Oliver	Oliver. And yours?
Tasha	My name's Tasha. It's short for Natasha, a Russian name. My mother's Russian. So, whereabouts in the US do you live, Oliver?
Oliver	I live in Canada, actually, in Toronto, but I'm staying in Denver for a couple of weeks, because of my job. And you? Are you on vacation?
Tasha	Yes, I'm going to Colorado to see some friends of mine. They live near Denver.
Oliver	Oh, I see. And your family?
Tasha	My father's working in London at the moment – until next June. He works abroad quite a lot. It's nice because my mother organizes her work so that she can travel with him. Even if they aren't at home, I go to Denver every year because I need to see other relatives and friends.

11.09

Tasha and Oliver continue their conversation. They exchange personal details and plan future contact.

Oliver	As I'm working in Denver for two weeks, we could … we could meet for a drink one evening, if you like.
Tasha	Yes, that would be nice.
Oliver	Can I give you my number? I'll give you both my cell and my office numbers – then you can phone me and we can arrange something
Tasha	OK. Just a minute. Where's my phone?

Tasha opens her bag and gets her phone.

Tasha	OK, What's your last name?
Oliver	Rees.
Tasha	Is that R, E, E, C, E?
Oliver	No, it's R, E, E, S actually, and my cell number is 769 189 4304.
Tasha	001 769 189 …?
Oliver	189 … 4304 and the phone number of the Denver office is 404-555-1212.
Tasha	404-555 …?
Oliver	1212. You can get me at my direct number, 159, I think it is. Yes, 159. Or you could email me. My email address is orees (O, R, double E, S) at starmail dot com.
Tasha	OK. When we land I'll send you a text and then you'll have my number. I can give you the number of my friend's house now, if you like.
Oliver	Why not? Then I can call you.
Tasha	My first name's Harrison, by the way. Tasha Harrison.
Oliver	Harrison, 'H', Tasha Harrison. And your friend's number is …?
Tasha	303-555-9866.
Oliver	303-555-9886.
Tasha	No, it's 303-555-9866 … Yes, that's it.
Oliver	When would you like me to call, during the day or in the evening?
Tasha	I don't mind. I'm going to visit relatives and do other things but I'm going to spend time at home with my friends, too. So, any time's all right with me, really. I'm on vacation!
Oliver	Great, I'll call you some time next week, Tasha, if that's OK.
Tasha	Yes, I'll look forward to it.
Oliver	Oh, look, the 'Fasten your seat belts' sign is on. We're landing in a minute.

 11.10

The plane is arriving at Denver International airport.

Pilot	Good morning, ladies and gentlemen. This is your captain speaking again. In a few moments, we will begin our descent into Denver International Airport. Please return to your seats and fasten your seatbelt. If you would like to adjust your watches, the time in Denver is now 6.50 in the morning and the temperature on the ground is 28 degrees. Our estimated time of arrival is 7.15. That's a quarter past seven on the ground in Denver. The forecast for today is cold … but bright.

11.11

Our story continues. Oliver and Tasha get off the plane.

a

Oliver	Well, it's been really nice talking to you, Tasha.
Tasha	Yes, and thanks for the help with the luggage.
Oliver	I'll be in touch next week, then.
Tasha	Yes, bye.
Oliver	Bye.

b

Oliver	Wow, this suitcase is a bit heavy – is that it now?
Tasha	The suitcase, the small bag and my purse – yes, that's everything.

c

Immigration officer	Thank you, madam. Sir, your passport, please. Thank you.

d

Oliver	Do you need a luggage cart?
Tasha	That would be a good idea – I've got quite a lot of luggage.
Oliver	They're right over here. Now, let's find the rest of the luggage.

e

Tasha	Would you mind waiting for just a minute, Oliver?
Oliver	Of course not. The suitcases aren't here yet, anyway.
Tasha	Could you look after my luggage cart – oh, and can you take my coat, please?
Oliver	Sure, go ahead.

Tasha asks for help at the information desk.

Airport employee	Can I help you?
Tasha	Yes, could you tell me where the restroom is, please?
Airport employee	Of course, madam. Just over there. Can you see the sign?

11.12

Our story continues. Oliver is in a shop in the airport.

Oliver	Excuse me, do you sell *Marketing Week*?
Seller	Yes, sir, they're here.
Oliver	And a package of mints – have you got Lifesavers?
The seller gets a package of Lifesavers.	
Seller	Three ninety-five, please, sir.
Oliver	Sorry, I haven't got any change. Is twenty dollars OK?
Seller	Sure, no problem. Sixteen dollars, five cents change.
Oliver	Thanks.

 11.13

Oliver is at the information desk at the airport. He needs to get into the city.

Airport employee	Can I help you?
Oliver	Yes, could you tell me how to get into the city, please?
Airport employee	You can go by taxi, limousine, rental car, or by bus. Where are you going in the city?
Oliver	I need to get to the Denver Tech Centre.
Airport employee	Then you can take a SkyRide bus. It goes all the way to the Tech Center.
Oliver	SkyRide. Good. And where do I get the bus from?
Airport employee	Just over there, sir. You follow the signs that say 'SkyRide'.
Oliver	Oh, I see! Do you know when the next bus leaves?
Airport employee	In ten minutes, sir – that's 8.05.
Oliver	And how long does it take to get there?
Airport employee	I'm not sure – the best thing is to ask the driver.
Oliver	Many thanks for your help.

 11.14

Our story continues. Oliver is walking towards the SkyRide bus. A man talks to him.

Man	Excuse me, can you tell me the time, please?
Oliver	Yes, it's five to eight.
Man	Many thanks.

 11.15

Tasha leaves customs. Who's there to meet her? What happens next?

Helen	Tasha, hi, how are you? It's lovely to see you again!
Tasha	Hello, Helen! It's great to see you too. How are things?
Helen	I'm fine. We're all fine. How was your flight?
Tasha	It was all right – 13 hours is a bit long and tiring, but I'm here now. Thanks for picking me up, by the way.
Helen	That's OK. We're glad you could come. The car's in the parking lot, this way. David and the children are at home, waiting for you.

11.16

Our story continues. Helen and Tasha go to the airport parking lot to get Helen's car.

Helen	The car's on level 2. We can take the luggage cart with us in the elevator. We have to pay on the way out, so I had better get the ticket and my money ready. Here's the ticket in my pocket. One hour – $11.00. Let me see if I've got the correct change.
Tasha	I'm afraid I haven't got any change. I've only got bills.
Helen	No, don't worry. I'll pay for this. I'm sure the attendant can make change. So, let's find the car.
Helen	There it is – it's the green Ford. Now, let's get your luggage in the trunk. Can I help you with your suitcase?
Tasha	No, really, it's all right thanks – I can manage. Could you just hold this bag for a minute while I get the suitcase in, then we can put the bag on top.
Helen	Come on! Let me help. Don't lift that suitcase on your own.
Tasha	OK – Thanks – it is quite heavy… Ready? One, two, three …
Helen	We can put our coats in the back seat.
Tasha	I think I'll keep mine on. I'm really cold.
Helen	I expect that's because you're tired after your long flight. Let's get home and you can have a rest.

 11.17

Oliver is at the hotel reservations desk in the tourist information center. He needs a room.

Assistant	Who's next, please?
Oliver	I think I am. I'd like to reserve a room, please.
Assistant	Yes, how many of you are there?
Oliver	It's just for me.
Assistant	How long is it for?
Oliver	I need a room from tonight until the end of next week.
Assistant	OK. So that's a single room for 14 nights altogether.
Oliver	Yes, that's right.
Assistant	In any specific area?
Oliver	I don't mind, as long as it's near the Tech Center.
Assistant	What sort of price are you looking to pay?
Oliver	Between $90 and $125 a night.
Assistant	There's the Courtyard, Denver Tech Center.
Oliver	How much is that one?
Assistant	$100 a night.
Oliver	That would be fine.
Assistant	I'll just see if they have any vacancies. Would you like to take a seat for a moment?
Oliver	Thanks.

11.18

Our story continues. The assistant telephones the Courtyard Hotel, then talks to Oliver.

Assistant	Sorry to keep you waiting, sir. I'm afraid the Courtyard has no vacancies.
Oliver	Have you got anything else?
Assistant	How about these two? Summerfield Suites or TownePlace Suites. Both are close to the Denver Tech Center.
Oliver	Are they about the same price?
Assistant	Let me see. Summerfield Suites is $95 a night and TownePlace Suites is a bit cheaper, $85. They both have the same facilities. Breakfast is included, of course, and all the rooms have private bathrooms, with free wifi, television and minibar in the room.
Oliver	Which one is closer to the Denver Tech Center?
Assistant	They are about the same but you may need a rental car.
Oliver	I think I'll take a room at Summerfield. It costs more and it might be a little more comfortable.

 11.19

Our story continues. Oliver arrives at the hotel. He checks in.

Receptionist	Good afternoon. Can I help you?
Oliver	Yes, I've got a room reserved.
Receptionist	In what name, sir?
Oliver	Rees, R – double E – S, Oliver.
Receptionist	Yes, here it is, a single room for 14 nights.
Oliver	That's right.
Receptionist	Could you sign this registration card, please?
Oliver signs ...	
Oliver	There you are.
Receptionist	Thank you. Here's your key. Room 508's on the fifth floor. Breakfast is served in the breakfast room downstairs from seven to ten o'clock and the elevator is around the corner to your right. Do you need help with your luggage?
Oliver	No thanks, I'm fine.
Receptionist	I hope you enjoy your stay with us, Mr Rees.
Oliver	Thank you.

11.20

Our story continues. Oliver is in his hotel room. He phones his mother.

Oliver	Hi, Mom! it's Oliver. How are you?
Mother	Hello, dear. Where are you?
Oliver	I'm in a hotel in Denver, the Summerfield Suites. I haven't stayed here before. It's quite nice – comfortable and quiet. I've just got here from the airport.
Mother	How was your trip?
Oliver	It went quite well, actually. First, I visited our new representative in Chile, and then on Tuesday, Wednesday and Thursday I went to the Computer Fair in Buenos Aires. I talked to a lot of people there and had lots of meetings. And then on the flight on the way back I met a very interesting girl.
Mother	Oh, did you?
Oliver	Yes, she's an English teacher in South America. She's on vacation here, staying with friends, just outside Denver. I've got her number there so I can contact her again. I'm going to call her one day next week. We might have dinner together, or something. Anyway, how are you?
Mother	Did you get my message?
Oliver	What message?
Mother	I left a message at your hotel in Argentina two days ago.
Oliver	What was it about, Mom? Come on – what's happened?

Index

"Global scale" of the Common European Framework of Reference for Languages: learning, teaching, assessment (CEFR)

Advanced	**CEFR LEVEL C2**	Can understand with ease virtually everything heard or read. Can summarise information from different spoken and written sources, reconstructing arguments and accounts in a coherent presentation. Can express him/herself spontaneously, very fluently and precisely, differentiating finer shades of meaning even in more complex situations.
Advanced	**CEFR LEVEL C1**	Can understand a wide range of demanding, longer texts, and recognise implicit meaning. Can express him/herself fluently and spontaneously without much obvious searching for expressions. Can use language flexibly and effectively for social, academic and professional purposes. Can produce clear, well-structured, detailed text on complex subjects, showing controlled use of organisational patterns, connectors and cohesive devices.
Intermediate	**CEFR LEVEL B2** (A Level)	Can understand the main ideas of complex text on both concrete and abstract topics, including technical discussions in his/her field of specialisation. Can interact with a degree of fluency and spontaneity that makes regular interaction with native speakers quite possible without strain for either party. Can produce clear, detailed text on a wide range of subjects and explain a viewpoint on a topical issue giving the advantages and disadvantages of various options.
Intermediate	**CEFR LEVEL B1** (Higher GCSE)	Can understand the main points of clear standard input on familiar matters regularly encountered in work, school, leisure, etc. Can deal with most situations likely to arise whilst travelling in an area where the language is spoken. Can produce simple connected text on topics which are familiar or of personal interest. Can describe experiences and events, dreams, hopes and ambitions and briefly give reasons and explanations for opinions and plans.
Beginner	**CEFR LEVEL A2:** (Foundation GCSE)	Can understand sentences and frequently used expressions related to areas of most immediate relevance (e.g. very basic personal and family information, shopping, local geography, employment). Can communicate in simple and routine tasks requiring a simple and direct exchange of information on familiar and routine matters. Can describe in simple terms aspects of his/her background, immediate environment and matters in areas of immediate need.
Beginner	**CEFR LEVEL A1**	Can understand and use familiar everyday expressions and very basic phrases aimed at the satisfaction of needs of a concrete type. Can introduce him/herself and others and can ask and answer questions about personal details such as where he/she lives, people he/she knows and things he/she has. Can interact in a simple way provided the other person talks slowly and clearly and is prepared to help.

© Council of Europe. www.coe.int/lang.
Extract reproduced with the permission of the Council of Europe, Strasbourg

WHAT'S YOUR NEXT LANGUAGE?

Learn a new language and discover a new world
with Teach Yourself Languages Online.

Enter code: **TYLO25X**
and receive a 25% discount
on your monthly subscription.

www.teachyourselflanguagesonline.com

/TYOpenroad   @TYOpenroad

Terms & Conditions: You can cancel your subscription at any time. Please refer to our standard terms and
conditions www.teachyourselflanguagesonline.com/terms&conditions for all other applicable terms